THE LIFE

OF

HENRY JOHN TEMPLE,

VISCOUNT PALMERSTON.

THE LIFE

OF

HENRY JOHN TEMPLE,

VISCOUNT PALMERSTON,

K.G., G.C.B., Etc.

With Selections from his Diaries and Correspondence.

BY THE

RIGHT HON. SIR HENRY LYTTON BULWER, G.C.B., M.P.

VOLUME I.

PHILADELPHIA:
J. B. LIPPINCOTT & CO.
1871.

TO THE

RIGHT HON. WM. F. COWPER-TEMPLE, M.P.

MY DEAR TEMPLE,—

Had Lady Palmerston been spared to us, my respectful dedication of this work would have been to her who felt so deep an interest in its subject, and who offered me the means for accomplishing the task which at her wish I undertook.

Alas! she has departed from a world which her noble and kind nature, her grace and her goodness, so long adorned.

To you I am, next to her, most indebted; and, in inscribing to you these volumes, I am testifying my gratitude for the help you have given me in recording the career of a statesman who rendered the name of Temple, already historical, one of the proudest illustrations of our country.

Yours, my dear Temple, very sincerely,

H. L. BULWER.

October 10, 1870.

PREFACE.

IT is difficult for any one who has not tried to write a work of this kind to anticipate the difficulties through which it is carried out, inasmuch as its proportions are being constantly changed according to the materials the writer receives.

My first idea was to sketch Lord Palmerston as I have sketched Mr. Canning in "Historical Characters." But when a large mass of his private letters were placed in my hands, they were so characteristic of the man, and so good as letters, that I thought they ought to be included in his biography. I still, however, contemplated finishing the work in two volumes, when I again was put in possession of such masses of private correspondence* connected with foreign policy, and this at a time when foreign

* I should say that the value of this hitherto unpublished correspondence consists in its showing not merely the outside which is contained in official documents, but the inside of public affairs for a very long period of time. From the letters of Lord Palmerston I have copied freely; from the letters to Lord Palmerston I have merely selected a very few, which neither the persons who wrote them nor their friends could feel the slightest dislike to see in print.

policy itself had become of such intense interest, that I found it again necessary to extend my plan; and finally, though I have endeavored to confine my quotations to such papers alone as peculiarly illustrated the policy of the statesman I was describing, and the manner in which he carried that policy out, I have not reached further than the fall of the Whig Cabinet in 1841 in the two volumes I now publish.

These two volumes, however, comprise Lord Palmerston's early and subordinate career, and carry us also through the period during which his reputation as a Foreign Affairs Minister was formed, and his talents as a statesman acknowledged. It begins with a certain struggle against the resistance of the Northern Cabinets to any liberal change in the affairs of Europe, and a struggle, at the same time, against that revolutionary spirit, sprung from the revolution of 1830 in France, which wished to change everything.

He succeeded in this struggle by moderating the two conflicting extremes; establishing a constitutional sovereign, and a neutral state in Belgium, and uniting France, Spain, Portugal, and England in an alliance favorable to constitutional monarchy. This he did with the aid of France, whose restless ambition he had nevertheless to restrain.

His wish, no doubt, would have been to maintain and perpetuate a cordial understanding with this Power, under whose union with England he wished the education of Europe to be achieved.

But, from causes which I have more or less explained, the French Cabinet had hardly connected itself formally with ours than it began to be uneasy under the connection, and to seek the sympathy of those states against whose policy we had been combating together.

At last arose one of those questions in which the interests of Great Britain were deeply involved. England could not allow the ruler of Egypt to be independent of the Porte under the protection of the French government.

The French government, notwithstanding, aimed at carrying out, more or less gradually, this project, and only wished to do so with such cleverness as not to give us an apparent cause for offense. Lord Palmerston did his utmost to open the eyes of Louis Philippe's ministers as to the futility of their plans, and he had to deal alternately with M. Molé, Marshal Soult, and M. Thiers. Finally, believing he had to do not so much with the ministers of the King of the French as with the king himself, he broke from an ally who wished (as he imagined) to make him a dupe, and successfully opposed France, with the aid of Austria, Prussia, and Russia, as he had previously opposed those three Powers with the aid of France. In both cases the policy of England triumphed under his auspices; and in both cases the policy of England was a natural policy in conformity with her principles in the one case and with her interests in the other.

It is not, however, to the success which attended his efforts so much as to the mode in which that success was obtained, that as his biographer I wish to draw attention.

There was nothing mean, shifty, underhand, or vacillating in his course. Whatever line he took, he pursued it openly, straightforwardly, firmly. There is hardly a paper he ever signed up to the time of which I am speaking, that every Englishman on reading it would not have said, "Well done, Palmerston!"

His brave yet gentle nature was, indeed, manifest in his boyhood; and I have just received a letter from one of his schoolfellows, which, coming too late to be inserted in the body of this work, shall close its Preface:

Letter from Sir Augustus Clifford.

"WESTFIELD, RYDE, September 21, 1870.

"When I went to Harrow in 1797, the late Lord

Palmerston was reckoned the best-tempered and most plucky boy in the school, as well as a young man of great promise. We were in the same house, which was Dr. Bromley's, who was then called 'Old Parr,' and by whom we were often called, when idle, 'young men of wit and pleasure.'

"The late Lord De Mauley—then William Ponsonby—Poulett, a son of Lord Poulett, and myself, were fags to Althorp, Duncannon, and Temple, who messed together; and the latter was by far the most merciful and indulgent.

"I can remember well Temple fighting 'behind school' a great boy called Salisbury, twice his size, and he would not give in, but was brought home with black eyes and a bloody nose, and Mother Bromley taking care of him. I went to sea shortly after, and though I cannot bear testimony to his future career, I can to the invariable kindness he has always shown me, and the happy hours I have spent in his society.

"Lord Lonsdale and Lord Headfort were also in the same house, and would, I am sure, confirm what I say.

"Believe me, yours very truly,

"AUGUSTUS CLIFFORD."

CONTENTS TO VOLUME I.

BOOK I.

BOOK II.

BOOK III.

APPENDIX.

LIFE OF HENRY JOHN TEMPLE,

THIRD VISCOUNT PALMERSTON, K.G., G.C.B.

BOOK I.

Character—Career—Landmarks in it—Parentage, birth, boyhood —Italy and Harrow—Letter from and to young Hare—Future life shadowed out in boyhood—Goes to Scotland and Cambridge —Stands for Cambridge University—Defeated, and comes into Parliament for Horsham; but is unseated—Becomes Junior Lord of the Admiralty—Stands again for Cambridge—Again defeated; but is returned for Newtown—Journal from 1806 to the Duke of Portland's Administration.

I HAVE undertaken to write the biography of a great statesman, under whom I long served, and for whom I had a sincere and respectful affection. I shall endeavor to perform this not ungrateful task with simplicity and impartiality, feeling certain that the more simply and impartially I can make known the character of Lord Palmerston, the more likely I am to secure for his memory the admiration and esteem of his countrymen.

The most distinguishing quality of the eminent Englishman whom I am thus about to describe was a nature that opened itself happily to the tastes, feelings, and habits of various classes and kinds of men. Hence a comprehensive sympathy, which not only put his actions in spontaneous harmony with the sense and feeling of the public, but, by presenting life before his mind in many aspects, widened his views and moderated his impressions, and led him away from those subtleties and eccentricities which solitude or living constantly in any limited society is apt to generate.

In the march of his epoch he was behind the eager, but before the slow. Accustomed to a large range of observation over contemporaneous events, he had been led by history to the conclusion that all eras have their peculiar tendencies, which a calm judgment and an enlightened statesmanship should distinctly recognize, but not prematurely adopt or extravagantly indulge. He did not believe in the absolute wisdom which some see in the past, which others expect from the future; but he preferred the hopes of the generation that was coming on to the despair of the generation that was passing away. Thus throughout a long political life there was nothing violent or abrupt, nothing that had the appearance of going backwards and forwards, or forwards and backwards. His career went on in one direction gradually but continuously from its commencement to its close, under the impulse of a motive power formed from the collection of various influences—the one modifying the other—and not representing in the aggregate the decided opinion of any particular party or class, but approximating to the opinion of the English nation in general. Into the peculiar and individual position which in this manner he by degrees acquired, he carried an earnest patriotism, a strong manly understanding, many accomplishments derived from industry and a sound early education, and a remarkable talent for concentrating details. This last, indeed, was his peculiar merit as a man of business, and wherein he showed a masterly capacity. No official situation, therefore, found him unequal to it; whilst it is still more remarkable that he never aspired to any situation prematurely. Ambitious, he was devoid of vanity; and with a singular absence of effort or pretension, found his foot at last on the topmost rail of the ladder he had been long unostentatiously mounting.

Born	20 Oct., 1784
Succeeded his father	17 April, 1802
M.A., Cambridge	27 Jan., 1806
Lord of the Admiralty	3 April, 1807—Oct , 1809
Secretary at War	28 Oct., 1809—26 May, 1828
Secretary for Foreign Affairs	22 Nov., 1830—15 Nov., 1834 18 April, 1835—31 Aug , 1841 3 July, 1846—22 Dec , 1851
Home Secretary	28 Dec , 1852—30 Jan., 1855
Prime Minister	20 Feb , 1855—20 Feb., 1858 30 June, 1859—18 Oct., 1865

Such were the ascending steps of a prosperous life, toward the end of which, fortune constantly accompanying him, the hero of this memoir reached the summit of public distinction.

It must be admitted, however, that he engaged in public affairs with advantages which are great at all times and in every country, but which were especially great in England during what may now be called "the old régime." He was of a good family, with a well-known name, and a fair fortune.

The Temples were gentlemen in the reign of Henry VIII. A Sir William Temple was the secretary of Sir Philip Sidney, and afterward of the unfortunate Earl of Essex. He seems to have been a man of letters, with the chivalric temperament that characterized his age. His son Sir John held posts of confidence and authority in Ireland, and Sir John's son was the celebrated diplomatist who had William III. for his friend, and Swift for his dependent. Lord Palmerston descended directly from a younger brother of the great diplomatist, this brother rising to be Attorney-General and Speaker of the Irish House of Commons. His son Henry, created a Peer of Ireland (March 12, 1722), was for several years a member of the English Parliament, sitting successively for East Grimstead, Bossiney, and Weobley. The heir to his title died young, but left issue, and thus the second viscount was grandson to the first. He was known as an accomplished and fashionable gentleman, a lover and appreciator of art, which made him, no doubt, an admirer of beauty. Of this he gave a proof in his second marriage* to a Miss Mee, the sister of a director of the Bank of England, and who is said to have been the daughter of a respectable Dublin tradesman, into whose house, in consequence of a fall from his horse, the peer had been carried. Our late Prime Minister was the son of this nobleman and of Miss Mee, who, though not of aristocratic birth, appears from all accounts to have been not only handsome, but accomplished and agreeable, and to have taken in a becoming manner the position in Dublin and London society which her marriage opened to her. Her husband's artistic tastes led him at various times into Italy; and it was thus that a portion of the future minister's boyhood was passed in that country, in the fate of which he always took an interest. He formed at this time an intimate acquaintance with a lad of the name of Hare, who became in after-years one of the best-known and most accomplished gentlemen of his time; and I happen to have a curious letter from young Francis Hare to young Harry Temple, then at Harrow, and a letter from Harry Temple in reply:

---

* His first wife, whom he married Oct. 6, 1767, was Frances, only daughter of Sir Francis Poole. She died June 1, 1769, without leaving issue.

Francis Hare* to Harry Temple, vale.

"BOLOGNA, Jan. 5, 1798.

"I hope, dear Harry, that you continue always well, and that you profit much at school, both in Greek and Latin. I make you this wish, as I think it the very best that a true friend can make, and I think I ought to believe that you place me in this number.

---

* Hare was the eldest of four brothers (Francis, Augustus, Julius, and Marcus), of whom Augustus and the Archdeacon—Julius—authors of the "Guesses at Truth," became the best known publicly, though all were remarkably accomplished, and held in high esteem by the scholars and poets of their time. In Mr. Forster's "Life of Walter Savage Landor," several notices occur of Harry Temple's correspondent Francis, who met Landor at Tours in 1815, and during their joint residence in Italy became his most intimate friend. When Hare first went to Christ Church, Cyril Jackson referred to him as the only rolling stone he had ever known which was always gathering moss; and Landor, of whom the same might with equal truth have been said, told Mr. Forster that from Hare's society he had derived the animation and excitement that had helped him most in the composition of his "Imaginary Conversations." Excepting a few remarks (signed F.) in the "Guesses at Truth," Francis Hare published nothing; but so accurate and extensive were his classical attainments that his brother Julius, a most distinguished scholar, told Mr. Maurice he owed as much to him as to any of his instructors. "I remember our Consul-General at Rome," writes Mr. Seymour Kirkup, "calling him a monster of learning." And Landor, in introducing him in 1827 to Southey and Wordsworth, dwells even less on his prodigious scholarship than on "his wit and the inexhaustible spirit and variety of his conversation." In April, 1828, he married Anne, eldest daughter of Sir John Dean Paul, and had with her £20,000. He died in Sicily in 1840, and there is an allusion to him in a poem by Landor as one—

. . . . "Who held mute the joyous and the wise
With wit and eloquence; whose tomb, afar
From all his friends and all his countrymen,
Saddens the light Palermo."

"I hope you take no part in those vices which are common to a public school, such as I suppose Harrow, as swearing and getting drunk; but I imagine the son of a gentleman so well taught cannot partake in things like these.

"Pray give a kiss to each of your two amiable sisters, but particularly to Fanny, and tell her to write me a letter whenever you answer mine. I still persist in my opinion of never marrying, and I suppose you think the same, as you must have read as well as myself of the many faults and vices of women.

"Perhaps I at Bologna may have learnt more Greek than you, and that you at Harrow may know best how to fight with your fist; however, if you challenge me I shall not hesitate to accept, for I remember I am an English boy, and will behave like a brave one. Pray salute for me Willie Ponsonby, whom you and I knew in Italy. Billy desires not to be forgotten by you. I have no more time for writing, so shall only add that I shall wait for your answer with impatience. I protest myself, with all my heart, your most affectionate friend,

"FRANCIS GEORGE HARE."

"HARROW, March 29, 1798.

"DEAR HARE,—

"I am just recovered from the measles, which, however, I have had very slightly, and am now very well. I am sincerely obliged to you for your kind wish, and trust that I make as much progress as boys in my situation at school generally do. I have begun Homer's Iliad, which I did in that beautiful episode, in the 5th* book I think, in which Andromache takes leave of Hector, when returning from

* Really 6th book, line 116.

the war to Troy, to order a general supplication to Minerva, at this line,

Ὣς ἄρα φωνήσας ἀπέβη κορυθαίολος Ἕκτωρ.

I suppose, however, that you have made considerable progress in your learning, more than is perhaps in my power, we having tasks regularly allotted for each day, as long as we stay in each form or class. I am now doing Cæsar, Terence, Ovid, Homer, Greek Testament, and a collection of Greek epigrams, and after the Easter holidays, which are now drawing near, I shall begin Virgil, Horace, and some more. I am perfectly of *your* opinion concerning drinking and swearing, which, though fashionable at present, I think extremely ungentlemanlike ; as for getting drunk, I can find no pleasure in it. I am glad to see that though educated in Italy you have not forgot old England. Your letter brings to my mind the pleasant time I spent in Italy, and makes me wish to revisit the country I am now reading so much about ; and when I am sucking a sour orange, purchased by perhaps eight biochi, I think with regret upon those which I used to get in such plenty in Italy ; and when eating nasty things nicknamed sausages, envy you at Bologna, who perhaps now are feasting off some nice ones. I have begun to learn Spanish, and have also begun to read Don Quixote in the original, which I can assure you gave me no small pleasure. Mr. Gaetano, if you remember him, desires to be remembered to you. I can assure you I have by no means left off my Italian, but keep it up every holidays with Mr. Gaetano, who has published a new Italian grammar, which has been very much approved of here in England. I cannot agree with you about marriage, though I *should be by no means precipitate about my choice.** Willy is come to Harrow, and sends

* This intention was literally carried out.

his love to you. I send you no news, as I know none. Adieu!

"Believe me ever your affectionate friend,

"HENRY TEMPLE."

It is amusing to find two boys, then about thirteen years old, discussing the question of marriage, on which Lord Palmerston does not like to compromise himself. He declares, however, stoutly against drinking and swearing—vices which he acknowledges to be *fashionable*, but condemns as *ungentlemanlike.* The distinction is not unimportant; for boys who do not think for themselves, fancy that to be fashionable is to be gentlemanlike.

We are glad to go back to the early years of those who in maturer age became eminent, and mark how much of the man was in the boy. A youth, whose English is far from perfect, admiring a beautiful passage in Homer, keeping up his Italian in an English school, feeling a greater interest in Latin literature from his recollection of the spots to which it frequently refers, voluntarily learning Spanish, stating that he had not made up his mind about wedlock, but that he regretted Italian oranges and Bologna sausages, ripened naturally into a man who would turn his attention to foreign affairs, admire the classic oratory of Canning, prove industrious in office, speak a good deal without compromising himself, keep race-horses, have a good appetite, and be generally at once what is so charming and so rare — gay and thoughtful, manly and refined.

The Harrovian did not on quitting the school so celebrated for producing statesmen move on directly to an English university. It was the fashion of the time for young men to take the University of Edinburgh as an intermediate preparation for that of Cambridge or Oxford; for Scotland at that period had acquired a reputation both in philosophy and history which she never previously possessed, and has not since fully maintained. This preeminence may be accounted for by the writings of Hume, Robertson, Dugald Stewart, and Adam Smith; and also by the variety of distinguished scholars who had been formed by such men as these, or by their works. Brougham, Horner, Jeffrey, Henry Petty (afterward Lord Lansdowne), had preceded Henry Temple; Lord John Russell and William Lamb (Lord Melbourne) were his successors.

The lectures that principally attracted attention were Dugald Stewart's on political economy and moral philosophy; and to these studies, than which none are better calculated to be the foundation of a statesman's education, it would seem that Mr. Temple especially applied himself. The notes which he made form, indeed, the principal part of the text which is now given as "Dugald Stewart's Lectures on Economical Science;" for it appears that the lectures in question were in a great measure *extempore;* and when Sir William Hamilton undertook to publish them he was obliged to consult the memoranda of the pupils by whom they had been attended, and he found none so complete as those taken originally in short-hand, and subsequently copied out, by Henry Temple, who, speaking of this time,* says, "I lived with Dugald Stewart, and attended his lectures at the University. In these three years I laid the foundation of whatever useful knowledge and habits of mind I possess."

It should be added, that if the scholar so highly es-

* Autobiography.—I had better mention here that this autobiographical sketch, as it was placed in my hands, will be found entire in the Appendix to this volume, but, to make a continuous narrative, I have inserted it in parts where the passages apply. This autobiographical sketch is entirely different from the Journal, which I also quote.

teemed the advantages he owed to his professor, the following letter will show that the professor entertained a high opinion of his scholar:

Extract from a letter of Professor Dugald Stewart to Mr. Blane, dated Edinburgh, April 27, 1801.

"With regard to Mr. Temple, it is sufficient for me to say that he has constantly confirmed all the favorable impressions of him which I received from your letter. His talents are uncommonly good, and he does them all possible justice by assiduous application.

"In point of temper and conduct he is everything his friends could wish. Indeed, I cannot say that I have ever seen a more faultless character at his time of life, or one possessed of more amiable dispositions."

In 1803 the student from Edinburgh went to St. John's, Cambridge. He says:*

"I had gone further at Edinburgh in all the branches of study pursued at Cambridge than the course then followed at that university extended during the two first years of attendance. But the Edinburgh system consisted in lectures without examination; at Cambridge there was a half-yearly examination. It became necessary to learn more accurately at Cambridge what one had learned generally at Edinburgh. The knowledge thus acquired of details at Cambridge was worth nothing, because it evaporated soon after the examinations were over. The habit of mind acquired by preparing for these examinations was highly useful.

"Dr. Outram, my private tutor at Cambridge, more than once observed to me that, as I had always been in

* Autobiography.

the first class at college examinations, and had been commended for the general regularity of my conduct, it would not be amiss to turn my thoughts to standing for the University whenever a vacancy might happen.

"My father had died in April, 1802, and I lost my mother in January, 1805.* The last misfortune delayed

---

* Henry Temple, now become Lord Palmerston, thus expresses himself as to this great loss:

"BROADLANDS, Jan. 31, 1805.

"MY DEAR SULIVAN,—

"You will, I am sure, not attribute to any other than the real motive my not having before this answered your very affectionate letter. The kindness and sympathy of friends afford indeed one of the few alleviations of which such afflictions as ours are susceptible, and I am confident none feel more than you do. Consolation is impossible; there are losses which nothing can repair; and griefs which time may fix and mellow, but never can obliterate. After the example, however, of fortitude and resignation set us by a being who was the model of every human excellence, it would be criminal in us not to imitate the resignation as well as every other perfection of her character.

"She was conscious, it is true, that she was but passing to that happiness which her virtues had secured her; and beheld with calmness and composure an event which, to the generality of mankind, comes clad with all the terrors of doubt. It will, I am sure, give you satisfaction to hear that my sisters are as well as after such a loss could be expected. William comes to-morrow. My uncle is gone to London to meet and bring him down here. Adieu. Pray remember me to Mr. and Mrs. Sulivan, and believe me ever yours affectionately,

"PALMERSTON."

Lord and Lady Palmerston left, in addition to the subject of this biography, one son, Sir William Temple, K.C.B., who died August 24, 1856, H.M.'s minister at Naples, and two daughters, Fanny and Elizabeth, the latter of whom married, December 6, 1811, Lord Palmerston's college friend, Mr. Sulivan, to whom the letter I have just quoted was addressed, and the former, August 9, 1820, Captain, afterward Admiral, Sir William Bowles.

a few months the taking of my degree as master of arts, which it was usual at that time for noblemen to take as an honor, conferred without examination, at the end of two years after admission.

"In January, 1806, Mr. Pitt died, and the University had to choose a new member, as well as the king a new minister.

"I was just of age, and had not yet taken my degree, nevertheless I was advised by my friends at St. John's to stand: the other candidates were Lord Althorp and Lord Henry Petty. I was supported by my own college, and by the exertions of the friends of my family; but the Pitt party in the University was broken up. Most men thought that the new government would for many years have the disposal of the patronage as well as the command of the power of the country; and I stood at the poll where a young man circumstanced as I was could alone expect to stand; that is to say, last:

*Petty...331
†Althorp..145
Palmerston 128

"It was an honor, however, to have been supported at all, and I was well satisfied with my fight."

Lord Palmerston (whom I henceforth designate by the title he had inherited) was no doubt right; to have stood for one of our great universities, before he had even taken his degree at it, with any chance of success, took a young

* Afterward Lord Lansdowne. He had just been appointed Chancellor of the Exchequer.

† Then a Junior Lord of the Treasury; well known as leader of the House of Commons and Chancellor of the Exchequer from 1830 to 1834, when he became, on the death of his father, Earl Spencer.

man at once out of the crowd of young men and brought him individually into notice.

Neither did his success as a candidate seem at one time improbable, if we may judge of his prospects by a letter written during the election, which seems pretty well charged with the electricity of youth and hope:

"ST. JOHN'S, Jan. 28, 1806.

"MY DEAR SULIVAN,—

"Things go on very well, thanks to you, Shee, and the Malmesburys. This morning's accounts from town were excellent; here we advance too, I think. Mansel* has promised not to oppose me. Pearce, Sumner, Milner, Turner are for me, and, I hope, the masters of Emanuel and Catherine Hall. I am very glad to hear Lord Spencer declares Althorp shall not yield to Petty. '*Divide et impera*' is true and applicable. The Duke of Rutland stands for the high stewardship against Lord Hardwicke;† and unless Charles Yorke comes forward in our support, St. John's will not support Lord Hardwicke, in which case the duke will certainly carry his point. If you know any of the Yorke faction, mention that I have written to

* Dr. Mansel was Master of Trinity, afterward Bishop of Bristol; Dr. Pearce, Master of Jesus, Master of the Temple, and Dean of Ely; Dr. Sumner, Provost of King's; Dr. Milner, President of Queen's and Dean of Carlisle; Dr. Turner, Master of Pembroke and Dean of Norwich, and also Vice-Chancellor that year.

† Not unjustly described in Cobbett's "Political Register," when Lord-Lieutenant of Ireland, as "a gentleman chiefly distinguished for his good library in St. James's Square, and understanding the fattening of sheep as well as any man in Cambridgeshire" Nevertheless, he beat the Duke of Rutland in the contest for the high stewardship of the university, and retained it till his death in 1834.

Charles Yorke,* and given him a broad hint about it. Wood has spoken decisively to some of his friends here. I wrote in the same strain the other day to the Bishop of Ely† (of course, very civil), but hitherto he has not taken the hint. The duke's declaration this morning, however, will bring things to a crisis. It is, on the whole, a good thing for me. The small colleges cannot but look with jealousy upon Trinity, when they see it start candidates for every honor in the gift of the university: the representation, the high stewardship, and the Duke of Gloucester for the chancellorship. Little Gill and I are as thick as three in a bed, and he talks of the great civilities experienced from his particular friend Lord Grantham.‡

"I am glad I know Petty and Althorp, as, since we run foul of each other perpetually, it would otherwise be awkward. I took my degree yesterday, and got a very short buttering. Outram was taken quite unawares, and did not expect to be called upon till to-day or to-morrow, as the Vice-Chancellor thought no other business could be done the day the king's answer was read. I heard that Percy§ was expected this week; I hope he may come, if he intends to be of use to me, of which I have no doubt, if the old Boy will let him.

"Pray thank Knox for his friendly communications.

---

* The Right Hon. Charles Yorke, half-brother of Lord Hardwicke, was afterward one of the Tellers of the Exchequer, and First Lord of the Admiralty from June 23, 1810, to March, 1812.

† The Hon. James Yorke, uncle of Lord Hardwicke, and of Charles Yorke.

‡ Cousin to Lord Hardwicke. He was afterward Earl De Grey.

§ Afterward third Duke of Northumberland, K.G., Ambassador Extraordinary in 1825 at the coronation of Charles X., King of France, and Chancellor of the University of Cambridge from 1840 till his death in 1847.

The election will probably come on this day week. I own I *entertain strong hopes of success*, if my two rivals do not coalesce, and even then do not despair. At any rate, whatever be the event, I shall consider my having stood as one of the most fortunate circumstances of my life, it having procured me such gratifying proofs of the warmth of my friends' attachment to me. Adieu! my dear Sulivan. I wrote to Shee* last night, but that with several other letters were, unluckily, too late for the confoundedly precise Cerberus of a fellow who guards the post-office.

"Ever yours affectionately,

"PALMERSTON."

"In November, 1806," continuing from the manuscript sketch just quoted,† Lord Palmerston says, "Parliament having been dissolved, a general election took place. Lord Fitz-Harris‡ and I stood for Horsham The borough was burgage-tenure, and the right of voting disputed.

"There was a double return; each party petitioned, and the committee seated our opponents.

"Fitz-Harris and I paid each about £1500 for the pleasure of sitting under the gallery for a week in our

* Sir George Shee, second baronet, was born June 14, 1784 (a few months before Lord Palmerston). He was the son of Sir George Shee, who filled successively the offices of Surveyor-General of the Ordnance, Secretary of the Treasury, and Receiver-General in Ireland, and Under-Secretary of State in England. The son was Under-Secretary of State for Foreign Affairs from 1830 to 1834, and was appointed in 1834 Minister at Berlin, and in 1841 was transferred to Stuttgart, where he remained till 1844. He died in London January 25. 1870.

† Autobiography.

‡ Afterward second Earl of Malmesbury, father of the present peer. He was Under-Secretary of State for Foreign Affairs for a few months in 1807.

capacity of petitioners. We thought ourselves very unlucky; but in a short time came the change of government and the dissolution in May, 1807, and we then rejoiced in our good fortune at not having paid £5000 (which would have been its price) for a three months' seat.

"I was at Broadlands at Easter, 1807, when, on the 1st April, I received a letter from Lord Malmesbury, desiring me to come up to town immediately, as he had found me a seat, if not in Parliament, at least at the Admiralty.

"The Duke of Portland* had been appointed First Lord of the Treasury. He was an old and intimate friend of Lord Malmesbury, who had been one of my guardians, Lord Chichester† being the other; and he had obtained from the duke that I should be one of the Junior Lords of the Admiralty."‡

Shortly after this we see young Palmerston standing again for Cambridge.

---

* He had already been Prime Minister, in 1783, of the administration which combined Fox and Lord North, and Lord-Lieutenant of Ireland in 1782. He died in 1809.

† Lord Chichester, as Mr. Pelham, had for many years been M.P. for Sussex. In 1788 he was secretary to Lord Northington, and in 1795 to Lord Camden, when they filled the office of Lord-Lieutenant of Ireland. He was Secretary of State for the Home Department from July 30, 1801, to July 17, 1803, and in 1807 Postmaster-General. His birth took place in 1756, and he died July 4, 1826. He was the father of the present earl.

‡ Lord Palmerston's father, who had represented East Looe, Hastings, Boroughbridge, and Winchester in the House of Commons, had occupied a similar post in the Duke of Grafton's administration in 1766.

"When Parliament was dissolved I stood again for Cambridge, and, having entered the lists when nothing perhaps could be reasonably expected but an honorable defeat, I had established a kind of right to support from the government and its friends in preference to any other ministerial candidate.

"It was, however, considered that one candidate against two would have no chance; and Sir Vicary Gibbs was sent down to assist me against Lord Euston* and Lord Henry Petty. But I soon found that my colleague was as dangerous as my opponents, and that every supporter of the government who had but one vote to give was requested to give it to Gibbs.†

---

* Afterward fourth Duke of Grafton, K.G., and grandfather of the present duke. His father was Chancellor of the University at the time.

† Attorney-General, and successively a Puisne Judge of the Court of Common Pleas (June, 1812), Lord Chief Baron (November, 1813), and Lord Chief Justice of the Common Pleas (April, 1817). He resigned November, 1818, and died February 9, 1820, aged 68. "Endowed by Nature with acuteness and an unlimited power of application, he became, to use his own somewhat unseemly expression toward as considerable a man as himself, and a far more amiable one (Mr. Justice Bayley), 'as good a lawyer as that kind of man can be.' Disciplined by an excellent classical education, the fruits of which stuck by him to the last, and somewhat acquainted with the favorite pursuits of Cambridge men, his taste was always correct, and his reasoning powers were as considerable as they ever can be in a mind of his narrow range. . . . In the House of Commons he really had no place at all; and, feeling his nullity, there was no place to which he was with more visible reluctance dragged by the power that office gives the government over its lawyers. He could only obtain a hearing upon legal questions, and those he handled not with such felicity or force as repaid the attention of the listener. He seldom attempted more than to go through the references from one act of Parliament to

"Our committees canvassed separately, and there was no coalition. The night, however, before the polling began, Gibbs and myself and the chairmen of our committees met to go over our returns. It appeared doubtful from the books who was the strongest, and there was no sufficient evidence to show who ought to give up in order to bring in the other; for Lord Euston was known to be stronger than either, and the only question was whether one of us could beat Lord Henry Petty. We therefore agreed to combine, and that each should give to the other the second votes of all his disposable plumpers.

"Toward the end of the polling Sir Vicary Gibbs came up to me in the Senate House, and said that my friends were not acting up to my agreement, and were going to plump for me. I said I would immediately see that this was not done, and went and placed myself at the bar through which the voters went up to poll, that I might beg each man as he went by to vote for Gibbs as well as for me.

"Dr. Outram,* my tutor, was standing there. He urged me to let my friends do as they chose. That they wanted to bring me in, and not Gibbs. That the votes had been counted by people in the galleries posted for that purpose. That Euston was far ahead, and Gibbs was running me hard. That my committee and a few more stanch friends had reserved their votes, and if they plumped for me I should certainly come in, but that if they split their votes

---

another; and though he was doing only a mechanical work, he gave out each sentence as if he had been gifted and consulted like an oracle, and looked and spoke as if when citing a section he was making a discovery."—*Statesmen of the Time of George III.* By Lord Brougham.

* Public Orator; afterward Canon of Lichfield and Archdeacon of Derby.

I should be thrown out. That they were no parties to the agreement of the night before, and were not to be bound by it.

"I said this would not do. I was bound in honor. Gibbs's friends had, I believed, given me their second votes; but be that as it might, and be the result what it might, I must insist, if they had the slightest regard for me, on their giving—every man of them—a second vote to Gibbs.

"They consented, though with much ill humor and grumbling; and Gibbs beat me by four votes.

"It turned out that I had no reason to complain of want of good faith, as Gibbs, after all, had only seven plumpers whilst I had twelve."

The following letter relates to the same circumstances that Lord Palmerston has just been recounting. Both illustrate his simple, straightforward way of looking at right and wrong, and display a character which was of more advantage to him on commencing life than a mere seat in Parliament.

"CAMBRIDGE, May 8, 1807.
"12 o'clock Friday night.

"MY DEAR SULIVAN,—

"We are beat by four votes.

Euston	324
Gibbs	313
Palmerston	310
Petty	265

"It is provoking to think that four men wished me in the Senate House to let them give me plumpers instead of giving their second votes to Gibbs. I did not conceive myself at liberty to recede from the agreement I had made, particularly as Gibbs had honorably adhered to it; and these four votes turned the scale. However, I did not certainly expect so large a number of supporters, and possibly at some future time I may meet with better success. The poll continued open till ten o'clock, and the votes have only just been declared. I mean to remain here two days longer, just to thank my voters, and shall then return to town. Adieu! many, many thanks for your kindness and labors.

"Believe me ever yours affectionately,

"PALMERSTON."

"Soon after this" (I quote again the autobiography) "I came into Parliament for Newtown in the Isle of Wight, a borough of Sir Leonard Holmes'. One condition required was, that I would never, even for the election, set foot in the place. So jealous was the patron lest any attempt should be made to get a new interest in the borough."

Lord Palmerston was thus at last in that great council wherein he sat so long, and played eventually so conspicuous a part. Nor was he altogether untrained for the career he entered upon, as may be proved by some extracts from a journal that he commenced in June, 1806, and carried on till the formation of the Portland ministry,—when he seems for a time to have abandoned it.

His observations in this journal on the policy of Napoleon, who, he says, instead of concealing his projects in order to take his enemies by surprise, published them purposely beforehand, in order that the world, being accustomed to expect them, might not be shocked when he executed them, are shrewd and profound; his description of the Prussian campaign, memorable for the defeat at

Jena, is well and graphically written. His remarks on the death of Fox are, for one who was so ardent an admirer of Fox's great rival, liberal and impartial; his accounts of the different election contests are interesting, as describing the parliamentary manners of the times; and his review of the conduct of the Whigs in the quarrel with George III., which ended by their dismissal,—though evidently that of a Tory partisan,—is an able and considerate statement for so young and decided an opponent.

EXTRACTS FROM JOURNAL.*

1806.

June 29.

ON the 12th of June, Lord Melville's trial in Westminster Hall was brought to a conclusion. The proceedings in the Hall had lasted fifteen days, after which the Lords had discussed the evidence for eight or ten with their doors shut. In the course of these discussions two questions were submitted to the judges, which were very material in influencing the ultimate decision of the Lords.

The first question was, whether, subsequent to the Act by which the office of Treasurer of the Navy was regulated, it was legal for the Treasurer to take money from the Bank and vest it in the hands of a private banker, provided that such money was drawn *bona fide* for naval purposes.

The judges were unanimously of opinion that there was no provision in the Act forbidding such a transfer of the public money.

The second question was, whether, previous to the passing of the above-mentioned Act, but subsequent to the issuing of the warrant by which the salary of the Treasurer of the Navy was increased upon condition of his not making

---

* *Note to this Journal by Lord Palmerston.*—The opinions and remarks contained in this volume are the exact expressions of my feelings at the moment when they were written. Upon many points, however, relative both to persons and things, cooler reflection, and a few more years' observation and experience, have, as is natural, very much altered my sentiments.—P., April 15, 1812.

use of the public money, his having made use of that money would subject him to a criminal or to a civil prosecution. Upon this the judges also unanimously declared that such an act would render the Treasurer liable to a civil prosecution only.

These two decisions led the public to expect the acquittal, which was pronounced by a large majority of the Lords on the 12th. The question of "Guilty or Not Guilty" was put by the Chancellor to each Lord in succession upon each article separately. But had it been put upon the whole case collectively, Lord Melville would still have been acquitted, as out of 135 who attended the trial, 57 acquitted him on every article. The Scotch evinced their joy upon this occasion by general illuminations.

July 9.

Fox's illness, which has for some time confined him, has within these few days assumed a more alarming appearance, and is supposed to be a decided dropsy; his legs were, a day or two since, scarified and much water taken from them.

The king's health is extremely good. He walks as firmly as anybody at his age (68) could be expected to do, and scarcely avails himself, when on the terrace, of the assistance of a stick which he holds in his hand. His eyes, however, are scarcely of the smallest use to him.

July 15.

Sir Henry Mildmay moved a vote of thanks to the volunteers, which was supported by Canning and Perceval; Sheridan, Windham, and Hiley Addington opposed it, and it was disposed of by "the previous question" being moved and carried. Sheridan then proposed a similar motion, which was seconded by Vansittart and opposed by Petty. This also was disposed of in the same way. Thus the same House of Commons which three years ago unanimously thanked the volunteers before they had done anything but manifest a readiness to step forward, now put the previous question upon a motion of thanks to them after they have, by their patriotic and unremitted exertions, contributed in the greatest degree to the preservation of their country; and this "previous question" is supported by Hiley Addington,* whose brother first set the volunteer system on foot!

Negotiations for peace appear to be going on with much activity. Messengers are continually passing backward and forward between Paris and London.

Fox is extremely anxious to conclude peace, having disapproved the war from its commencement; but how Lord Grenville can join in that wish is not easy to conceive.

Neither do the acts and language of Bonaparte bear a very pacific appearance. The establishment of Louis as King of Holland,† and a declaration implying that he will insist upon the restitution of the Dutch colonies, present some difficulties to any negotiation; but, indeed, if we are to have peace now it seems very immaterial what the terms may be, as any peace at present would be ruinous. To disband our forces and dismantle our navy would be, in the existing state of things, impossible, as no reliance could be placed on Bonaparte's pacific professions; and if a large military and naval establishment has to be kept up, *we should suffer all the expenses of a war without enjoying any of its advantages.*‡

---

* The Right Hon. John Hiley Addington, one of the Commissioners of the Board of Control, younger brother of Henry, first Viscount Sidmouth. He died June 11, 1818.

† On July 5, 1806.

‡ The correspondence of Napoleon, recently published, shows the justice of this argument, which at the time was not unreasonably disputed.

Fox has lately been better, and is said to be in no immediate danger; but such a complication of disorders as he now labors under cannot fail, at his time of life, to prove fatal.

LONDON, July 23.

Parliament was this day prorogued by commission. The speech was short, and contained little. It thanked both Houses for their zeal and attention to the public business; for their new military plans; their care for economy; and the regulation for auditing the public accounts; it then thanks the Commons for raising so large a portion of the supplies within the year, and promises frugality in the administration of them. It concludes by saying that "His Majesty, being always anxious for the restoration of peace on just and honorable terms, is engaged in discussions with a view to the accomplishment of this most desirable end."

The Parliament was prorogued till the 28th of August.

A change has taken place in the Russian Cabinet. Czartoryski* has resigned, and is succeeded by Count

* Prince Adam Czartoryski, descended from the Jagellons, was born in 1770, and educated in England. He fought against Russia in the war on the second partition of Poland in 1793, and on the defeat of the Poles was taken to St. Petersburg, where he was patronized by the emperor Paul, and became the friend and favorite of the emperor Alexander, who intrusted him for a time with the department of Foreign Affairs, which post he filled till the peace of Tilsit. The high places he had occupied in the Russian government had never alienated him from his own country, and in the Revolution of 1830 he suffered himself to be placed at the head of the national government; risking thereby his immense fortune and estates in Poland, which, after the suppression of the insurrection, were confiscated. He, however, escaped to Paris, where he died a few years ago at a very advanced age, devoted to

Budberg. The former was a favorite with the young empress. But a reconciliation having taken place between her and the emperor, the minister is dismissed, and a lady whom the emperor is said to have preferred sent to travel.

July 29.

A separate peace has been signed between France and Russia at Paris.*

Gaeta still continues to hold out under the Prince of Hesse, and Sir Sidney Smith has thrown some succors into the town, which have restored the spirits of the besieged. Joseph Bonaparte has taken possession of Naples and declared himself King of the Two Sicilies. He will not find the island so easy a conquest as the continent. Our force there amounts to near ten thousand men, and a reinforcement is now fitting out from Ramsgate.

Minto, August 2.

This day Lord Lauderdale left London for Paris, in order to carry on the negotiations which had been commenced between the two courts. Professor Stewart accompanied him; but it is not known whether he went in any official capacity, or merely as a private individual. The selection of Lord Lauderdale as a negotiator does not lead one to form any favorable conjectures as to the termination of the negotiations. A man who has professed such violent principles,† and has shown himself such an advocate for France,

---

the last to the cause of his country and the relief of the poor and exiled of his countrymen.

* On the 20th of July by M. d'Oubril, afterward disavowed by Russia.

† Thought at that time to be what we should now call a great radical, and even to have sympathized with the Irish rebels. He was an intimate friend of Mr. Fox. He died in 1839, in his eighty-first year.

cannot be supposed to be very hearty in the cause he has undertaken, or likely very strenuously to uphold the honor and interests of his country; and though, probably, but little would be left to his discretion, yet the anxiety displayed by ministers to send a man who should be the most agreeable to Bonaparte and Talleyrand indicates a spirit of concession not very consonant with the dignity of the country they govern.*

EDINBURGH, August 21.

Nearly three weeks have elapsed since Lord Lauderdale set out for Paris, during which nothing has transpired respecting the object of his mission. On the whole, however, the aspect of affairs grows more warlike.

August 26.

It is a singular circumstance in Bonaparte's political conduct that, so far from concealing his designs, he purposely publishes even the most violent of his projected innovations some time before they are put in execution; and the consequence has uniformly been, that, instead of being alarmed and prepared to resist, the world has, by anticipating conquests and changes, become by degrees reconciled to them, and submitted almost without a murmur to the mandates of the tyrant. It is thus that for some years he has thrown out hints of some grand confederated European system of which he is to be the head, and of which the hitherto independent states around him are to be the subordinate members. At length his plans have been more boldly exhibited, and, by a sort of manifesto

* *Subsequent Note by Lord Palmerston.*—Lord Lauderdale's judicious and spirited conduct during his embassy fully justified the appointment. But so far from his being agreeable to Bonaparte, the latter is said to have asked, when Lord L. was named to him, "Pourquoi m'envoie-t-on ce Lor Jacobin? Croit-on que j'aime les Jacobins?" (April, 1812.)

lately issued from the Cabinet of St. Cloud, the whole German Constitution is declared to be dissolved, and a union, called the "Rhenish Confederacy," is established,* of which France is the protector. The Constitution is digested into about thirty articles, enumerating the states which are included,—namely, France, Bavaria, Wirtemberg, Baden, etc.; inviting others to join, and instituting an alliance offensive and defensive among all the members of the league, settling the quotas of troops to be furnished by each of the parties, and providing, among other arrangements, that if any neighboring state or states shall arm, the Confederacy shall do the same as a matter of precaution.

The election of Cardinal Fesch as Arch-Chancellor of the Empire gave rise to a remonstrance on the part of the Emperor of Austria, to which Bonaparte has since replied —that as there now exists no empire there can be no cause or pretext for complaint. The emperor was, indeed, immediately upon the formation of the Rhenish Confederacy, required to resign his crown, with which demand he has without hesitation complied; and in a public instrument published at Vienna the 7th of this month, he declares the German Constitution dissolved, and renounces a title which, he says, the present state of Europe renders useless. Thus has that confederacy of states, which has for ages occupied the attention of statesmen, been annihilated by the decree of a man who, little more than ten years ago, might have considered it as the summit of his ambition to equal in power the smallest of its independent princes.

Gaeta, after an obstinate resistance, has been obliged to capitulate.† The Prince of Hesse was wounded by a cannon-ball while inspecting the breach, and his absence

---

* July 12, 1806.

† July 12, 1806.

was soon followed by a capitulation. The Calabrians still continue to hold out against King Joseph.

Fox has been tapped, and has, of course, received immediate relief from the operation; but the dropsy is an incurable complaint, and he will, probably, not survive another year.

Sept. 10.

The Emperor of Russia has refused to ratify the treaty signed at Paris by D'Oubril.* It was submitted to his council for discussion, and, after much deliberation, rejected.† The terms were reported to be so disgraceful to Russia that a ratification would have been submission to France.

Sir John Stuart has gained a splendid victory, near Maida, on the plain of St. Euphemia, in Calabria. He landed at the town of that name with four thousand men. Regnier, who commanded in that district, fell back in order to concentrate his forces, and was posted with seven thousand men at Maida. Sir J. Stuart advanced to attack him, and, after an obstinate engagement, totally routed him. The French fled in all directions, leaving a thousand dead on the field. Those who were taken in the battle, and picked up among the woods and mountains afterward, amounted to three thousand; the last accounts which came away from Messina state that on the 25th Regnier was at Colrone, surrounded by the Calabrian levy in mass, and that by the assistance of the English he would probably be obliged to surrender. The Calabrians appear to have harassed the French excessively, and to be actuated by

* D'Oubril, though deprived of his post and left out of employment, was not disgraced, and doubts have been entertained as to whether he had really exceeded his instructions, or as to whether it was deemed advisable to say he had done so.

† It has been alluded to before as a fact accomplished.

the most violent detestation of their new masters. The above-mentioned victory was gained entirely by the undaunted bravery of the British troops. Two corps of equal force were opposed to each other at the distance of a hundred yards; after a few rounds had been fired, they, as it were, by mutual agreement ceased firing, and advanced to the charge. When, however, their bayonets were just crossing, the French were panic-struck, and fled with precipitation, but too late to prevent their entire annihilation. This decided the fate of the day; our loss was trifling.*

Walcot Park, Sept. 16.

On Saturday last, Sept 13, Mr. Fox expired. He had been tapped three times. His last moments were free from pain, and he retained his faculties till a very short time before his death. He had transacted business three days previous to this event with as much coolness as if he had been in perfect health. It is singular that the two great rival statesmen should have died in the same year; that the one should have obtained that high station to which he aspired only by the death of the other, and have found in the attainment of this object of his wishes the cause which accelerated his own demise. Had Fox lived in times less troublesome than those in which he was thrown—or had he not been opposed to such a rival as

---

* *Note by Lord Palmerston.*—January, 1807.—This victory was not followed by any of the important consequences which we were led to anticipate. Sir John Stuart re-embarked and retired to Sicily, where he was soon after superseded by General Fox. Had our force in Sicily been as numerous as it ought, there is no doubt but that after the affair at Maida we might have expelled the new King of Naples. But the pending negotiations seemed to have completely paralyzed all the energies of ministers, as they sent out no forces anywhere until Lord Lauderdale's return.

Pitt—he would, undoubtedly, have been ranked not only among those statesmen the brilliancy of whose genius has reflected honor upon the country that produced them, but among those illustrious patriots whose names, consecrated by the applause of a grateful people, are held up to the admiration of posterity as fathers of their country and benefactors of the human race. He set out in life by being the supporter of the royal prerogative, and took part with the Crown against Wilkes. But, being thrown into opposition by Pitt, he quitted a line in which he saw his rival would eclipse him, and became a strenuous advocate for the rights of the popular part of our constitution. In this course the ardor of his temper carried him further than prudence could justify; and, as it generally happens in controversies, he frequently in the violence of debate supported doctrines which, perhaps, his cooler reflection would have led him to disavow. With this impetuosity of temper, it is less to be wondered at than regretted that, in the general delirium produced by the French Revolution, he should have been infected with the disorder, and have connected himself with the most frantic of the reformers. It was well remarked in one of the papers of the day, that there scarcely ever lived a statesman *for whom as an individual the people felt more affection, or in whom as a politician they placed less confidence.*

PARK PLACE, Oct. 5.

Sir Samuel Hood, with two seventy-fours and a sixty-four, the "Mars," fell in,* off Rochefort, with a French squadron, consisting of five frigates and a sloop. The French, it is supposed, mistook our men-of-war for Indiamen, as they allowed themselves to be overtaken. As

* September 25.

soon as our headmost ship came up, a severe engagement took place, which terminated in the capture of four of the frigates. The other having escaped, in company with the sloop, one of our men-of-war was detached in pursuit. The loss on our side was nine killed and thirty-two wounded. That of the enemy must have been great, as they had on board two thousand land troops, destined, it is supposed, for the West Indies. Another French frigate was taken at the same time by another squadron. They are all fine ships of the first class. Sir Samuel Hood was the only officer wounded. His right arm was shattered by a bullet, and was immediately amputated.

The new ministerial arrangements are at length completed. Lord Howick* succeeds Mr. Fox in the Foreign Department; T. Grenville† goes to the Admiralty instead of Lord Howick, and is succeeded at the Board of Control by Tierney. Lord Sidmouth‡ is made President of

* Afterward Earl Grey, of the Reform Bill.

† T. Grenville, brother to Lord Grenville, well known as a man of the world and a great friend and follower of Mr. Fox, who employed him, when Minister of Foreign Affairs, in 1782 on a mission to France,—his complaints during which, of the intrigues of Lord Shelburne, were among the causes of Fox's rupture with that statesman.

‡ Created Viscount Sidmouth Jan. 12, 1805, after having been, as Mr. Addington, Mr. Pitt's successor in 1801. His nickname of "the Doctor," derived from his sedate manner, and also from his being the son of a physician, stuck to him during life; and the necessity of pleasing George III., which introduced him into so many administrations, justified Mr. Canning's witticism that he was like the smallpox, that every one was obliged to have once in their lives. His character and ability are best described by Sir Henry Holland in his interesting volume of Recollections: "When he told me, as he often did, that no events of the day had ever ruffled his night's sleep, he described one effect of that tem-

the Council instead of Lord Fitzwilliam, who resigns, but retains a seat in the Cabinet; and Lord Holland becomes Privy Seal in place of "the Doctor." General FitzPatrick* goes to some inferior situation, and is succeeded by Whitbread.† The administration will not gain much strength by this arrangement: the only new acquisition is Tierney, who is undoubtedly an able and useful man. T. Grenville they had already in the Board of Control; and that situation would have sufficed for him. Whitbread would have been as much at the disposal of ministers in debate, although no office had been given him; and indeed his oratory is much better suited to the violence of opposition than to the grave and dignified office of defending ministerial measures. The only accession of numerical strength which Lord Grenville has made since last session has been the Northumberland interest, which he has succeeded in conciliating. The Duke of Northumberland, who had long been a partisan of Fox, was much offended last year at not being consulted upon the subject of the ministerial arrangements that took place upon the death of Mr. Pitt, and complained that the first intelligence he received of the formation of the government was from his porter. During the whole of the last session he appeared undecided in his politics; and in the debates that took place upon Windham's military plan, his members were actually ordered to

---

perament which protracted his life to nearly ninety" (he died in 1844), "but left little else of lasting history to the world."

* General FitzPatrick was one of those men who occupy no place in history, but are so interesting in memoirs. Brother of Lord Ossory, he was Secretary at War in 1783; he spoke well, wrote society verses, served with distinction in America, and, to crown his reputation in the drawing-rooms and clubs, went up in a balloon when those aerial vehicles were coming into fashion.

† This last arrangement never took place.

divide with the Opposition. Toward the latter end of July, however, Lord Percy came into Parliament for the borough of Buckingham, one of the Marquis of Buckingham's seats, thus proclaiming in the most public way the duke's union with the Grenvilles. It is only upon the supposition that it was meant to be an open declaration of his political opinions that it is possible to account for a step so disgraceful to the family of Percy; and indeed one could hardly have supposed that any consideration would have induced the Duke of Northumberland—having, it is said, seven seats at his command—to owe it as an obligation to Lord Buckingham that his son is a member of Parliament. This affair is the more extraordinary as he had, it seems, resolved that Percy should stand for Westminster on the death of Fox, and he must have foreseen that the latter event would, in all human probability, take place before the meeting of Parliament. Accordingly, as soon as Mr. Fox was dead, Lord Percy offered himself as his successor at Westminster, supported by Lord Grenville's party. Sheridan had always been destined by the Foxites to succeed to Fox's seat, if by any event it became vacant; and it excited some surprise that the Grenvilles should set up a candidate to oppose him. The excuse given by Lord Grenville was that he had been told by some third person that Mr. Sheridan did not mean to stand. It was for some days doubtful whether Sheridan would contest the point or not, and the Grenville papers gave him some hints not to "*quarrel with his bread and butter.*" Finding, however, that the rest of his party preferred remaining in office to supporting him, and that the whole ministerial influence would be exerted against him, at a meeting of the electors he pronounced a beautiful panegyric upon Fox, detailed some well-invented reasons which prevented him from standing, and concluded by recommending his friends to concur in supporting Lord Percy. The electors, however, were not so easily satisfied; and after resolving that Sheridan was a proper person to be elected, that they regretted he had declined, and that in their opinion Lord Percy was not a proper person, they adjourned the meeting in order to find some eligible man. Sir Francis Burdett, Mr. Curran, and Mr. Paull* were successively applied to in vain; none chose to enter into a contest with a man supported by Grenvillites, Foxites, and Pittites, and at length, for want of any other candidate, the Westminster electors were obliged to choose Lord Percy.

Oct. 11.

A telegraphic dispatch was received yesterday at the Admiralty from Deal, stating that a messenger was just come over from Paris with the intelligence that Lord Lauderdale was immediately to return; that he had got his passports, and was to leave Paris on the 8th. A bulletin was sent to the Lord Mayor, who immediately went to the Exchange, where he read it to the merchants. They received the news with *three cheers*, and in every part of London it occasioned the most lively demonstrations of joy—so firmly is everybody impressed with the conviction that none but a dishonorable peace could have been obtained, and that continued war is preferable to an ignominious treaty. It is said that our government did

---

* Paull had returned from India with charges against Lord Wellesley's administration, for which he had failed to obtain the hearing he desired, but which attracted to him for a time much popularity, ending at last in a bitter disappointment. He ran Sheridan very closely in the Westminster election of 1806; quarreled and fought a duel with Burdett shortly before his victory over Sheridan in the contested election of 1807; and in 1808 died by his own hand.

not expect Lord Lauderdale's return so soon, but that it arose from some categorical demand on his part.

In a work by F. Gentz, entitled "Fragments upon the Political Balance of Europe," published in 1806, is the following excellent definition of the meaning affixed to *peace* by Bonaparte:

"What, in his vocabulary, is meant by *peace*—the liberty of doing whatever is suggested to him by the feelings of unbounded power or momentary desire, and the unconditional subjection of his neighbors to every form of his increased and insupportable domination."—*Vide* p. 323.

Dec. 30.

A succession of events as rapid and extraordinary as those which occurred in the close of the last year, have marked the termination of this. In 1805, Europe saw with astonishment the ancient and powerful empire of Austria laid in the dust in the course of three months. The battle of Ulm, the consequent surrenders of the Austrian army, and the battle of Austerlitz, reduced the emperor to the abject conditions of the treaty of Presburg. This year one single battle has annihilated the former rival of Austria.

Prussia and France had for some time been upon terms less friendly than their usual good understanding—when the publication of the Rhenish Confederacy and the demand of Bonaparte for some of the smaller possessions of Prussia, in order to complete his confederate system, opened the eyes of the latter; and convinced the Prussian court that the unprincipled system of aggression, which they had assisted France in enforcing against every other state of Europe, would at length be applied against itself, and that it had no choice left but resistance, or an unconditional acknowledgment of vassalage and submission. The King of Prussia sent, therefore, to Bonaparte three demands; to which he required an answer by the 8th of October. These were, that the French troops should retire from Germany, that no opposition should be made by France to the establishment of a *Northern Coalition,** *of which Prussia should be the chief and protectress,* in order to counterbalance the Rhenish Confederacy. In the mean time both parties prepared for the contest, which now became inevitable, since it was very obvious that Bonaparte could not with honor accede to the requisitions of Prussia. By the 8th both sides were in the field. The Prussians commanded by the Duke of Brunswick, the French by Bonaparte. After some partial skirmishes, in one of which Prince Louis of Prussia was killed in defending the passage of a bridge, a general and decisive battle took place on the 14th between Jena and Auerstadt, which ended in the total defeat and annihilation of the Prussian army. The force on each side was nearly equal, amounting to about 120,000 men. The two armies had for some days been near each other; but the Prussians were so destitute of intelligence that they did not know where the French were till a day or two before the action. The reason of this is stated to have been the spirit of desertion prevalent in the army, which rendered it useless to send out patrols, who generally joined the enemy instead of returning with intelligence. Two days before the battle 10,000 French penetrated between the center and left wing of the Prussians, got to Naumburg in their rear, and burnt their magazines. The two armies were at that time in the

---

* A project which it seems had even then been formed, and, as it usually happens with plans long meditated, was ultimately consummated.

following positions: the French at Mühlhausen, Eisenach, and Gotha; the Prussians at Erfurt, Jena, and Zeist. Upon finding that a body of the enemy had got into their rear, and that the main body of the enemy were making a demonstration to turn their left wing, the Prussians threw that wing back. In the mean time the French fell upon them, and an action commenced, which lasted from eight in the morning until three in the afternoon, when victory declared in favor of the French. The loss of the Prussians—killed, wounded, and prisoners—amounted to fifty thousand men, and the rest of the army was entirely dispersed. Mr. Ross, who went as secretary to Lord Morpeth, said the rout of the Prussians exceeded belief. The flying troops were scattered in all directions. Corps without their officers, and officers without their corps, cavalry and infantry, cannon and wagons, were all mixed in one general confusion. To rally or reassemble them was impossible, and the only limit to the captures and slaughter of the Prussians was the inability of the French to pursue them. The king fled to Berlin, whence he retired immediately to Custrin.*

This day, the last of the Prussian monarchy, was also fatal to its veteran hero, the Duke of Brunswick. His regiment of grenadiers, a favorite corps, refused to charge. Enraged at this disgrace, and determined not to survive the calamities of the day, he seized a standard and rode

---

* *Note by Lord Palmerston.*—He fled from thence to Osterade, in the neighborhood of Dantzic. Such was his apathy with regard to his affairs, that when Count M. Woronzow, who was sent from Petersburg on a mission to him, reached Osterade, he was immediately invited to attend the king on a hunting-party. They had good sport, and killed a wolf and an elk. The queen, though ill and disgusted with this ill-timed amusement, was forced to join the party.

headlong into the midst of the enemy. A French chasseur shot at him with his musket at a few yards' distance. The ball pierced the bridge of his nose, and he was carried off the field, senseless, by some of his officers, who had followed their commander. He was conveyed to Altona, where he languished some weeks in the greatest agony, having been blinded by the wound, and at length expired, worn out by the sufferings of his mind as well as the torture of his body. Before his death he wrote a letter to Bonaparte, entreating that the neutrality of his states might be respected, since they had taken no part in the war, and urging that he acted as a general in the Prussian service, and not as Duke of Brunswick. Bonaparte having read the letter threw it down upon the table, and haughtily replied to the officer who brought it, "*Cette excuse ferait très-bien pour un conscrit, mais pas pour un prince souverain; ni lui ni aucun de ses enfans ne mettront jamais le pied dans le Duché de Brunswick.*" After his death, permission was requested to bury the duke in the tomb of his ancestors, which the usurper arrogantly refused, saying he was unworthy to lie with them.

Lord Morpeth, with his two secretaries, Ross and Frere, had been sent by government, as soon as hostilities commenced between Prussia and France, to open a communication with the former. Lord Morpeth reached the headquarters at Erfurt a few days before the battle, and finding the King of Prussia was preparing to withdraw, and that a general engagement was expected, he resolved to retire also. Instead, however, of following the king, he allowed himself to be taken in by Haugwitz, who desired he would follow him, and having described the way he meant to go, took another road. Lord Morpeth discovered the trick, pursued Haugwitz, and, overtook him at Weimar the night before the action. Haugwitz, however, went off again early in the morning; and Lord Morpeth, after having been detained some time by a want of horses, set out to return to England by Nordhausen and Osterhausen; a step, this, extremely unjustifiable in a man who was sent to remain with the King of Prussia. It is true that the action commenced before he left Weimar; and by the approach of the noise of firing he could clearly distinguish that the Prussians were giving way; and before he got far he was overtaken by a hussar, who informed him of the fate of the day: but the more evident the defeat the more necessary was it to have somebody with the king, to prevent, if possible, its probable consequence, the signature of an ignominious peace. Lord Morpeth,* however, was a very improper person to be intrusted with so difficult a mission. A young, inexperienced fine gentleman could not know how to act with firmness when surrounded by artillery on one side and cunning diplomatists on the other. Soon after Lord Morpeth returned, ministers determined to send a military man, and Lord Hutchinson was selected; but a whole month at the most critical period was suffered to elapse before he sailed, and by that time the French had made such progress in Prussia that it was uncertain where Lord Hutchinson† would be able to land. Dantzic was believed to be the only place where it was practicable for him to disembark.

---

* Afterward sixth Earl of Carlisle, K.G. He was 33 at the time.

† A general officer, Colonel of the 18th Foot, G.C.B., and Governor of Stirling Castle. He succeeded to the command of the British army in Egypt in 1801, on the death of Sir Ralph Abercromby, and for his services was raised to the peerage, and granted a pension of £2000 a year. He inherited the earldom of Donoughmore on the death of his brother, in 1825, and died without issue in 1832.

After such a signal overthrow as that of Jena, it is natural *to endeavor to find out reasons in the treachery or incapacity of the officers concerned, and it often happens that much injustice is in this manner done to men whose only fault has been a want of success.* In the present instance there can be no doubt that to the above-mentioned causes, in part, the defeat of the Prussians may be ascribed. All possible allowances being made for superior skill and generalship on the part of the French, still, had the Prussians done their duty, the catastrophe could not have been so complete. It is, however, known that they did not. In the first place, Haugwitz and Lombard, the two ministers of the king, were traitors. Lombard is a Frenchman by birth, a man of very low origin, and introduced by Haugwitz to the king; he was a known spy of the old French government. If any circumstantial proof were wanting of Haugwitz's perfidy, the following account, given by Count Woronzow, ci-devant ambassador here from Russia, would be sufficient for his condemnation: When first the Emperor of Russia found in the Cabinet of Berlin a disposition to break with France, he sent an offer to renew his alliance of last year, and to put 150,000 men at the disposal of Prussia; the only request he made was, that General Zastrow, on whom he could rely, might be sent to Petersburg to arrange the march, etc. of the troops. For three weeks Haugwitz sent no answer to this offer, and at length sent, not Zastrow—whom it was alleged the King of Prussia could not spare—but some colonel, a creature of Haugwitz. This envoy, on his arrival, said that 150,000 men were too many by far; that for so large a force they had no magazines or supplies, but that if the emperor would send 50,000 men they should be glad to receive them; the Russians, however, were by this time on their march; and subsequent events proved that had the emperor waited for Haugwitz's answer, or complied with his requests, the only chance of recovering Prussia would have been lost.

It is said that some of the Prussian generals, among whom were Mollendorf and Hohenlohe, strongly urged the expediency of attacking the French as soon as possible after the 8th, the day fixed by the king as the last on which he should wait for an answer to his demands. The Duke of Brunswick, however, was for delay, and wished to wait the attack of the enemy, and his opinion prevailed. The duke was a man who carried personal courage even to rashness,* but wanted that firmness and decision of character so necessary for a great commander. No one could execute with more ability and courage the orders of others, but, placed at the head of an army on which depended the fate of a kingdom, he shrunk from the responsibility of his situation, and lost in hesitation and doubt those moments which should have been employed in vigorous exertion. Had the Prussians attacked the French earlier, before they had collected and assembled their whole force, the event might have been very different; and at any rate, if they had been defeated, their army would not have been so entirely cut to pieces. By this delay, too, they suffered the

---

* *Note by Lord Palmerston.*—His uncle said of him, when he served as a young man in the Low Countries, that he was the only person he had met with who really loved danger. Lord Malmesbury, when ambassador from England at the Hague, hearing that the duke, who was then commanding in the Low Countries, exposed himself unnecessarily, wrote to him to request he would recollect the importance of his own life, and take more care of it. The duke thanked him for his attention as one would thank a person who desired one not to catch cold, and added that with regard to his life he was very indifferent about it, as he knew he should lose it "*par un coup de feu;*" a curious prophecy.

French to take possession of a small knoll which commanded the field of battle, and on which the French established a battery of one hundred and twenty pieces of cannon, whose fire mowed down whole ranks of the Prussians, and in a great measure decided the fate of the day. Of this they might have made themselves masters in the first instance; but when once the enemy had fortified it, it became impregnable, and we find in the bulletins that the Prussians failed in several attacks which they made upon it. But such was the treachery of some of the officers and the cowardice of most of the men, that at whatever time the battle had been fought, its fate would probably have been the same. The Duke of Brunswick's aide-de-camp, who caught him in his arms when he fell, and afterward brought over his blue ribbon, said that as soon as the *Feu de Mitraille* commenced, the Prussians fled *comme des perdreaux.* A strong proof how inefficient mere parade discipline is toward making good soldiers, and that nothing but actual service will accomplish that end.

After the action, the Prussian army being, as has been already observed, entirely dispersed, and having the enemy interposed between them and the Oder, it could not make again any general stand. Some few corps got into Magdeburg, but the largest number that escaped in a body were about twenty or thirty thousand under Prince Hohenlohe and General Blücher. Finding it impossible to get to the Oder in a straight line, Hohenlohe attemped to reach Stettin by a circuitous march. By uncommon exertions he succeeded in getting as far as Prentzlow, only seven German miles from Stettin, when the French overtook him; and, his troops being worn out by excessive fatigue, and totally destitute of provisions, he was obliged to surrender with the main body of his corps, amounting to above sixteen thousand men. The rest, under Blücher, were at Liechen, behind him ; and, hearing of his surrender, Blücher, despairing altogether of escape, determined to render his country all the service he could, and saw that the only thing in his power was to draw off a portion of the French army from the pursuit of the flying Prussians. Accordingly he began to retreat to the northwest, and having defended himself with the greatest skill and courage against three French divisions, each much superior in numbers to his own corps, he reached Lubeck. Here he meant to make a stand ; but the town was forced, in consequence of the treachery of the officers who commanded one of the gates. Blücher had now no alternative but to violate the Danish territory, or sustain an attack by a force infinitely superior to his own. The first, for obvious reasons, he declined doing ; and his men being reduced in numbers by the various actions they had been compelled to fight, and weakened by the fatigues of three weeks' incessant forced marching, without having during that period tasted bread, and being almost starved, he was obliged to surrender. His force was reduced to nine thousand men, and he had the glory of having drawn from the Marches of Brandenburg to the shores of the Baltic three large divisions of the French army. Had all the Prussians behaved like Blücher, Bonaparte would have found the road to Berlin not quite so easy as he expected. The disaster at Jena was soon followed by the surrender of Magdeburg, Stettin, Custrin, and Gros Glogau. The easy capitulation of these places afforded another decisive proof of treachery somewhere. If, as was alleged by the officers commanding them, they were destitute of provisions and other supplies for sustaining a siege, Haugwitz deserved to be hanged for not taking his measures beforehand ; if that be untrue, and they were able to make a defense, the officers who surrendered ought to be shot for their cowardice. Magdeburg is very strong, but Custrin is almost impregnable, being surrounded by the Oder and the Waarta on two sides, and on the other by deep morasses. Bonaparte, having nothing to oppose his progress, marched to Berlin, and thence to Warsaw. The Russians, who had come with the expectation of joining a large Prussian army, found themselves too weak to resist long, and although they had advanced as far as Posna when the French got to Berlin, as the latter advanced they were obliged to retire and fall back upon their reinforcements.

The Parliament, which had been summoned to meet for the dispatch of business at the end of October, was unexpectedly dissolved. The country was taken completely by surprise, for although rumors of a dissolution had prevailed during the whole of the summer, the proclamation summoning Parliament for the end of October convinced people that, if dissolved at all, it would not be till the spring. It was, indeed, a sudden determination, and the king was not made acquainted with it till a week before the event took place. That it was a sudden resolution, or at least, if settled beforehand, not made known to the whole Cabinet, is proved by two advertisements from Windham to the Norfolk electors. In the first, published during the summer, he assured them that government had not any intention of dissolving Parliament; and in the second, which immediately followed the dissolution, he said it was a measure unknown to him till a few days previous to its publication, contrary to his wishes and prejudicial to his interests; a singular declaration, certainly, from a Cabinet minister. The method adopted by ministers with regard to their borough seats was very politic and ingenious. They purchased seats from their friends at a low price, making up the deficiency probably by appointments and promotions. These seats they afterward sold out at the average market price to men who promised them support; and with the difference they carried on their contested elections. The sum raised in this manner was stated by a person who was in the secret to be inconceivably great, and accounts for an assertion afterward made by Lord Grenville in the Lords, that "not one guinea of the public money had been spent in elections."* It may be imagined that if seats were bought for two thousand five hundred, or even two thousand, pounds, and sold again for five thousand pounds, a comparatively small number of such transactions would furnish a considerable fund; and government had so many seats passing through its hands that, at last, in one or two instances, it sold them to people who only professed themselves in general well disposed toward them, without exacting a pledge of unconditional support.

The elections were in general carried on very quietly; the principal contests were in Westminster, Middlesex, Southwark, Norfolk, and Hampshire. In the first, Sheridan and Hood stood upon the government interest against Paull. Sheridan, at first relying upon his popularity, refused ministerial assistance, asserting that he should walk over the course. He soon, however, found how uncertain the *popularis aura* is. Paull, being the greatest blackguard of the two, quite supplanted him in the affections of the Covent Garden electors; and if Sheridan had not received timely assistance from Hood, he would have been shamefully distanced. Even as it was, his majority above Paull was very trifling; and the general opinion is that it

* Lord Palmerston's observation seems to imply that the spending public money for party elections would not have been deemed, on the part of any government, a very extraordinary occurrence.

will not stand the test of an examination by a committee, before whom Paull has pledged himself to bring it.* Paull's failure was, in a great degree, owing to his uncalled-for adoption of Sir F. Burdett's principles, which rendered it quite impossible for any well-disposed person to give him their support. Sheridan's unpopularity was said to have arisen chiefly from his never having paid his debts. Numbers of poor people crowded round the hustings, demanding payment for bills which he owed them. Mr. Sloane mentioned a curious fact relative to the election. Having gone one day to Covent Garden to see what was going forward, among the cries of Sheridan, Hood, and Paull forever! he heard several voices in the mob exclaiming, Pitt forever!

At Southwark, Sir Thomas Turton, the old antagonist of Tierney, drove him out of the field. The latter had to contend with all that violence of popular clamor which had so often on former occasions been exerted in his favor; and he was scarcely allowed to speak during the whole election. Few people would have believed ten or twelve years ago, that the time would ever have arrived when Sheridan and Tierney would be objected to by their electors as candidates, and would complain of the clamor and violence of the mob!

The Middlesex election was conducted with the greatest quiet. The candidates were Byng,† Mellish, and Burdett; and the latter having previously declared that he would

---

* Sheridan was not, however, unseated, but in the following year Burdett and Cochrane were returned over him and Elliot.

† Mr. George Byng, a type of the country gentleman in the time of Mr. Fox and Mr. Pitt, and the last M.P. who was seen in the House of Commons with the top-boots that formed part of the costume of that epoch. He represented Middlesex in Parliament for fifty-six years—from 1790 till his death in 1846.

give neither cockades nor post-chaises, his former voters, who were not of a description to sacrifice much to disinterested affection, deserted his cause, and the two first candidates were returned by very large majorities. The mob also, who were so outrageous in their demonstrations of regard for Sir Francis at the two former elections, not being paid at this one for making a riot, were peaceably disposed; and it was no longer dangerous to appear at Brentford in any colors but purple.

The Norfolk election did not afford a very striking proof of the popularity of ministers. Windham was brought in solely by the great influence of Mr. Coke,* assisted by all the exertions of government. Windham† had, indeed, rendered himself so generally odious in the country, by his ungrateful conduct toward Pitt, and the incessant abuse and ridicule which he had lavished upon the volunteers, that it was with the utmost difficulty that even Mr. Coke's friends could be induced to vote for him.

His triumph, however, will be but short, as both Coke and himself will be turned out upon the Treating Act. All the candidates had agreed not to take advantage of that Act, and accordingly opened houses for their electors. But two ladies, friends of Wodehouse (Coke's and Windham's opponent), having appeared every day in a barouche

---

* Afterward created Earl of Leicester.

† It would be absurd in any one not a young politician enthusiastically attached to Fox's rival, to talk of such a man as Mr. Windham as ungrateful to Mr. Pitt; but this statesman, though so celebrated for his attainments as a scholar and his wit and delivery as a speaker (the grandfather of the present Lord Lansdowne told me he was the most agreeable speaker he ever listened to), was so uncertain as a politician that each party alternately abused him, and in his own county he was never spoken of by the farmers without the nickname of "weathercock" being applied to him. He died June 3, 1810, in his sixtieth year.

and four at the hustings with his colors, the friends of Windham determined to drive them away, and accordingly put two women of the town in another barouche, decorated with the same ribbons, and drew them alongside the carriage of the ladies.

This unmanly insult so incensed those who were the objects of it, that they determined to be revenged. They consequently prevailed upon some of the electors to petition against the sitting members; and, as the fact of their having treated is notorious, there is no doubt of their being turned out.

With regard to the county of Hants, the old members were Sir William Heathcote and Mr. Chute, both for many years attached to the politics of Pitt. Neither, however, had at any time taken a violent part in public affairs. Sir William Heathcote, a quiet country gentleman naturally of a retired disposition, and married to a very penurious wife, lived like a recluse at Hursley; and Chute, a hospitable squire, preferred entertaining his neighbors at "The Vine" to mixing with much zeal in parliamentary disputes. The latter, however, had in the course of the last session voted three times in opposition to ministers: on the American Intercourse Bill, on the repeal of the Defense Bill, and on Windham's plans. This was an offense not easily to be forgiven; and it was determined to turn him out. Accordingly, in the month of September Lord Temple rode to Hursley, and said to Sir William Heathcote, that Mr. Chute having gone into a systematic opposition to ministers, it could not be expected that they should give him their assistance, but that as Sir William had not attended last session, if he would now declare himself favorably disposed toward government they would vote for him; but that if he and his friends intended to make a common cause with Chute, government must set up two candidates instead of one.

This communication Lord Temple gave to understand came from Lord Grenville. Had Sir William acted with becoming spirit, he would immediately have taken down what Lord Temple had said, desired him to read it, and then ordered the servant to show him the door. However, he answered, that with regard to himself, he never would pledge himself to support any administration, not even that of Pitt, were he alive; and that as to his friends, he must consult them before he could give any answer with regard to them. He then, when Lord Temple was gone, wrote down the substance of what had passed, and laid it before the County Club. The indignation excited by this attempt to dictate to the county members was universal; and it was immediately determined to support the two sitting members, and in them the freedom and independence of the county. Two candidates, however, were now set up by ministers, Mr. Herbert and Thistlewaite; the former, a clever young man, but third son of Lord Carnarvon, and in no way connected with the county; the latter, a very stupid but respectable young man, possessing considerable property near Portsmouth. Hereupon Sir William Heathcote, alarmed at the trouble and expense of a contest, declined standing, upon pretense that his age and infirmities would not allow him to attend Parliament any longer; and though Sir H. St. John Mildmay, after hesitating ten days, was prevailed on to stand in conjunction with Chute, the delay, however, produced by these arrangements gave the ministerial candidates a fortnight's start in their canvass, and this, and the great mass of voters in Portsmouth at the command of government, decided the fate of the contest.*

* This story is curiously illustrative of the manners of the times.

Jan. 20.

The new Parliament met a little before Christmas, but no business of any importance was transacted till the 2d of January, when the papers relative to the late negotiation with France, which had been laid before Parliament, were discussed in the House of Lords. Lord Grenville opened the debate by an excellent speech, in which he detailed the progress of the negotiation and the causes which led to its rupture. The speech appeared, however, more intended for Europe than the audience to which it was addressed, as it consisted chiefly in a labored defense of the rupture of the negotiation and a proof of the insincerity of the French government,—two subjects upon which, probably, not one of his auditors was likely to disagree with him. Lords Sidmouth and Lauderdale spoke on the same side with Lord Grenville. Lords Hawkesbury* and Eldon concurred in the address moved by Lord Grenville, but contended that the assertion made in the first paragraph of the declaration, that France had proposed to treat on the basis of the "uti possidetis," was not proved by the papers before the House, inasmuch as Talleyrand not only never admitted that basis during the whole negotiation, but in the first communication from him that can be considered as an overture, he distinctly made an offer to treat upon the basis of the stipulations of the Treaty of Amiens, which certainly is not the "uti possidetis" of the present day. Lord Grenville, in reply, contended that ministers were not called upon to prove that assertion by the papers in question; that they had proved by Lord Yarmouth's declaration in the House of Commons that Talleyrand had admitted verbally the basis of the

---

* Succeeded as Earl of Liverpool Dec. 17, 1808. Prime Minister June, 1812.

"uti possidetis;" that after Lord Yarmouth's return he was particularly instructed to insist upon a written admission to the same effect, and ordered not to produce his full powers till that writing was obtained. That, however, Lord Yarmouth thought proper, contrary to his instructions, to produce his powers before he had obtained this document, and that this was the reason it did not appear among the papers on the table. This statement Lord Yarmouth afterward denied in the House of Commons; and it does not appear that he was ever ordered to keep back his full powers till a written admission of the "uti possidetis" was given him; but the condition on which that production was to depend was the abandonment of a demand of Sicily, set up by the French government subsequent to the commencement of the negotiations.

About the end of last December died the Duke of Richmond. His death put four good appointments into the disposal of ministers. The command of the Blues, which was given to the Duke of Northumberland; that of the Sussex militia, given to Lord Chichester; and a Blue Ribbon and the lord-lieutenancy of Sussex, which were given to the Duke of Norfolk. To the last appointment great objections were made, on the ground that the man who was struck out of the Privy Council for disloyalty to his sovereign should not be made lord-lieutenant of the county the most likely to be invaded. Nor did the duke get the Blue Ribbon, it being necessary in point of form that he should ask it of the king, a degradation in his opinion to which he would not submit.

Feb. 5.

This day Lord Grenville moved the second reading of the Slave Trade Abolition Bill, which was carried after a long debate by a large majority. The numbers were 100 contents, 36 non-contents; majority 64. The time fixed for the importation to cease was the 1st of January, 1808.

Feb. 8.

Yesterday arrived the Russian official account of the battle of the 26th of December. The Russians had continued retreating till they arrived in the neighborhood of Pultusk, beyond the Vistula.

Here, on the 26th, an action took place, in which the French under Bonaparte, having attacked the Russians under Benningsen, with a view to cut them off from their magazines, were completely defeated and repulsed with the loss of 4000 killed and 6000 prisoners. The two armies amounted each to about 50,000. The Russians were, however, unable from want of provisions to pursue their advantage, and both armies fell back, the French to Warsaw and the Russians to Ostrolenka and Rozau. The French army has suffered dreadfully from the dysentery occasioned by damp and fatigue; it is also believed that they have got the plica polonica among them. Bonaparte is gone into winter quarters at Warsaw, and Benningsen will probably attack him if he can advance through the country lying between them, which has been rendered a perfect desert by the retreating Russians.

The uncommon mildness of the winter renders operations less difficult.

Oct. 1.

There has seldom happened in this country so sudden and unexpected a change of ministers as that which took place last March. The broad-bottomed administration (or, as they were called, from a foolish boast they made when first they came into power, "All the Talents") appeared in the beginning of the month so strong that it seemed beyond the power of events to shake them.

They had called a new Parliament, in the elections for which the influence direct and indirect of government had been exerted to an extent and with a success beyond ex ample. They and their adherents had so long and assiduously made the country re-echo with the boast that they alone were fit to conduct the affairs of the nation, that the multitude—who seldom take the trouble of judging for themselves, and are apt to believe what they perpetually hear—began at length to give them credit for the abilities of which they claimed such exclusive possession; and keeping the king as a sort of state prisoner, by allowing none but themselves to approach him, they began almost to consider themselves a fourth branch of the government of the country. From this height of power nothing but their own conduct could have brought them down.

The question as to the propriety of taking off from the Catholics in these kingdoms those restrictions which prevent them from holding various offices of trust and power is one of a very important, extensive, and difficult nature. But it must divide itself into two parts; the one relating to the general and abstract expediency of doing this at some time or other; the second confining itself to the policy of an immediate relaxation of the existing laws, taking into consideration the present state of our affairs and the actual bias of the public mind. These are two questions so different and distinct that it is quite possible that any one may think with the Catholics upon the first, and be adverse to them upon the second. But it is obvious that whenever any proposition tending to what is called (but very improperly) Catholic emancipation is submitted to Parliament, it is the latter of the above-stated questions upon which we are called to decide. That a set of men in opposition to ministers, and convinced of the justice of the claims of the Catholics, should, even at the risk of exciting and reviving the animosities of opposing sects, endeavor to obtain the opinion of Parliament and of the country upon the pretensions which they favored is natural, and perhaps not much to be blamed; and upon those grounds one cannot certainly be surprised at the agitation of the question by Lord Grenville and Mr. Fox in 1805. But after the very decided rejection of their proposition by both Houses of Parliament, after the general disapprobation expressed at this proposition throughout the country, and more especially after it was universally known that the king had invincible conscientious objections to it—people did not expect that the Opposition leaders, having become ministers, would re-enter upon a course in which they were certain to be confronted by insurmountable obstacles. Yet so confident was the late administration of its firmness and omnipotence, that they flattered themselves they should be able to overcome all the difficulties that hindered the accomplishment of their wishes. Aware, however, of the impossibility of forcing the whole extent of the measure which they had in 1805 submitted to Parliament, they resolved to carry it by subdivisions; and the first proposition with which they began related to the admission of Catholics to the higher situations in the army. By the existing laws Catholics may, in Ireland, hold any commission below that of major-general on the staff; but this privilege, which was conceded to them by the Irish Parliament in 1793, never was granted to the Catholics of England; so that a man entering the army legally in Ireland might, upon the removal of his corps to England, become subject to severe penalties. This is certainly an absurdity in theory, although the inconsistency has been remedied in practice, the penal laws having been suffered to sleep in England as far as they have been abrogated in Ireland. This inconsistency, however, was what ministers resolved first to correct; and some insignificant disturbances that took place about this time in some counties of Ireland, occasioned by disputes about tithes, and carried on by a set of people calling themselves

"Threshers," afforded a pretext for what was to be called a measure of conciliation. In point of fact these disturbances were totally unconnected with religious differences, since the "Threshers" were many of them Protestants; and at any rate no legislative concession could be required to quiet them, since it was a boast of the Duke of Bedford's friends that he had suppressed these commotions by the ordinary course of law. The truth, however, probably was (as indeed is almost acknowledged) that the coalition had so deeply pledged themselves to the Catholics when out of power, that now they were in office they found it impossible wholly to withstand the solicitations they received in consequence of their former professions. In fact, the language held by Lord Grenville when he brought forward the petition in 1805 rendered it impossible for him ever to put it off upon the ground of circumstances. "It is urged," he said, "that this is not a proper time to bring this question before Parliament. I answer, this year is the proper time—next year is the proper time—the year after, and every year, is the proper time. It is a question that cannot be too often discussed and brought under the consideration of Parliament and the country."

Finding it, therefore, difficult altogether to refuse the Catholics their support, and at the same time feeling that a full concession of their demands would be impracticable, the ministers thought that by granting some smaller boon they should, for the present, satisfy one set of people without going so far as to alarm another. It was thus that they determined to extend to both countries the provisions of the Irish Act of 1793. When the proposal was made to the king,* he expressed a considerable repugnance to

* The draft of a dispatch, accompanied by a Cabinet minute, was dated Feb. 9.

accede to it. But after a correspondence with the Cabinet,* at length he was finally induced to consent to it. He accompanied this consent, however, with the following written declaration: "That while his Majesty agreed to the measure proposed, particularly adverting to the provisions of the Act of 1793, he felt it necessary to declare that *he would not go one step further.*" Lord Howick then gave notice that he should propose certain clauses in the *Mutiny Bill* to enable the Catholics to hold *certain* commissions in the army; and a dispatch† was sent to Ireland, containing those clauses, which Mr. Elliot, the secretary, was to communicate to the Catholics. In the conference which took place upon this subject, the Catholic deputies asked Mr. Elliot whether it was meant merely to extend to England the Irish Act of 1793, or whether *all commissions* in the army and navy were to be opened to them. To this question it appears Mr. Elliot was unable, from the want of precision in the dispatch in which the views of the government had been explained, to give a decisive answer, and consequently he wrote back to ascertain clearly the intentions of the Cabinet. Another dispatch was then sent to him, and this dispatch clearly expressed that his Majesty was to be empowered to confer *any commission* or appointment in the army or navy upon *all descriptions* of his subjects, *without any exception whatever;* it added that this concession was no longer to be made by a clause in the Mutiny Act,‡ but by a separate enactment. This second dispatch was sent to Windsor to the king, and,

* The second Cabinet representation was dated Feb. 10.

† Dated Feb. 12.

‡ The measure extending now to the *navy*, to which the Mutiny Act does not apply, it became obviously necessary to make it the subject of a separate bill.

being returned without comment, was transmitted to Ireland.* On the following Wednesday,† the day on which the Mutiny Bill was to be committed and the separate bill brought in, Lord Howick had an audience with the king upon the business of his office, and after it was over the king asked him what was coming on that day in the House of Commons. Lord Howick said that the committee on the Mutiny Bill stood as the order for the day, and explained to the king the nature of the change that had taken place, and the reasons which had induced it. The king then asked whether the separate bill intended to be brought forward was not the same as the Irish Act. Lord Howick, in reply, stated the degree in which they differed, observing that this difference had been explained to his Majesty in the last dispatch which had been submitted to him. Lord Howick also stated the reasons why he conceived the measure, in the extent to which it was intended to be carried, to be of the utmost importance to the welfare and security of the government of the country. "And here, sir," said Lord Howick, in his explanatory speech on the 26th of March,‡ "I must acknowledge that his Majesty, upon that occasion, did express a general dislike and disapprobation of this measure—I mean to state everything frankly—but I did understand our conversation to conclude by the king giving his consent—a reluctant consent, I admit—or perhaps it would be more correctly stated by *not withdrawing the consent which he had originally given* —to carrying out the views of his government. I conceived, therefore, that I had still sufficient authority, as a

* Lord Howick sent it to the king on the night of Monday, March 2, and it was returned the next morning.

† March 4.

‡ From which the account of this audience is taken almost verbatim.

member of that government, for the introduction of the bill that had been prepared."

In consequence of this conception, Lord Howick, the next day or the day after, introduced the said bill, and some discussion took place between him and Perceval, who opposed it. About the same time Lord Sidmouth sent in his resignation. On the following Wednesday,* Lord Howick did not attend the levée, on account of the death of a near relation; but the king signified to Lord Grenville his decided disapprobation of the measure that had been brought forward, and the misconception of its extent, under which his consent to it had been originally given, having before expressed his objections to it; and in consequence of this explanation Lord Howick on the next day postponed the further reading of the bill, which ministers finally resolved to drop altogether. A minute was accordingly transmitted to the king, stating this determination, but making three demands—1st, that they should be allowed when they dropped the bill to state the strong persuasion they entertained individually of the advantage which would result to the empire from a different system of policy toward the Catholics of Ireland; 2d, that they should be allowed openly to avow these sentiments, not only on withdrawing the bill, but in the possible event of the discussion of the Catholic petition in Parliament; and, 3d, that notwithstanding the deference which they had thought it their duty to show on the present occasion to the opinions and feelings expressed by his Majesty, they should be free to submit from time to time, as their duty was, for his Majesty's decision, such measures respecting Ireland as the course of circumstances should appear to require. In answer to this minute, the

* March 11.

king expressed some dissatisfaction that the ministers should feel it necessary as individuals to express their opinions on withdrawing the bill, and in the event of the discussion of the Catholic petition, but required them absolutely to withdraw the latter part of their declaration, stating that he never would consent to any concessions to the Catholics which they might in future propose to him, and requiring a positive assurance in writing, which, as they conceived, would not only preclude them from proposing concessions to the Catholics, but from all measures connected with such concessions. The ministers refused to withdraw their statement, or to give the written assurance demanded; and the king communicated to them his intention of intrusting the management of his affairs to other ministers. Lord Grenville and Lord Howick then asked and obtained from the king permission to state to Parliament the circumstances which led to the change of ministry; and their statements, made in the Lords on the 26th March, and in the Commons on the same day, were subsequently published.

In reviewing this transaction, it must immediately strike one as a singular circumstance that there should so long have existed upon so important a subject such a wide misunderstanding, not only between the king and his ministers, but even among the very members of the Cabinet in which the measure originated; that in submitting to the king a proposition connected with a subject upon which he was known to entertain such a decided opinion, sufficient care should not have been taken by Lord Howick to avoid the possibility of a misconception on either side, is certainly extraordinary; but that some of those colleagues in office, with whom he and Lord Grenville must have discussed, digested, and arranged the measure, previous to its being communicated to the king, should almost to the last have mistaken its nature and extent, is wholly inexplicable. Such, however, was the fact. Lord Sidmouth declared in the House of Lords that he understood the first dispatch precisely as the king did, and never conceived till the second was drawn up that anything more was in contemplation than to extend to England the Irish Act of 1793; on the other hand, Lords Grenville and Howick not only assert that from the beginning their intentions were to open to the Catholics and all descriptions of persons all ranks and appointments in the army and navy, but seemed to wonder that any person could have mistaken their meaning; their partisans of course go further, and scruple not to affirm that the king fully understood the extent of the measure to which he assented, that he retracted his word in consequence of private representations made to him by interested persons, and that the ministers were the victims of secret intrigue and cabal. In matters of this nature facts are more to be depended upon than the most confident assertions of the parties concerned; and, however high the characters of Lord Grenville or Lord Howick may stand, we are perhaps more likely to arrive at the truth by a deduction from admitted facts, than by trusting implicitly to their explanations of their own views and intentions. Now certainly from such a review there are very strong grounds for believing that when they first laid their proposition before the king they themselves only meant to extend the Act of 1793; that the king, Lord Sidmouth, and the other two Cabinet ministers rightly understood its nature; and that the subsequent misunderstanding arose from a change of plan on the part of the two lords, rather than any original mistake of the king. If it were not so, how happened it that the dispatch was so ambiguously worded that neither the king, nor many of the Cabinet, nor the Irish deputies, nor Mr. Elliot should hit upon its real meaning ?* Is it possible that Lord Grenville or Lord Howick are so unused to composition, or so ignorant of the force of words, as not to be able to draw up a dispatch without leaving doubtful and ill explained so very material a point as that upon which the essence of the measure they were about to adopt depended ? It is but a poor excuse for them to say that the king misunderstood them. It was their bounden duty to take care that he should not misunderstand them; and suffering him to misconceive their proposal was nearly as culpable as an attempt to deceive him with regard to it would have been. Moreover, if the government from the first intended to admit all persons into the army and navy, is it not singular that Lord Howick should propose to do so by a clause in the Mutiny Bill ? A measure so new and important is not usually introduced as a clause to any bill, because some stages of discussion are by that means cut off. If, however, on the other hand, the extension of the Act of 1793 had been all that was meant, to introduce such a proposition into the Mutiny Bill was natural and proper.

A circumstance upon which the partisans of the ministry lay great stress, as proving them to have been warranted in their supposition that they were acting with the king's consent, is that the second dispatch to the Lord-Lieutenant was sent to the king with the amended clauses, and returned by him the next day without comment. The explanation of this circumstance is, that whenever any business is in progress, the dispatches relative to it which are sent to the king are considered as sent merely *pro forma*,

---

* The change in the extent of the bill was probably owing to the conversation between Mr. Elliot and the Irish deputies; when Lord Grenville found, from what passed in that interview, how far the wishes of the Catholics extended, he did not choose that his bill should fall short of their expectations.

and are not read by him, unless there is a note in the box, specifying that the dispatch contains new matter, and requesting his attention to it. What, then, was more natural than that, seeing this dispatch and the clauses to be merely explanatory of those which he had already seen, and that there was no note inclosed, he should either run them carelessly over, or not look at them at all? The omission of an accompanying note proves more against the ministers than the want of any comment does against the king. Lord Grenville in his speech dwells much upon the length of time which elapsed between the notice of the separate bill, which was given in the House by Lord Howick the day of his first conversation with the king (the 4th), and the notification of the king's decided objection to it, which was not made till the following Wednesday (the 11th). The king, argues Lord Grenville, must have heard by the newspapers that the bill had been introduced; and is it not singular that a week should be suffered to elapse before he informs his ministers that they had mistaken his sentiments, and acted in opposition to his wishes? but, on the other hand, the king, being at Windsor, might not for some days hear of the debate in question; and as he only came to town on Wednesdays, and the second reading was not to come on till the next Thursday, he might naturally think that it would be time enough for him to put a stop to further proceedings when he next went to town, and that there was no necessity for inconvenient hurry.

But if ministers cannot be acquitted of some degree of insincerity in their transactions with the king previous to the explanation, neither can their subsequent conduct be in any way reconciled with the respect which they owed to their sovereign, or the constitutional principles by which it was their duty to have been guided. When, from deference to the king's opinions, they dropped the obnoxious bill, there were but two lines of conduct which they could with propriety pursue. If they thought that the safety of Ireland was consistent with the king's ideas respecting the Catholics, they should have adopted those ideas without reserve; but if it appeared to them that nothing could permanently secure the tranquillity of the country but such an enlargement of the political privileges of that description of its inhabitants as it was contrary to the king's determination to grant, it was incumbent upon them to resign situations which they could no longer hold without compromising their own honor, or sacrificing the public advantage. *But they viewed the matter in another light, and insisted upon retaining both their places and their opinions.* They asserted that nothing but their strong conviction of the imperious necessity of adopting some measure to relieve the Catholics from the restrictions under which they labored would have induced them to propose the measure which they had framed for that purpose; and yet, though nothing had occurred to diminish that imperious necessity, they consented to withdraw their proposals and retain their places, thereby taking upon themselves all the responsibility of any of those fatal effects to the country which they prophesied would be the inevitable consequences of rejecting their advice. It is idle to contend that, by stating in Parliament the opinions on which they did not act, they exempted themselves from the responsibility which might result from the sovereign's disregard of those opinions, since ministers are and must be responsible for any policy, whether active or passive, that is adopted while they remain in power. If this were not so, an unprincipled minister might sanction and give effect to the most profligate policy by his acquiescence, and yet secure himself from punishment by saying that he had disapproved of it. The course, therefore, which till this instance has invariably been pursued is, that so long as the king and his ministers think together, or the former is willing to give way to the latter, the administration goes on; that upon points not concerning the great interests of the country, the latter may even concede to the opinion of the former; but that whenever discussions arise between the sovereign and his Cabinet upon great and important questions, if a difference of opinion should unfortunately take place, and neither party succeed in convincing the other, the ministers are bound in honor to retire from their situations and give the king an opportunity of ascertaining whether he can find other servants who will enter more readily into his views. Should he succeed, and the new ministers begin to execute his ideas either by proposing or omitting to propose any particular measure, then those who went out may properly as individual members of Parliament oppose to their utmost what they resisted when in office. Should he fail in his search, then comes into operation one of those salutary checks which the practice of the Constitution has imposed on the royal prerogative, and he must necessarily abandon a line of conduct which he cannot find men of character and ability willing to pursue.

The new ministerial arrangements were completed by the end of March, and were as follows:

First Lord of the Treasury.	Duke of Portland . . .	*vice*	Lord Grenville.
Lord of the Admiralty . . .	Lord Mulgrave	"	Mr. Grenville.
Chanc. of the Exchequer . .	Hon. Spencer Perceval	"	L'd Henry Petty
Sec. of Foreign Affairs . . .	G. Canning	"	Lord Howick.
War and Colonies	Lord Castlereagh . . .	"	Mr. Windham.
Home Department	Lord Hawkesbury . . .	"	Lord Spencer.
Lord Chancellor	Lord Eldon	"	Lord Erskine.
Lord Privy Seal	Lord Westmoreland . .	"	Lord Holland.
President of the Council . . .	Lord Camden	"	Lord Sidmouth.
Pres. of the Board of Trade	Lord Bathurst	"	Lord Auckland.
Master-General of the Ordnance	Lord Chatham	"	Lord Moira.

The above formed the Cabinet.

Attorney-General	Sir V. Gibbs	*vice*	Sir A. Pigott.
Solicitor-General	Sir Thomas Plomer .	"	Sir Sam'l Romilly.
Board of Control	Hon. S. Dundas . . .	"	Mr. Tierney.
Treasurer of the Navy . . .	G. Rose	"	Mr. Sheridan.
Secretary at War.	Lt.-Gen. Sir James Pulteney	"	Gen. FitzPatrick.
Master of the Horse.	Duke of Montrose . .	"	Lord Hertford.
Lord-Lieut. of Ireland . . .	Duke of Richmond .	"	Duke of Bedford.
Secretary for Ireland	Sir A. Wellesley . . .	"	Rt. Hon. W. Elliot.
Chanc. of the Exchequer for Ireland	Mr. Forster	"	Sir. J. Newport.
Postmasters-General	Lord Sandwich.		
	Lord Chichester.		
Paymasters of Forces. . . .	Rt. Hon. C. Long . . .	"	Lord Temple.
	Lord C. H. Somerset.		
Lords of the Treasury . . .	Lord Titchfield.		
	Mr. Sturges Bourne.		
	Hon. R. Ryder.		
Lords of the Admiralty . .	Lord Gambier.		
	Sir R. Bickerton.		
	Capt. W. J. Hope.		
	Mr. R. Ward.		
	Lord Palmerston.		
	Mr. James Buller.		

BOOK II.

Now in Parliament, and speaks with credit in defense of the government in regard to the Copenhagen Expedition—Visits his Irish estates—Is offered the Chancellorship of the Exchequer, after the Canning and Castlereagh quarrel; refuses, and becomes Secretary at War—Becomes, on the dissolution, Member for Cambridge University—Makes a successful speech on bringing forward the estimates—Cites passages from the dispatches of Lord Wellington, then driving Massena out of Portugal—Describes a shooting-party in Essex—Correspondence with the Commander-in-Chief as to the position of Secretary at War.

I HAVE stated that Lord Palmerston, after once more failing at Cambridge, had been returned for Newport. There was not so much and such constant talking in the House of Commons then as there is now. People did not take up the morning's reports of the debates and again put them down, lost amid the wilderness of commonplace remarks of commonplace men on commonplace subjects, which, in the flattering way it has become the fashion to adopt in speaking of ourselves, we call business-like speaking, but which, in reality, is for the most part twaddle, and prevents or impedes the transaction of business.

The ordinary affairs of government, which after all have to be gone through as a matter of course, with little or much speech about them, were permitted to pass off quietly, without every member making a speech which no other member wanted to hear. Any great affair was debated in a great manner by the leading men. When a new member was animated by ambition, he made a trial of his strength, and was judged by the assembly he addressed as fit or unfit to be one of the select to be listened to. The ordeal was a severe one. But the novice who passed it with tolerable credit in the judgment of those men whose opinion was the test of success and failure, and who knew at once how to detect mind—which, if accompanied by energy, ends in giving ascendency in any body of men who live much together—was henceforth classed, and almost certain, if he persevered in a parliamentary career, to obtain place and distinction.

A first speech under such circumstances was an important affair. Lord Palmerston thus speaks of his own:

"In September of this year (1807), Copenhagen was taken, and the Danish fleet carried off.

"The Danish expedition was the great subject of debate at the beginning of the session in 1808. Papers relating to it were laid before Parliament. At that time lay Lords of the Admiralty had nothing to do but to sign their name. I had leisure, therefore, to study the Copenhagen papers, and put together a speech, on which I received many compliments. Robert Milnes,* better known as Orator Milnes, had made a splendid speech on the first night of the discussion.

"He chose to make a second speech on a following night, to show that he was as good in reply as on preparation. His speech was a bad one, and my first speech was thought better than his second."

He thus writes modestly to his sister:

To the Hon. Miss E. Temple.

"Admiralty, Feb. 4, 1808.

"My dear Elizabeth,—

"You will see by this day's paper that I was tempted

* Father of the present Lord Houghton.

by some evil spirit to make a fool of myself for the entertainment of the House last night; however, I thought it was a good opportunity of breaking the ice, although one should flounder a little in doing so, as it was impossible to talk any very egregious nonsense upon so good a cause. Canning's speech was one of the most brilliant and convincing I ever heard; it lasted near three hours. He carried the House with him throughout, and I have scarcely ever heard such loud and frequent cheers. Ponsonby* was dull and heavy, and neither Windham nor Whitbread were as good as usual; in fact, Canning's speech was so powerful that it gave a decisive turn to the debate. Lord Granville Leveson† made a very good speech, and stated an important fact—that all the impartial people in Russia, and other parts of the Continent, as far as he had any opportunity of collecting their sentiments, highly applauded, instead of condemning, our Danish expedition. Our division was not so large as I expected.‡ The Opposition were not more numerous, but we were less so than I expected. I thought we should have had three to one, but during this weather it is difficult to get people to come up to town.

"Adieu! my best love to all.

"Ever your affectionate brother,

"PALMERSTON."

---

* Described in the "Whig Guide," it is said by Palmerston, as a "squat gentleman, prolific in commonplaces."

† Then Secretary at War. He became ambassador at St. Petersburg, and afterward at Paris, and was created Earl Granville. He married a daughter of the fifth Duke of Devonshire, and was the father of the present earl.

‡ For the motion	108
Against it	253
Majority for government	145

To the Hon. Miss E. Temple.

"Admiralty, Feb. 6, 1808.

"My dear Elizabeth,—

"Many thanks for your congratulations. I certainly felt glad when the thing was over, though I began to fear I had exposed myself; but my friends were so obliging as to say I had not talked much nonsense, and I began in a few hours afterward to be reconciled to my fate. The papers have not been very liberal in their allowance of report to me; but the outline of what I said was as follows. In the first place, that the House was, to a certain degree, pledged by the address, in which they expressed their approbation of the expedition; but that the papers were in themselves improper to be produced, as they would betray the sources from whence we obtained intelligence, and expose the authors to Bonaparte's vengeance. That they were unnecessary, because the expedition could be justified without them. That Zealand and the Danish fleet was an object to France; that the neutrality of Denmark would have been no protection, as Bonaparte never did respect neutrality, and was not likely to do so now, when the temptation was the strongest, and his facility the greatest; and that in fact it was evident he did intend to seize the fleet. That Denmark was unable to resist; but, if she had possessed the means, was unwilling to have exerted them, since it was evident from various circumstances that she had determined to join France. Her refusal to accept our offers of alliance proved this. If we could have defended Denmark, the crown prince proved his hostility by refusing our guarantee; if we could not, how could the Danes have defended themselves without our assistance? on either supposition ministers were equally justified. . . . In conclusion I adverted to the slight inconsistency in those who, having sent out orders to Lord St. Vincent to do the same thing at Lisbon which we did at Copenhagen, although subsequent events prevented these orders from being executed, now blame ministers for having acted at Copenhagen on their own principles. I was about half an hour on my legs; I did not feel so much alarmed as I expected to be. I saw Emma to-day, and mean to dine with her to-morrow at Peggy's. William, as you will see by a letter from him, is returned to Cambridge. I do not know what we shall do for a house; how far upward should you mind going? There is a nice house in Manchester Square, but it is, to be sure, sadly out of the way.

"Adieu! my dear Tilly.

"Ever your affectionate brother,

"PALMERSTON."

The speech to which this correspondence alludes was evidently composed with much care, and in those parts which had been carefully consigned to memory was spoken with great ease and facility; but in others there was that hesitation and superabundance of gesture with the hands, which were perceptible to the last when Lord Palmerston spoke unprepared and was seeking for words; for though he always used the right word, it often cost him pains to find it. This marred, no doubt, the continued effect of his delivery, and made him doubtful, as we have seen, at first as to the impression he had produced; but every one recognized that a clever, well-instructed young man had been speaking, and made ready allowance for defects which might not remain, and to which if they did the House would become accustomed.

If there are any still entertaining doubts as to the necessity of the action which the orator defended, it may be as well to direct their attention to two letters to be found in the recently-published correspondence of Napoleon:

"**A M. de Talleyrand.**

"SAINT-CLOUD, 31 Juillet, 1807.

"Le même courrier continuera sa route sur Copenhague, et sera porteur d'une lettre à mon ministre, par laquelle vous lui ferez connaitre mon mécontentement de ce que les promesses qu'a faites le Danemark n'ont point d'effet, et que la correspondance continue avec l'Angleterre.

"Dimanche, au plus tard, vous aurez une conférence sur ce sujet avec M. de Dreher. Vous lui direz que, quelque soit mon désir de ménager Danemark, je ne puis empêcher qu'il ne se ressente de la violation qu'il a laissé faire de la Baltique; et que si l'Angleterre refuse la médiation de la Russie, il faut nécessairement qu'il choisisse, ou de faire la guerre à l'Angleterre ou de me la faire.

"NAPOLÉON."

"**Au Maréchal Bernadotte, Gouverneur des Villes Hanséatiques.**

"SAINT-CLOUD, 2 Août, 1807.

"Je ne veux pas tarder à vous faire connaitre mes intentions, qu'il faut tenir secrètes jusqu'au dernier moment.

"Si l'Angleterre n'accepte pas la médiation de la Russie, il faut que le Danemark lui déclare la guerre, ou que je la déclare au Danemark. Vous serez destiné, dans ce dernier cas, à vous emparer de tout le continent danois.

"NAPOLÉON."

I here insert another letter to his younger sister, which, though it relates to matters strictly private, shows in the most agreeable manner Lord Palmerston's business-like habits and generous and liberal views, and might serve as a lesson to English landlords having Irish estates.

To the Hon. Miss E. Temple.

"CLIFFONEY, September 12, 1808.

"MY DEAR ELIZABETH,—

". . . The rain, which had commenced the morning we left Dublin, and had continued with little intermission, was more particularly violent this day, and William,* who was not so much interested in seeing the estate as in keeping himself dry, returned home very soon. We, however, persevered, and saw the greatest part of the estate. Thursday, 8th, I employed in walking and riding about the town of Sligo with Chambers, and Friday, 9th, we took another ride over the whole of that part of the estate which lies connected by the seacoast. I find there is a great deal, I may almost say, everything, to be done, and it will be absolutely necessary for me to repeat my visit next summer, and probably make it annual for some time. I have in this part of the country about ten thousand acres, of which between eight and nine lie together to the north of Sligo. It is a tract of country about two miles broad and six long, bounded on one side by the sea, and on the other by bog and high, craggy mountains. It is wholly unimproved; but almost all the waste ground or bog is capable of being brought into cultivation, and all the arable may be rendered worth three times its present value. This, however, must be the work of time, and to accomplish it much must be done. The present objects which I must in the first instance set about, are to put the parish church in a state of repair, so as to make it fit for service; to establish schools, to make roads, and to get rid of the middlemen in some cases where it can be accomplished. After that, as opportunities occur, I mean to endeavor to introduce a Scotch farmer, to teach the people how to improve

* Mr. William Temple, his brother.

their land; to establish a little manufacturing village in a centrical part of the estate, where there are great advantages of water and stone; and to build a pier and make a little port near a village that stands on a point of land projecting into Donegal Bay, and called Mullaghmore.

"The schools and roads, however, are the most important points at present, and the condition of the people calls loudly for both. The thirst for education is so great that there are now three or four schools upon the estate. The people join in engaging some itinerant master; they run him up a miserable mud hut on the roadside, and the boys pay him half a crown, or some five shillings, a quarter. They are taught reading, writing, and arithmetic, and—what, from the appearance of the establishment, no one would imagine—Latin, and even Greek.

"I mean to build three good school-houses on the estate, and attach to each three or four acres of land, which will keep a cow and grow potatoes without making the schoolmaster into a farmer. Then, if the salary paid by the boys is not sufficient, the deficiency may be made up in money; and as the masters will be under my control, to be turned off at pleasure, I shall have security for their good conduct. I fancy they must be Catholics, for the people will not send their children to a Protestant.

"Roads are the first necessity for the improvement of the land. The seacoast abounds with a shelly sand, which is the best possible manure for boggy ground; and roads of communication between the shore and the upper country will enable the inhabitants of the bogs to reclaim their waste ground with this manure, and the people on the seaside to get turf for fuel from the bogs; and both are in need of a ready communication with Sligo market.

"The worst circumstance attending the property is that it is so populous. Every farm swarms with little holders, who have each four or five, or at the utmost ten or twelve acres. They are too poor to improve their land, and yet it is impossible to turn them out, as they have no other means of subsistence. Their condition, however, will be improved as I gradually get rid of the middlemen, or petty landlords.

"These people take a certain quantity of ground, reserve to themselves a small portion, and let out the rest to under-tenants. They make these unfortunate devils pay the rent of the landlord, and an excess, which they keep themselves, and call a profit-rent, while they live upon the part they reserve without paying any rent for it. In my last ride the day was very fine, and the whole tenantry came out to meet me, to the number, in different places, of at least two or three hundred. The universal cry was, 'Give us roads, and no petty landlords.' . .

"What admirable news from Portugal! Last night we heard of the surrender of Lisbon and the fleet by an express from Cork to Dublin; but it was a necessary consequence of the battle, and one did not feel anxious about it. What will the croakers say now? They have not a twig left to perch upon. I only hope Saumarez* will fall in with the Russians in the Baltic, and then I think we shall have beat Alexander into the warmest friendship and regard for us. What a triumph to the orders in Council is the opening of the Dutch ports! It is a complete confession of defeat by Bonaparte in the commercial as well as military contest he is waging with us; and I doubt not of equal success in both.

"Adieu! my dear Elizabeth. Our best love to all.

"Ever your affectionate brother,

"PALMERSTON."

---

* The distinguished admiral, afterward created, for his brilliant achievements, Lord de Saumarez. He was Nelson's second in command at the battle of the Nile. He died in 1836.

A new era now takes place in Lord Palmerston's life. He had spoken but once since his entry into the House of Commons, and he was but twenty-five years of age, when, by a singular combination of circumstances, he had an offer which would have turned most heads, but seems to have steadied his own.

The well-known quarrel between Lord Castlereagh and Mr. Canning had led to the necessity of a change of ministry, though not to the downfall of the party in the possession of power. Mr. Perceval became Prime Minister, and had to fill up important places without any very ready means of doing so with men of established reputation. He turned, not unnaturally, therefore, to those young men who had given promise of ability; and among these was undoubtedly the Junior Lord of the Admiralty, who could hardly, however, have expected the proposal which he now received, and to which he thus alludes:

"I was at this time (the breaking-up of the Portland Ministry) at Broadlands (October, 1809), and received a letter from Perceval, desiring me to come to town immediately, as he had a proposal to make to me which he thought would be agreeable: I went up to town, and he offered me the Chancellorship of the Exchequer. I was a good deal surprised at so unexpected an offer, and begged a little time to think of it, and to consult my friends.

"Perceval said that if I declined to be Chancellor of the Exchequer he should perhaps be able to offer me the War Office; but he felt bound to offer it first to Milnes.

"I wrote to Lord Malmesbury, then at Park Place, and consulted with Lord Mulgrave,* then First Lord of the

---

* Afterward Earl of Mulgrave, G.C.B., a general officer, and Lord-Lieutenant of the East Riding of Yorkshire. Grandfather of the present Marquess of Normanby. He died in 1831.

Admiralty. The result was that I declined the Chancellorship of the Exchequer, as too hazardous an attempt for so young and inexperienced a man, and accepted the offer of Secretary at War."*

I have obtained, through the kindness of Lord Malmesbury, the interesting correspondence to which Lord Palmerston here alludes :†

"BROADLANDS, Oct. 15, 1809.

"MY DEAR LORD MALMESBURY,—

"I have just received the inclosed letter‡ from Perceval, and am, in consequence, setting off for London, where I shall be early to-morrow morning.

"We have been spending three days very pleasantly on a sailing-party, from which we returned last night; the weather has been remarkably fine for our purpose, with plenty of wind and sunshine; and, although the latter was not quite so strong as the former, it made everything look very bright and cheerful, and, by dint of boat-cloaks, one can always keep out the cold."

"Oct. 16, 1809.

"MY DEAR LORD MALMESBURY,—

"I got to town this morning, and went to Perceval's, and was, as you may imagine, infinitely surprised at the proposal he had to make to me. He stated that, having

---

* On the 28th of October, and sworn a member of the Privy Council on the 1st of November.

† These letters—which came into my possession in the way I have stated—were in print when I heard they were about to be published by Lord Malmesbury himself, with other correspondence of his distinguished grandfather. Had I known this before, I might not have given them in extenso. As it is, I cannot avoid doing so; and at all events they have an appropriate place in Lord Palmerston's biography.

‡ The letter of Mr. Perceval here alluded to has not been preserved.

been deprived of the assistance of Huskisson* and Sturges Bourne, he felt much in need of some one to take off his shoulders part of the labor of his offices in and out of the House; that he meant for that purpose to divide the situations of Chancellor of the Exchequer and First Lord of the Treasury, and proposed to me to take the former. He said he had previously offered it to Vansittart, who declined taking it unless Lord Sidmouth formed part of the administration, and they had decided that it was not expedient to take Lord S. in. Annexed to this office he offered a seat in the Cabinet if I chose it, and he thought it better I should have it. I, of course, expressed to him how much honored I felt by this very flattering proof of the good opinion he was pleased to entertain of me, but also my great fears that I should find myself wholly incompetent for the situation, both from my inexperience in the details of matters of finance, and my want of practice in public speaking. To this he replied that he should of course take the principal share of the Treasury business, both in and out of the House. That in the office Harrison and his own secretary would be able to afford me great assistance, and that in the House practice would soon enable me to get on well enough for the purposes of business. He said that he felt great difficulty in finding any one to take the situation, and that he did not at the moment know of any one else to whom he could offer it. He named Milnes, Member for Pomfret—the man who made so great a figure as a speaker—as the only other person he had thought of. Upon further conversation, he appeared to think it possible that I might come in at first as a Lord of the Treasury, and afterward, if upon fagging at the business between this and the meet-

---

* Huskisson had been Secretary of the Treasury, and Sturges Bourne one of the Lords of the Treasury.

ing of Parliament, I found it likely I could take the Chancellorship, I could be promoted to it. The inconvenience, however, of this arrangement would be, that if I declined it ultimately, he might not be able to find any one else in the short interval which would possibly elapse, and that then I should not be of so much use to him in the House, as not carrying so much weight as if I held the Chancellorship. Thirdly, he suggested that it was possible that if I felt objections to either of these proposals, the office of Secretary at War* might be to be disposed of, if I chose to take that.

"I own I feel the most extreme embarrassment to know what answer to give. Of course one's vanity and ambition would lead one to accept the brilliant offer first proposed; but it is throwing for a *great stake*, and where much is to be gained, *very much* also may be lost. I have always thought it unfortunate for any one, and particularly a young man, to be put above his proper level, as he only rises to fall the lower. Now, I am quite without knowledge of finance, and never but once spoke in the House. The approaching session will be one of infinite difficulty. Perceval says that the state of the finances of this country, as calculated to carry on the war, is very embarrassing; and from what has lately happened in public affairs, from the number of speakers in opposition, and the few debaters on our side of the question, the warfare of the House of Commons will certainly be for us very severe. I don't know upon which of the two points I should feel most alarmed. By fagging and assistance I might get on in the

* This office, which had to deal with the accounts of the War Department, was distinct from the Secretary for War, who was, properly speaking, the war minister — an office usually coupled with some other appointment.

office, but fear that I never should be able to act my part properly in the House. A good deal of debating must of course devolve upon the person holding the Chancellorship of the Exchequer; all persons not born with the talents of Pitt or Fox must make many bad speeches at first, if they speak a great deal on many subjects, as they cannot be masters of all, and a bad speech, though tolerated in any person not in a responsible situation, would make a Chancellor of the Exchequer exceedingly ridiculous, particularly if his friends could not set off against his bad oratory a great knowledge and capacity for business; and I should be apprehensive that, instead of materially assisting Perceval, I should only bring disgrace and ridicule upon him and myself. The second proposal of coming in first as simply a Lord of the Treasury, at first sight is liable to fewer objections of the above sort. I might, to a certain degree, qualify myself for the other office in the interval between this and the meeting of Parliament; but still the same objections hold good as to the parliamentary part if I ultimately take the other—and it would not be fair to Perceval and the government to come into the Treasury unless with a pretty determined view of taking the Chancellorship, as it might be difficult, if not impossible, when near the opening of the session, for Perceval to make the division of his offices which he wishes. There are now two seats in the Treasury vacant, and of course one* must be filled by the Chancellor of the Exchequer, whoever he may be; it would therefore be impossible, probably, to keep one vacant for any great length of time; so that I think I am in a great degree called upon to make my determination as to the office now. And thus the second proposal, I think, reduces itself to a choice between taking

* The other was filled by Mr. Snowden Barne.

the office now, or being raised to it gradually by a previous seat at the Treasury board. I should myself strongly incline to being Secretary at War. From what one has heard of the office, it seems one better suited to a beginner, and in which I might hope not to fail, or in which one would not be so prominent if one did not at first do as well as one ought to do. Perceval said, however, that he must see me again before he could positively say that this was at his disposal. He has given me till *Wednesday* to consider. He at first proposed to have my answer to-morrow, but I begged to have till the next day, as I thought by that time I could have your sentiments upon the subject. I think the choice lies between being Chancellor of the Exchequer and Secretary at War, since the latter I should certainly prefer to being a Lord of the Treasury simply, another being the Chancellor and Perceval First Lord. Perceval did not mention whether the seat in the Cabinet would go with the War Office; but that, though a great honor, and certainly an assistance in debate, should not, I think, alone determine my choice. One consideration not to be wholly overlooked is, that we may probably not remain in long enough to retrieve any blunders made at the outset; and the ground of the War Office is, I think, *quite* high enough for me to leave off upon. Our party is certainly ill off for second-rates, but if Perceval cannot find another as good as me for the Exchequer, it's clear, I think, that we are too weak to stand. Milnes would probably not take it unless his ambition got the better of his partiality to Canning and his aversion to Perceval; and though a man of very brilliant talents, I should much doubt his steadiness; but there must be many well fitted for the office.

"I send you a duplicate of this letter by Broadlands in case it should by any accident miscarry, as the time of deliberation is so short that I cannot wait for another post-day. Should you be too late for the Christchurch post, my groom can take your answer, as our post does not go till near five, and even then it could be sent to Winchester at a later hour, as the mail does not pass through there till seven or eight o'clock.

"Yours most affectionately,

"Palmerston."

"New Hall, Oct. 17, 1809.

"My dear Harry,—

"I had just answered your letter of the 15th, and put my answer into the post, when your servant, who had sought for me in vain at Heron Court, brought me the one written yesterday explanatory of the reason which induced Perceval to send for you in such haste. As you wish to have my answer by to-morrow morning, I have little time (it is now a quarter-past seven) to bestow on perusing it; but although the subject is a very important and serious one, yet it strikes me so manifestly what is best for you to do, that I think I can venture to give an immediate opinion, without any great apprehension that I should deviate from it on more mature consideration.

"Nothing can be more flattering to you, nor of course more pleasing to me, than Perceval's offer to you. In different times, and under less perplexing circumstances, I should not demur as to the propriety of your accepting the Chancellorship of the Exchequer; for although it is a post which requires great labor and knowledge of finance, yet you would easily get habituated to the first, and soon acquire the latter. By what I say of the 'times,' I do not refer to the probable short duration of this government—that consideration would be a narrow and selfish motive for refusing to become a member of it; but I mean the peculiarly irritated state of the country, and the dangers which menace it from abroad; and I cannot wish you to be placed at once *in the breach*, to experience all the buffetings to which this would expose you, without the adequate means of resisting and counteracting them. I therefore am decidedly of opinion that you would not act fairly either by Perceval, by the public, or by yourself, were you to undertake the Chancellorship of the Exchequer, either in the first instance, or after the sort of preparatory seminary in which he proposes to place you; since, by taking the one post, you would virtually pledge yourself to accept the other; and if, at the expiration of the time stated, you were to decline it, you would increase the difficulties you are desirous to alleviate. Without hesitation, I advise you to decline the greater office, and I do it more confidently, since every reason I could possibly urge you have anticipated in your very judicious and most rational remarks.

"But, on the other hand, I am strongly inclined to recommend you to take the Secretaryship at War (with the Cabinet). It is a very reputable situation, which, without bringing you too forward at *once*, will, if you hold it a short time, infallibly lead you to the higher posts in the Cabinet, and one from which if you are dismissed you will not fall from a perilous height, or quit with any discredit.

"I have not time to add a word more. I can have no objection, if it be of any use to you, for you to tell Perceval my opinion. *I* wish his government to be strong and lasting, from the bottom of my heart.

"Ever, my dear Harry,

"Most truly and affectionately yours,

"M.

"I will return your letter to me to-morrow."

"Admiralty, Oct. 18, 1809.

"My dear Lord Malmesbury,—

"I have many thanks to give you for your very kind letter, which afforded me great satisfaction, by confirming the opinion which I had at first entertained of Perceval's very flattering proposal, and which had been strengthened by all the reflection I had been able to bestow on the subject during the time that has elapsed since I wrote to you. I am just returned from Perceval, to whom I stated the result of my deliberation; and that, fully sensible of the honor he did me in offering me the Exchequer, I thought it most prudent to decline it, but should, however, feel much gratified by the appointment of Secretary at War, if it should be at his disposal. He then told me very frankly that, as he had mentioned in our former interview, it depended upon certain other arrangements whether he should be able to give me the office. That, conceiving that Milnes would be a very great acquisition to government, if the bias he had in favor of Canning did not prevent him from joining us, he had written to him to say that he had to offer him such an official situation as (if inclined to take any) he would probably be disposed to accept. That, should Milnes come up in consequence, he meant to offer him the Chancellorship of the Exchequer. But that it was possible Milnes might decline so responsible a post, and that then, rather than run the risk of losing his support, he wished to offer him the War Office, which, in case he declined the other, he possibly might accept. That in such a case he would only have it in his power to offer me a seat at the Treasury, which he still hoped I would take, as it would let me more into business, and, if we stood our ground, pave the way to some further advance. He said he felt that this preference of Milnes might not appear very flattering to me but he trusted I should view it in its right light, as proceeding from his great anxiety to secure a doubtful friend who might be of essential service to our cause. I assured him that my principal wish was that his government should receive every possible accession of strength, and that no personal considerations would prevent me from acquiescing in any arrangement which could conduce to that end, but that in point of fact the first offer he had made me of the Exchequer was so very flattering, that, having declined that, I could not in any case object to giving Milnes the preference as to the War Office; and that should he decide to take it, I should very willingly take a seat at the Treasury. I trust you will approve of this resolution. It may not at first sight appear worth while to move from hence to the Treasury; but in as far as it will initiate me into Treasury business, and give me better opportunities of communicating with Perceval and others as to the matter and conduct of debates which may arise, it will be a desirable move. Perceval then told me, in strict confidence (which, however, I do not consider myself as violating in mentioning it to *you*), that there was an idea of making George Rose Chancellor of the Exchequer; that the king had objected to it upon the ground of his being Clerk of the Parliament —an office he thought inconsistent with the other; that this objection, however, might perhaps be obviated; that this appointment would, however, be considered as temporary, and that if the administration lasted, I might still look forward to the situation. Whatever may be the result of this business, it must always be a source of great pride and gratification to me to have been thought worthy of so splendid an offer; and I am persuaded that no afterthoughts will diminish the satisfaction I feel of having been right in declining it.

"Milnes' answer cannot be received for some days; but

I shall not fail to let you know as soon as I hear anything more upon this subject.

"Ever, my dear Lord Malmesbury,
"Yours most affectionately,
"PALMERSTON.

"There is a hitch in Dundas' appointment to the War Department, arising from Lord Melville, who probably wants it himself. Perceval seems, however, to think the general feeling against Lord Melville too strong to render it advisable to take him in; and probably when he finds that object unattainable, he will let his son accept what is tendered to him.

"Lord Mulgrave has sent to offer my seat at this Board to Percy—but that, of course, is not to be mentioned. I had immediately communicated Perceval's offer to Lord Mulgrave, who talked to me about it in the kindest and most handsome manner, saying that, in his opinion, the only objection to my accepting it at once would arise from my own feelings upon the subject; and that, if I was not nervous about it, he advised me to take it."

"ADMIRALTY, Oct. 23, 1809.
"6 o'clock.

"MY DEAR LORD MALMESBURY,—

"I have time only just to tell you that Milnes has come to town; and having had a long conference with Perceval, and also one with Canning, he has determined, upon hearing both sides, heartily to support Perceval, but declines office altogether. This latter resolution, which surprised me exceedingly, is founded upon real and unaffected diffidence. I think it a great pity, both for him and for us, as he would be more useful in office than out of it. The War Office has consequently come to me, conditionally, however, upon arrangements I will presently mention. In the mean time, Perceval having very handsomely given me the option of the Cabinet with the War Office (if I go to it), I thought it best, on the whole, to decline it; and I trust that, although you seemed to be of a different opinion at first, you will not, on the whole, think I was wrong. The office is one which does not invariably, or, indeed, usually, go with the Cabinet. A seat there was consequently not an object to me for appearance' sake, and, considering how young I am in office, people in general, so far from expecting to see me in the Cabinet by taking the War Office, would perhaps only wonder how I got there. With the Exchequer it would have been necessary, but with the War Office certainly not; and the business of the Department will, I take it, be quite sufficient to occupy one's time without attending Cabinet Councils. It would undoubtedly have been highly interesting; but for all purposes of business or debate, Perceval will of course keep one sufficiently informed to answer all one's wishes, at first at least. The arrangements on which the doubts I mentioned in the first page depend are, the determination of Rose upon the Exchequer, which, in consequence of Milnes' refusal, has been offered to him, and the final decision of Dundas about the War Department, which it seems not impossible Lord Melville may not let him take. Lord Melville is, I fancy, in high dudgeon at a letter, more candid perhaps than cautious, which Perceval wrote to him, explaining as delicately as possible, at the same time without reserve or limitation, the reasons which had induced him absolutely to decline offering Lord Melville an official situation, but concluding by the proffer of an earldom as a testimony of the approbation of the king of his long and distinguished services. This offer Lord Melville refuses rather sulkily, and, upon the reasons and decision of Perceval, observes that they are unfounded in fact, and unwise in policy; alluding to the ground on which Perceval placed his resolve —the apprehension of the popular clamor which his taking office might create against the government. The situations which Perceval wishes to keep unsettled till to-morrow, with the intention of giving me one or other, according as it may best suit his other arrangements, are—the War Office, the Treasurer of the Navy, and the Board of Trade, should Rose take the Exchequer. If Dundas does not come in, Ryder will probably have the War Department. Dundas will be a great loss.

"Adieu! my dear Lord Malmesbury.

"Ever yours most affectionately.

"PALMERSTON."

"ADMIRALTY, Oct. 25, 1809.

"MY DEAR LORD MALMESBURY,—

"Nothing is settled as yet; but Dundas has positively refused the War Department, and, I am told, Rose also the Exchequer, and that Perceval means to offer the latter to Charles Long. The defection of Dundas may be hurtful, as it will a little shake the allegiance of the Scotch members, but he will certainly support us, though he does not take office. The idea of having recourse to 'the Doctor' seems again revived in consequence of this circumstance, but I know not upon what foundation. I am to dine to morrow at Perceval's, to meet Milnes and Lowther, and shall probably hear something more about my own fate. We have had very bad accounts this morning from Flushing. There are but three thousand five hundred men fit for duty out of the whole garrison, and the enemy are rapidly increasing their preparations for attack. The Cabinet have not yet decided whether the island is to be, or, indeed, can be, retained or not. The officers of the two services have given twenty different and contradictory opinions on the subject, and Strachan himself has changed his mind three or four times about it. His present opinion is, that it is not tenable without an enormous naval force, amounting to what would be equivalent to at least eighteen sail of the line, besides the same fleet which would be necessary for the blockade if we had not the island. The navy continues perfectly healthy, but the land sickness seems rather to increase than abate.

"Ever, my dear Lord Malmesbury,

"Yours affectionately,

"PALMERSTON."

"ADMIRALTY, Oct. 27, 1809.

"MY DEAR LORD MALMESBURY,—

"Upon Rose* declining to be Chancellor of the Exchequer, and Long,† I believe, giving the same answer, it was yesterday settled that I should be Secretary at War, and I accordingly entered upon my functions this morning. There appears to be full employment in the office, but at the same time not of a nature to alarm one, and I think I shall like it very much. Lord Melville has relented, and Dundas accordingly yesterday agreed to take office; but he has preferred returning to the Board of Control. It is Richard Ryder to whom the War Department was offered, and I should think he will, or indeed must, take it, as there is no one else in fact to whom it can well be given, as we want a Secretary of State in the House of Commons. Lord Harrowby has agreed to take the Foreign Department if Lord Wellesley declines it.

---

* The Right Hon. George Rose was Vice-President of the Board of Trade, and Treasurer of the Navy.

† The Right Hon. Charles Long was joint Paymaster-General of the Forces.

"I dined yesterday at Perceval's at Ealing with Milnes and Lowther. The former I am almost inclined to think will remain stanch to us. His present opinion at least is very strong, for on returning he expressed his hopes that we 'should be able to fix this *honest little fellow** firmly in his seat, as it is a struggle of principle on the one hand, against trimming and political intrigue on the other.' He seems very much steadier than he used to be, and I should not be surprised if he were to fag very hard in Parliament; and then if he acquires, as he will, a certain confidence in himself, and Perceval still keeps the office open for him, it is not impossible that he may take it before the session is over. Percy has, as I expected, refused the Admiralty, and Lord Mulgrave has offered it to Lowther, who will most probably take it. He seems to wish it himself, and Lord Lonsdale will no doubt be glad to get him employed, with the hope of taking him a little way from the turf. The Jubilee seems to have been very happily celebrated everywhere. Nothing could be better than its effect in London, and the town appeared in the evening to be as quiet and orderly as could possibly be wished. The public offices and a few other buildings were illuminated, and the mob were occupied the whole night in gaping at them, and cheering as any carriage passed by. The only exercise of their sovereign authority was compelling all the coachmen and servants to pull off their hats as they passed the illuminated crowns over the Admiralty gate. We were the great attraction, and the bulk of the

* Mr. Milnes was, as it has been seen, at one time very hostile to Mr. Perceval and very friendly to Mr. Canning. But he was a high-minded, impressionable man, who always found something to condemn on all sides, and on this occasion, after being a partisan of Mr. Canning, he became a partisan of Mr. Perceval, but not enough to join his ministry.

mob were stationed opposite this building the whole of the night. Nothing seems yet to be known of the terms of peace, although no doubt can be entertained of its having been signed. But Stahremberg,* two days before the news arrived, was presenting papers, containing assurances from persons at his court that peace would not take place, and that they were resolved upon breaking the armistice.

"Adieu! my dear Lord Malmesbury.

"Ever yours most affectionately,

"PALMERSTON."

"WAR OFFICE, Nov. 9, 1809.

"MY DEAR LORD MALMESBURY,—

"I understand that Lord Wellesley has agreed to take office, but under an impression as to what has happened which is not quite correct, and therefore it is just possible that when, upon his arrival, he finds himself to have conceived the case to be stronger than it is, his inclination toward us may be weakened. He understands that a distinct proposition to place him at the head of the government had been rejected by Canning, and that was the point on which he went out; now, in point of fact, what did take place was so nearly tantamount to this, that I cannot conceive it probable that any change can take place in his determination. He clearly understands that the offer now made him is, not to be at the head of the government, but to join it. It has at length been determined to abandon Walcheren. I fear it could not possibly have been retained without an expense infinitely beyond its value; and the peace between France and Austria will at least furnish a pretense for the measure. It is only to be regretted that this decision was not sooner taken, as the

---

* Prince Stahremberg, Austrian ambassador in London.

Cabinet have for a month had all the documents before them on which it is founded, and in the mean time a great number of lives have been lost by the disorder in the island. I am going to Cambridge this evening, to vote at an election for a public orator to-morrow, and return to town on Saturday or Sunday. I continue to like this office very much. *There is a good deal to be done; but if one is confined it is some satisfaction to have some real business to do; and if they leave us in long enough, I trust much may be accomplished in arranging the interior details of the office, so as to place it on a respectable footing.*

"Its inadequacy to get through the current business that comes before it is really a disgrace to the country; and the arrear of Regimental Accounts unsettled is of a magnitude not to be conceived. We are now working at the Treasury, to induce them to agree to a plan proposed originally by Sir James Pulteney, and reconsidered by Granville Leveson,* by which I think we shall provide for the current business, and the arrear must then be got rid of as well as we can contrive to do it.

"Adieu! my dear Lord Malmesbury.

"Ever yours most affectionately,

"PALMERSTON.

"William is come to town to begin his law."

"WAR OFFICE, Nov. 24, 1809.

"MY DEAR LORD MALMESBURY,—

"I regret much to find that it is not in my power to execute my intention of going to Park Place to-morrow, as some arrangements respecting the Clerical Establishment, which I had hoped to get settled, are still undecided; and

* The two Secretaries at War who had held that office in succession immediately before Lord Palmerston.

it would not be convenient for me to leave town until some determination is made upon them, as perpetual reference is necessary with the Treasury and Sir David.* I trust, however, that I shall be able to accomplish my visit next week, and shall in that case probably be able to bring Sulivan, who could not have left London to-morrow.

"I am glad to find Lord Wellesley has so readily accepted the offer made to him, and that he does it with such cheerful views of the prospect before him. He writes to Arbuthnot that, although the present situation of affairs in Europe was certainly far from promising, he yet hoped that much might still be accomplished, and felt, at all events, confident that as much could be done as had been performed by any ministry since the death of Mr. Pitt. He was to set out in the 'Donegal' immediately, and may be expected to arrive in the course of a week or ten days. It was in consequence of reading all the papers and correspondence which had passed among the different actors in the late comedy of errors, conveyed to him by Mr. Sydenham, that he determined to join Perceval. Arbuthnot† told me yesterday that Canning or his friends give out that *he* persuaded Milnes not to take office, that Milnes asked his opinion of the propriety of his doing so, and that on his advising him not, Milnes said that nine reasons out of ten which had occurred to himself weighed against the acceptance of office, and that Canning's opinion had finally turned the scale. How far anything of this sort may have passed between them it is impossible to say; but I am quite convinced that, if there is any faith to be placed in human nature, Milnes left London zealously

* Sir David Dundas.

† Secretary of the Treasury.

resolved to support Perceval, and that whatever considerations might have operated in persuading him to decline office, a leaning to Canning was not among the number. I find old Dundas has a strong national propensity to a job. He sent me a letter the other day to say that the king having signified his pleasure that *General Delancey* should be made a commissioner for managing Chelsea Hospital, he requested I would make out a warrant appointing him one accordingly. It struck me that this was so very objectionable a thing, and one for which I should perhaps be held so personally responsible, that I communicated the thing to Perceval, who fully agreed with me as to the impropriety of the appointment, and the affair has in consequence been stopped. I wonder that Dundas was not aware of the impolicy to himself and General Delancey of bringing the latter again under public discussion, when the best he can hope is to have his conduct forgotten.*

---

* Lord Palmerston here alludes to the first report of the Commissioners of Military Enquiry, presented in 1806, "from which it appeared that General Delancey, late Barrack-Master General, who filled that office from 1793 to 1804, had been accustomed, in making up his accounts with the public, to take credit to himself for one per cent. on the whole expenditure of the barrack department, under the title of *contingencies for additional charge and responsibility for unsettled accounts.* It appeared also that he had charged the public twice in one year with his pay and allowances; from the whole of which it followed that, supposing his accounts, not yet audited, to be in other respects correct, but subducting these charges, which on no account could be allowed, he was indebted to the public in the sum of £97,415, instead of £6865, which was the balance he acknowledged to be due by him."—*Annual Register*, vol. xlviii. p. 79. He was also, according to the third report of the Commissioners, somewhat mixed up with Mr. Alex. Davison, Treasurer of the Ordnance, whose fraudulent transactions with the public money were brought before the notice of

The Treasury are endeavoring to sound the disposition of members by letters announcing the time fixed for the meeting of Parliament; but, generally speaking, they do not seem apprehensive of any great defalcation. Some speculating politicians will probably not attend at first, and some votes will be unavailable the first day or two, from their seats being vacant by office; but it appears to be thought that if we stand the first brunt of attack we shall rather gain than lose strength. Petty's elevation to the Upper House is a great circumstance for us, not so much from the harm which he would have done us by his individual attacks as from the unity and vigor the Opposition would have acquired by placing him, ostensibly at least, at their head; a situation for which he was well qualified, but into which there is not another individual among them whom they can with equal advantage elect.

"It is supposed that Tierney will succeed Ponsonby, who decidedly retires; but Tierney is not the man whom many on that side of the House would willingly follow; they neither respect nor trust him.

"Adieu! my dear Lord Malmesbury.

"Ever yours affectionately,

"PALMERSTON."

"WAR OFFICE, Dec. 21, 1809.

"MY DEAR LORD MALMESBURY,—

"I am very fearful it will not be in my power to visit you at Park Place this Christmas, as, if I am able to leave town for a couple of days, I must go down to Cambridge. This is the best time for seeing the Johnians collected, and under the present circumstances it would be

---

Parliament in 1807.—*Vide Annual Register*, vol. xlix. pp. 100–102.
Sir David Dundas was his son-in-law.

unwise to lose an occasion of maintaining one's ground among them. There is, I believe, no foundation whatever for the rumors of resignations and disputes; of the latter the Cabinet appear to have had enough to satisfy them. Nor is there any truth in the report of overtures having been received from France for a congress, or other negotiation. There has been some sort of communication about an exchange of prisoners, but it is doubtful whether it will lead to anything.

"Perceval seems to feel very confident as to the meeting of Parliament. It is intended to lay before the House all the official correspondence relative to the expedition,* but to resist any further inquiry, unless in the course of debate anything should be urged, by persons connected with either of the two services, which should place the question in a different point of view from that in which it now stands.

"Adieu! my dear Lord Malmesbury.

"Ever yours most affectionately,

"PALMERSTON."

The acceptance of the War Office, as detailed in the above correspondence, is perhaps the most remarkable circumstance in this biography. Nineteen out of twenty young men either hastily grasp at the highest post they can get, or, shrinking from the temptation to be great in their youth, consent to embrace mediocrity in after-years. It requires more than an ordinary lantern to discover a man who is daily testing his own strength with confidence and without vanity; ready to use it to the full extent of its powers, and wary as to exerting it beyond them. But, though Lord Palmerston had declined the brilliant offer to

* Walcheren.

accept the safe one, the addition which his position received from his new post was still considerable, and he was about to increase it by becoming member for the University which he had twice already essayed to represent; he was also in a foremost post in that great fight which was waging between the universal tyranny of Napoleon and the spirit of liberty which still defied him in Great Britain. The following letters to his sister relate to these two subjects and the ordinary occupations of a gay though busy man's existence. He is playing whist and drinking punch with the fellows at Cambridge. He is making, with considerable success, his first speech on the war estimates in the House of Commons. He is reading dispatches from Lord Wellington in Portugal; he is shooting, and nearly shot by a spring-gun, at Mr. Conyers'; he is lending one of his comical hats for the hunting-field to his brother William at Broadlands. He is going in for life at every corner of it.

To the Hon. Miss Temple.

"ADMIRALTY, Jan. 4, 1810.

"MY DEAR FANNY,—

"I inclose some little *billets-doux* for you and William, which came in a very questionable shape.

"I went to Cambridge on Monday evening, and spent Tuesday and yesterday in paying visits and playing whist and drinking punch with the fellows. I found everything looking very well, although a number of new candidates have been showing themselves; but I am not much apprehensive of their doing me much harm. Law,* a son of Lord Ellenborough, who is also of St. John's, has been about with Lord John Townshend,† intending to stand

* The present Earl of Ellenborough, G.C.B., Governor-General of India from 1842 to 1844.

† Lord John Townshend had formerly represented the Uni-

upon Petty's interest; but among my friends I do not find that he has made any way, and, though it has been expected that from being a Johnian he would draw off much of my strength, I do not much fear him. He is, besides, only nineteen and a half, so that at all events he cannot stand for a year and a half. I left Cambridge last night, and arrived here between six and seven this morning. The weather has been remarkably favorable for my purposes, being both mild and dry; and I suppose it has been equally propitious for William's snipe-shooting. . . . . . . The state of things in India is unpleasant, but there is not the slightest foundation for the reports of the murder and imprisonment of Sir George Barlow* and Lord Minto.†

"Adieu! my dear Fanny.

"Ever your affectionate brother,

"Palmerston."

"Lower Grosvenor Street, Feb. 27, 1810.

"My dear Fanny,—

"I am glad to hear that Elizabeth's cold is so much better, and hope that, with this beautiful weather, it will soon get quite well. I have been of late so busily engaged in preparing the army estimates, that I really have not had time to write to you. However, that ordeal is now nearly

---

versity in Parliament from 1780 to 1784. He sat for Westminster from 1788 to 1790, and for Knaresborough from 1793 to 1818, when he retired from public life. He died Feb. 25, 1833, aged 76.

* A distinguished member of the H.E.I.C. Civil Service, at that time Governor of Madras.

† Then Governor-General of India. As Sir Gilbert Elliot, he was, in 1779, Envoy Extraordinary to Vienna; Viceroy of Corsica, 1797, when he was made a peer; President of the Board of Control in 1806; Governor-General of India from 1807 to 1813, when he was raised to an earldom. He died in 1814.

over, though there is still hanging over me some little discussion on the report. It is very gratifying to me to find that I got through the business in a manner that was generally considered satisfactory. My friends were of course bound to say that I had acquitted myself well; but I have received expressions of commendation from the Opposition, which are the more flattering, as they may be considered as conveying the real opinion of those from whom they proceed. Windham was pleased to make honorable mention of me in his speech; and, what I certainly least expected, Whitbread, with whom I had never before exchanged a word, took occasion, as he met me entering the House yesterday, to say some very handsome things to me about perspicuity and information. The 'Courier' gives a very good report of what I said, barring a few mistakes in figures, of which, however, it is only surprising there are so few.

"We had last night a most extraordinary display of folly, coarseness, and vulgarity from Fuller, who, because Sir John Anstruther,* Chairman of the Committee, would not take notice of him, when he several times attempted to rise, in order to put some very gross and absurd questions to Lord Chatham, flew out into such a passion, and swore, and abused the Chairman and the House to such a degree that it became at last necessary to commit him to custody. As he went out he shook his fist at the Speaker, and said he was a d——d insignificant little puppy, and, snapping his fingers at him, said he did not care *that* for him or the House either. He is now amusing himself with the sergeant-at-arms, and I think was very lucky in not being sent to Newgate or the Tower.

---

* A distinguished lawyer, who had been Chief Justice of Bengal from 1798 to 1806.

"I shall not be able to get down to Park Place this week, but I have ordered a new pair of *pumps*, and as soon as they are ready I shall take the first opportunity of running down to join your dancing-parties. . . . . .

"Did you see the following epigram the other day in the 'Chronicle'? If you did not, it is a pity you should miss it, and I send it you; it is by Jekyll:*

"'Lord Chatham, with his sword undrawn,
Stood waiting for Sir Richard Strachan;
Sir Richard, eager to get at 'em,
Stood waiting—but for what?—Lord Chatham!'

"It is very good, I think, both in rhyme and point.

"Yorke, you see, has succeeded poor Eden† as Teller of the Exchequer. I cannot help thinking, on the whole, that it is almost a pity he has taken it, as he stood so high as an independent character; and the other day in the House, having said that he should support every and any government during the life of the present king, he added, in answer to a taunting cheer from the Opposition, that he did it from independent conviction of what was right, and that he had nothing *to hope* or fear from any set of ministers. On the other hand, he is a very fit man for any mark of favor, and is, moreover, very poor. At all events, it is a great instance of self-denial and disinterestedness on the part of Perceval that, with his large family, he did not give it to his son. It certainly would have made an outcry; but there is not a man, I am persuaded, on the Oppo-

---

* Afterward a Master in Chancery, a post which the Prince Regent obtained for him by personally soliciting it from Lord Eldon.

† The Hon. Wm. F. Eden, eldest son of the first Lord Auckland, was found drowned in the Thames, Feb. 24, 1810.

sition side who would not have taken it under the same circumstances.

"Adieu! my dear Fanny; my best love to all.

"Ever your affectionate brother,

"PALMERSTON."

"WAR OFFICE, Friday, Oct. 19, 1810.

"MY DEAR FANNY,—

"Dispatches are just arrived from Lord Wellington, dated the 5th inst. The French had pushed on their outposts towards Coimbra on the 30th; and on the 1st Lord Wellington fell back by Pombal to Leyria and Alcobaça, where he arrived the 5th, and on the 7th, the day on which Walsh, the messenger, left Lisbon, he was expected at Rio Mayor, near Santarem.* Lord Wellington says† the army are within a few leagues of the ground on which he means them to fight the enemy; and, as the French were advancing with the evident intention of fighting, a battle

* "When Massena retired, he took up a defensive situation before Santarem. He was now blockaded by the British forces, and had to depend for his supplies on the bare country behind him.

"On the 6th of March, Wellington, who long maintained, contrary to general opinion, that Massena would be forced to retire from want of provisions, received information that he had retired, and immediately put his troops in motion in three columns. He pursued the enemy with skill; and on the 6th the French crossed the Aquado into Spain."—KNIGHT'S *History of England*, vol. vii. p. 539.

† *Note from an Officer in the Guards.*—"As Lord Wellington said, the army at the time he spoke of was within a few miles of the spot where it was intended to fight a battle. But we met with no provocation from Massena, whilst the game of our chief was a defensive one. We were covered by the lines of Torres Vedras in a triple defense. These lines were maintained harmlessly for six weeks, when Massena broke up and retired, Nov. 16, 1810."

must ere this have been fought, which will decide the fate of Portugal, and probably of Spain. The French were at Condexa. Nothing of consequence had happened in the retreat, only a few skirmishes between the cavalry and light troops. Stuart sends an intercepted letter from Massena, dated Viseu, September 27th, which gives a striking picture of the state of his army. He complains dreadfully of the roads : '*Nous passons par des chemins affreux hérissés de rochers.*' His artillery and baggage have suffered much, and must, he says, rest two days at Viseu to repair damages. He says he means to go to Coimbra, where he hears the English and Portuguese army is. He says : '*Monseigneur, nous passons à travers un désert ; on ne rencontre nulle part une âme ;*' that consequently he could get no guides ; that his men lived on potatoes they dug up, and grain they gathered in the fields. Our army were in high health and spirits.

"Adieu ! Love to all.

"Ever your affectionate brother,

"PALMERSTON.

"This wind must bring us news in a day or two."

"WAR OFFICE, Oct. 29, 1810.

"MY DEAR FANNY,—

"Still no news from Portugal, and, as the wind blows, no probability of any for some days.

"I went down to Conyers' on Monday morning to breakfast, shot there on Monday, and returned to town on Tuesday morning. The party consisted of William and Lady Caroline Lamb, and a Dr. Dowdeswell. The day was terribly stormy ; it blew an absolute hurricane, and *therefore* I killed only one brace of pheasants. Lamb*

---

* Afterward Lord Melbourne.

was luckier, and always found the wind *lower* when he fired, by which means he killed four brace.

"Mrs. Conyers and Julia were as delightful as usual, and Mr. Conyers as entertaining as ever. The chief objection to the shooting is that it is all wood shooting, the fields being entirely grass; and those woods contain more spring-guns and steel-traps than pheasants. I was unpleasantly disturbed in my progress by the wire of a spring-gun, which on looking round I saw staring me full in the face. Luckily, however, it was not loaded, or at least the powder in the pan was quite wet and useless; but I did not feel quite comfortable during the rest of the day whenever a bramble caught my legs. Old Conyers says he is sure some dreadful accident will happen some day with them, but he is overruled by the *youthful ardor* of his sons; in the mean time he dares not go into any of his woods, and, though fond of planting, is afraid of putting foot into any of his numerous plantations, lest he should leave it behind him.

"Sulivan has told you I have made Shee Agent-General to Volunteers and Local Military. It is a very good appointment, being worth £1000 per annum. There is a good deal to do, and a good deal of pecuniary responsibility attached to the office; but I have no doubt he will get through it very well, and he was dying for employment; and, between ourselves, I suspect some excuse for seeing a little less of dear Mrs. Shee, notwithstanding his animated eulogiums of her at Walcot. I was very glad to be able to do it. Hassel, the former agent, being rich and idle, has resigned.

"Adieu! my dear Fanny.

Your affectionate brother,

"PALMERSTON."

"War Office, Dec. 29, 1810.

"My dear Fanny,—

"My cold is quite well, and has been so for the last two days. I inclose a draft for £50 for clothing for the Romsey people, as usual. Will you tell Elizabeth to let me know what I owe her? Tell William he may hunt Pitch whenever he likes, and I am sure he will be well and pleasantly carried; and whenever he goes out it will do Highlander good to let young John Ashley ride him. I am much amused at William becoming a Nimrod, and complaining, the first time he goes out, of the hounds pottering about the covers. I expect to hear of his leading the field next. *He may wear any of my various comical hats if he likes them.*

"Pray tell Emma how glad I am to hear of her acquisition, as I always must be at anything agreeable that happens to her.

"The king is a little better, but has been, I believe, very dangerously ill. We are, I think, all on the *kick and the go,* but have probably a month to run.

"Adieu! My love to all.

"Ever your affectionate brother,

"Palmerston."

In allusion to what is said of the speech—much noticed at the time—on the estimates, I quote a passage, though in some of the many biographical sketches it has been already quoted, because it shows our force at that time in arms; indeed, if I were not cautious of overloading these volumes with already published matter, I should make further extracts from a speech which bears ample evidence of the careful preparation that had such a favorable effect, not only on the argumentative merit of Lord Palmerston's speeches, but also on their delivery.

"Our military force is at this moment as efficient in discipline as it is in numbers; and this not only in the regular army, but in the militia, volunteers, and other descriptions of force. We have six hundred thousand men in arms, besides a navy of two hundred thousand. The masculine energies of the nation were never more conspicuous, and the country never at any period of its history stood in so proud and glorious a position. After a conflict for fifteen years against an enemy whose power has been progressively increasing, we are still able to maintain the war with augmenting force and a population, by the pressure of external circumstances, consolidated into an impregnable military mass. Our physical strength has risen as the crisis that required it has become more important; and if we do not present the opposition of those numerous fortresses to invaders which are to be found on the Continent, we do present the more insuperable barrier of a high-spirited, patriotic, and enthusiastic people."

I have just observed that I was tempted to make further extracts from this very able speech, and the indulgent critic might probably have pardoned me if I had done so, whereas it may be thought, on the other hand, that I have injudiciously quoted letters which may seem frivolous when introduced into the biography of a veteran statesman. But I have dwelt, I confess, with detail and pleasure on this early epoch of Lord Palmerston's life, because, to those who only saw or knew him in his old age, there is something that freshens and brightens his memory in recurring to his youth, when we see him stepping on to the platform of life with the same gay and somewhat jaunty step, and yet with the same serious and business-like intent, that carried him on cheerfully and steadily along a sunshiny path through his long career.

That, indeed, to which I here wish more particularly to

call attention, is the universality of the man, who makes the business-like speech, writes the lively letter,—of the "new pumps," etc. He was not a prig or a coxcomb, but naturally grave and naturally gay; hearty in any pursuit, whether of business in the senate or of pleasure in the ball-room; taking pains to please without seeming to expect admiration. Hence he never made those enemies who are aroused by high pretensions, and he gathered round him that general good will which gives a slow but steady current to a statesman's fortunes. There were, moreover, under the apparent mixture of seriousness and frivolity which marked this portion of Lord Palmerston's life, a steady pluck and character, and a reliance on the strength of a right cause, which contrast favorably and singularly with the diffidence shown when, the question being merely a personal one, he put aside the temptation of a seat in the Cabinet and one of the first offices of state. These qualities were tested in a very trying manner not long after his entry into his new office.

There existed at that time a Secretary *for* War, who had little or nothing to do with details, but to consider the general war policy and the direction of the great military operations of the country. He was usually the Minister of the Colonies, or at times of another department. There was then the Commander-in-Chief of the army, who was exclusively charged with the discipline, recruiting, and promotions of the army; and there was then the Secretary *at* War, who was charged with and responsible for the expenses and accounts of the army, or, in other words, with controlling the military disbursements and superintending the settlement of the military accounts.

On the whole, these duties were pretty clearly separated and defined. The one nevertheless ran in certain instances into the other, especially in respect to forms; and I may mention two cases occurring almost immediately after Lord Palmerston's installation at the War Office, concerning which the Commander-in-Chief and the Secretary at War came into conflict.

1st. Generals on the home staff had the right to a certain number of aides-de-camp, for whom the government paid; and they often got paid for aides-de-camp whom they never had. The Secretary at War, deeming this a question of expense, required a return from the Horse Guards of all generals on the staff and their aides-de-camp on duty, in order to make his payments accordingly.

2d. The colonels of regiments were allowed so much to clothe the men, the sum granted being paid to their agents. But the Secretary at War said that he ought to have proof that the clothiers who had furnished the articles required were satisfied with the public money being paid to the colonels' agents, and not to themselves—that is, in fact, he ought to be satisfied that they were paid, or were satisfied they would be paid, for the goods delivered.

There can be no doubt that what the Secretary at War required in both instances was essentially for the public service, and intimately connected with the military expense. But Sir David Dundas, who had been appointed* Commander-in-Chief after the temporary retirement of the Duke of York, deemed that Lord Palmerston had greatly overstepped his province in interfering on his own authority in these matters. He contended that the Secretary at War was his subordinate, that all orders ought to come from him; but, admitting that a general ought not to be paid for aides-de-camp when he had not got them, he undertook to inform the Secretary at War when this was the case. With respect to the clothiers, however, he objected alto-

* March 25, 1809.

gether to any interference. It was something, in his own language, "so novel, so extraordinary, and likely to lead to such consequences," that he could not attempt to answer it off-hand. He applied on the subject to Mr. Perceval, advancing as his theory, that though the payment made to the colonels was public money, to be applied for a public purpose, they were to deal with it as private money; owing the persons they employed for regimental clothes as they would for their own clothes; and that the War Office, if the clothes, etc. were approved, had no business to inquire as to whether the persons who furnished them were paid or not.

He complained, moreover, generally that the War Office was becoming too arrogant and independent. The Secretary at War, however, would not recede. He maintained that with respect to the clothiers he was merely fulfilling his duty according to a recent Act of Parliament, and that as to his general position he held, as the representative of Parliamentary control over the military expenditure, and as the civil servant of the Crown in military matters, an independent post, which, though inferior to that of Commander-in-Chief, was not subordinate to it.

"I have always understood," he says, "and the doctrine seems also recognized in the sixth report of the Commissioners of Military Inquiry, that the Commander-in-Chief presides over the discipline, and the Secretary at War over the finance, of the army; that each are responsible and competent to act independently on matters which concern their respective provinces; but that on questions in which the two are blended, previous mutual communication should take place." On the one hand, Lord Palmerston referred for his independence to an order, November 1, 1804, which says, "All applications relative to military disbursements or to pecuniary claims to pay allowances, etc., and all letters which have for their object the construction and explanation of Acts of Parliament regarding the military service, or which have reference to the civil police of the country, are as formerly to be addressed to the Right Hon. the Secretary at War."

On the other hand, Sir David Dundas founded his superiority on the instruction given in the Secretary at War's commission under the sign manual: "You are to observe and follow such orders and directions as you shall from time to time receive from us or the general of our forces for the time being, according to the discipline of war, in pursuance of the trust reposed in you and your duty to us."

There were certainly two sides to the shield. But Mr. Perceval refused to decide which was the right one, and contented himself with begging both parties to pocket their differences. This Sir David, however, refused to do; and though when the Duke of York returned to his post* he was more moderate and courteous in his language than Sir David, he persisted in the same theory; and the views of the parties were ultimately brought before the Prince Regent, to whom Lord Palmerston clearly stated that he considered himself placed "as a sort of barrier between the military authority of the officers in command of the army, and the civil rights of the people," stating that "no alteration could take place in this situation *without the interference of Parliament.*"

This consideration, in fact, regulated his Royal Highness's decision, which was to leave things as they were, without saying what they were; adding, that if anything new was suggested by the Secretary at War relative to his functions, then it should be communicated to the Com-

* In May, 1811.

mander-in-Chief, and adopted if the two authorities were agreed; whilst, if they disagreed, the nature of the disagreement should be placed before the First Lord of the Treasury, who would take the pleasure of his Royal Highness the Regent thereupon.

This, in fact, solved none of the questions that had been raised; but it prevented the entire subordination of the civil authority to the military one—a result of which Lord Palmerston may fairly claim the merit.

An explanation that he wrote at this time of the historical character and position of the Secretary at War is one of the ablest papers in the War Office, and will be found in the Appendix

BOOK III.

Perceval's death—Palmerston remains in Lord Liverpool's government—Speaks in favor of Catholic Emancipation—Turn in the war—Speech on army estimates—Policy as to colonies—State of England—Alarm—Escape from assassination—Correspondence at Horse Guards—Speeches in Parliament—General position—Without party friends—New party formed—Election for Cambridge separates him from the old Tories—Correspondence.

A CONSIDERABLE space now intervenes in the private correspondence in my possession. Meanwhile the ministry of Perceval, which, as may be seen by one or two of the letters I have quoted, was but a rickety one, terminated by the melancholy death of that statesman, May 11, 1812. The general desire produced by this event was to see a government formed equal to the critical situation of affairs; this desire the public and private differences existing at that time among leading statesmen rendered abortive, and the country was disappointed by the advent of an administration universally considered the weakest that ever undertook to hold the helm of a great state, but which suffered less from opponents, and was more favored by events, than almost any other that has conducted the affairs of England. In this administration Lord Palmerston, having refused—before the offer was made to Mr. Peel—the Secretaryship for Ireland, maintained, without rise or fall, during fifteen years, the post which he had received in 1810 from Mr. Perceval, uniting during this period the pleasures of a man of the world with the duties of a man of business. No one went more into what is vulgarly termed "fashionable society," or attended more scrupulously to the affairs of his office; no one made better speeches on the question, whatever it was, that his place required him to speak on, or spoke less when a speech from him was not wanted. His ambition seemed confined to performing his peculiar functions with credit, without going out of the beaten track of his office as a volunteer for distinction. To this general rule, however, there was one exception; when Mr. Grattan, in 1813, brought forward the question of Catholic Emancipation, he made an eloquent oration in support of it. Still, the line he took was cautious. He did not assert that the state had not the right to exclude the Catholic body from participation in its affairs;—a consideration for the public interests was, according to him, supreme over all other considerations; but in this case he contended that the state imperiled itself by the measures it adopted for its security.

"If I think," he said, "that there is no real danger in the removal of these disabilities, accompanied by such other corresponding regulations as the House may ultimately adopt, I do think there is both inconvenience and danger in the continuance of the present anomalous state of things.

* * * * *

"Is it wise to say to men of rank and property, who, from old lineage or present possessions, have a deep interest in the common weal, that they live in a country where, by the blessings of a free constitution, it is possible for any man, themselves only excepted, by the honest exertion of talents and industry in the avocations of political life, to make himself honored and respected by his countrymen, and to render good service to the state;—that they alone can never be permitted to enter this career; that they may indeed usefully employ themselves in the humbler avocations of private life, but that public service they never can perform, public honor they never shall attain? What we have lost by the continuance of this system it is not for man to know; what we might have lost can be more easily imagined. If it had unfortunately happened that, by the circumstances of birth and education, a Nelson, a Wellington, a Burke, a Fox, or a Pitt, had belonged to this class of the community, of what honors and what glory might not the page of British history have been deprived? To what perils and calamities might not this country have been exposed? The question is not whether we would have so large a part of the population Catholic or not. There they are, and we must deal with them as we can. It is in vain to think that by any human pressure we can stop the spring which gushes from the earth. But it is for us to consider whether we will force it to spend its strength in secret and hidden courses, undermining our fences and corrupting our soil, or whether we shall at once turn the current into the open and spacious channel of honorable and constitutional ambition, converting it into the means of national prosperity and public wealth."

He argued in this manner; for his nature was not one that lingers over abstract rights or speculative theories: the broad fact which struck him practically, and which struck him the more forcibly as being one of a school which considered the power and greatness of his country the main object of a statesman, was, that the discontented condition of a large portion of British subjects weakened, when their contentment would strengthen, England. He saw, in the one case, Ireland a snarling cur worrying our heels; in the other, a gallant and faithful mastiff standing by our side.

The war in the mean time took a sudden turn; light penetrated the gloom that had long obscured the prospects of Europe: the great conqueror became the conquered; and he who had refused to have his sway limited by the Rhine accepted as his empire a microscopic island in the Mediterranean. In such a position it was certain he would not long remain; but in a new struggle with fortune he was again overpowered; and in the last and fatal battle which decided his fate and that of Europe, a British commander at the head of British troops had been victorious. This was a proud time for England, and the more severe and exciting labors of the Secretary at War were over. But if he had lighter work at the War Office, he had heavier in the House of Commons, with which it was easier to deal when the minister who had to ask for the means to support a large army could plead we were engaged in a gigantic conflict, than when, with an army which still seemed large to those who had to pay for it, he could not pretend it was wanted for a foreign foe.

On one of these occasions (in 1816) he had to deal with Mr. Brougham, who had just been making one of those powerful but discursive harangues with which he used to overawe the Treasury bench; and one cannot but admire the readiness and courage with which the usually silent Secretary at War puts aside the arguments of a speech it would have been difficult to answer, and retorts the sarcasm of an antagonist whom most would have feared to provoke. We can see him rising, with an undisturbed and half-careless air, as he says, "The honorable and learned member has made an accusation which I certainly cannot retort upon that honorable gentleman himself, namely, that *he very seldom troubles the House with his observations.* I, at all events, will abstain from all declamation, and from any dissertation on the Constitution, and confine myself to the business at present on hand—the Army Estimates of the current year."

It may be interesting to notice the extent and employment of our army at this period. Exclusive of the troops in India, and the army in occupation of France, the total number of men proposed in the votes was 99,000. These were divided under four heads: those stationed in Great Britain; those in Ireland; those in our old colonies, that is, the colonies we had possessed previously to the war; and those in our new colonies, which we had acquired during the progress of the war. It was proposed to have 25,000 troops in Great Britain, the same number in Ireland; 23,800 in our old colonies, and 22,200 in the new. Add to these 3000 as a reserve for reliefs to the colonial garrisons.

"With respect to the old colonies, the estimates provided only," says Lord Palmerston, "7000 men more than had garrisoned them previously to the outbreak of the war. In the whole of our North American possessions, the Bahamas included, there were only 4000 men more than there had been in 1791. There were many causes," he urged, "for this augmentation. The increasing population required larger means of defense—*certainly not to be used against the inhabitants*. Upper Canada had been almost entirely peopled and settled since the war commenced. He did not insinuate any suspicions of broils with the United States. He hoped that each country had equally made the discovery that peace was the preferable policy. Still, as a matter of political prudence, we must always provide for possible contingencies. He was firmly convinced that among nations weakness would never be a foundation for security. The navigation between the two countries was moreover suspended during the winter, and, in the case of a rupture, *many months might elapse ere reinforcements could be sent.* At Antigua there had been established a considerable naval arsenal, which involved the presence of an additional military force.

"The new or captured colonies were Ceylon, Mauritius, the Cape, the African Settlements, Trinidad, Tobago, St. Lucie, Demerara, Berbice, Essequibo, Malta, and the Ionian Islands. In all, the enemy's garrisons there had capitulated to the number of 30,000. This was after all their losses by deaths in action and from sickness. The government only proposed 22,000 for these colonies, not two-thirds of the garrisons that the enemy had kept up. The 25,000 men for the home station exceeded by 7000 the numbers in 1791. But the large increase in our colonial possessions rendered it necessary to keep up a considerable increased reserve at home.

"The plain question for the House to consider was, whether they should reduce all the military establishments of the country below their just level; and whether, if they did so, the saving would bear any comparison with the injury that it might produce. For, after all, even if the plans of retrenchment so loudly called for were adopted, the diminution of expenditure would not be half so great as the country and the House seemed to imagine. Would it, therefore, be a wise or expedient course, under these circumstances, to abdicate the high rank we now maintained in Europe, to take our station among secondary Powers, and confine ourselves entirely to our own island? He would again repeat that the question was not whether we should carry into effect such diminution of the military establishment of the country as would save the people from the income-tax,—for he contended that no possible reduction in those establishments could accomplish that end,—but whether we should compel the Crown to abandon all our colonial possessions, the fertile sources of our commercial wealth, and descend from that high and elevated station which it had cost us so much labor, so much blood, and so much treasure to attain."

A discussion no doubt was then commencing which is still going on, and which will pass through many phases during the present generation, before it is terminated by the decision of posterity. I myself remember saying, when speaking in favor of the American Union to an American audience, before the struggle for Southern independence began, that you should not ask the opinion of a healthy man as to the value of health; it was the invalid alone who could estimate it. You should not ask a great and powerful state in the height of its prosperity what are the advantages of being great and powerful. It is a state that finds its greatness fallen, its power diminished or menaced, that feels the loss it has incurred, or thinks it is about to sustain. In fact, it was only when the consolidated power of the United States was in serious peril that the resolve of preserving it intact, at any sacrifice, became intense. So, there has been a tendency of late years in England among a certain class of politicians to underrate the advantages of vast empire and great consideration. This is natural; men, as I have just said, undervalue what they possess. Who has not seen statesmen fatigued with office and pining to lay down its burdens, and found them, after a brief repose in obscurity, willing to undergo any amount of toil and responsibility in order to reach once more that point in the political ladder from which they not unwillingly descended? It is just so with a people. What efforts has not Poland made, what efforts did not Italy make, to regain the independence and recover the glory of past but unforgotten years! The expense of dignity and influence is, however, more frequently brought before a popular assembly than their importance.

No doubt a great gentleman, let him be a distinguished peer or commoner, is the same individual, whether he opens his house and keeps up a large establishment, or whether he lodges in a cottage and never offers a glass of wine to a friend. His ability is the same, his rank is the same, his wealth is the same; but his influence is different. A certain degree of show and hospitality gives influence—quietly, insensibly, but irresistibly. Lord Palmerston himself, in later years, gained much by a conspicuous mansion and frequent dinners and assemblies. It is all very well to sneer at these things; they affect us in spite of our philosophy.

As three or four servants in livery and a large house place a man in this world of ours higher than he would be placed if inhabiting a small lodging with a dirty maid to open the door, so a nation has its servants in livery, its large house, its large establishments—things not absolutely necessary to its existence, but the accompaniments of its position, and without which its position would not be duly represented and sustained. I may be mistaken, but I believe every Englishman has a certain pride and interest in the figure made by the English nation. He likes that it should be "the great nation" and appear "the great nation." All that seven-eighths of us ask is, that the proper effect should be obtained without needless or improper cost.

No man is thought the more of for muddling away his money. He should have for his expenditure what his expenditure ought to bring him. The minister who is careless as to what he spends, and the minister who is niggardly as to what he ought to spend, are equally acting against the instincts of our country; and they who think to acquire an honorable or durable popularity by bringing down this country from its traditional rank among the leading states of the world, do not know the spirit which still burns in the breasts of their countrymen.

If, indeed, the member of Parliament who affects to despise prestige or consideration as an object for the government of his country, would merely look into his own breast, and examine the motive which brings him into the House of Commons and directs his conduct there, he would find, unless actuated by the mere vulgar hope of official emolument, that it was the desire for prestige or consideration that induced him to submit to the toils and undergo the expense which our election petitions sufficiently demonstrate to be among the penalties attached to public life. It is this desire which is at the bottom of our individual honesty, our individual energy—which is, in short, our great individual characteristic. It is, and should be, our national characteristic also; for a nation which has no longer a wish for distinction has already a propensity to decline.

These were the ideas of Lord Palmerston; they were the guiding stars of his political life. He wished to make and to keep England at the head of the world, and to cherish in the minds of others the notion that she was so.

In the speech I have just quoted, especial reference is made to our colonies. Every age wishes to assume to be wiser than its predecessor; and inasmuch as there was formerly a somewhat exaggerated value attached to colonial possessions, without any distinct or accurate idea as to the profit to be derived from them, so there is now a supercilious and narrow-minded tendency to underrate their importance. There are many places presenting no peculiar advantage to us by their possession, but of which the loss would be exceedingly disastrous if they were in the hands of an enemy. From most of the others, though we derive no direct revenue, we indirectly feed our national resources. The wealth of nations is frequently formed and nourished by means only perceptible in their results, as you see the vital energies of the human body maintained or restored by certain springs, the analysis of whose waters gives no indication of the nature of their powers. An encouragement to enterprise, to navigation, to speculation produced by those relations which the colonist entertains with the mother-country, often carries capital into particular channels through which it would not otherwise flow, and enriches those by whom it is employed, and who by their residence and their expenditure in their native land add to its riches and its revenue.

Nor does wealth, though it is one of the main contributors to national greatness, alone or in itself constitute that greatness. Commercial prosperity soon vanishes when political importance departs, and no small portion of political importance depends on political prestige. When Mr. Webster says, "There is not an hour in the day in which the British drum is not beating in some region of the earth," he not only fills the minds of others with a vast idea of the power and majesty of Great Britain, but he gives us, the British people, an elevated sense of our own dignity; animating us thereby to noble achievements, and bracing up our minds for great deeds on great occasions.

The power of the imagination is not to be overlooked by those who assume to direct the destiny of empires; and it is singular to find so many of the gentlemen who cite to us as a model the great Transatlantic commonwealth altogether forgetful of the imperial spirit which, since the extent of its dominions was menaced, is the peculiar characteristic of the American republic. Whilst we, talking about the United States, are daily loosening the bonds which formerly bound our empire together, the people of the United States are strengthening, enforcing, and fighting for the permanent solidity of theirs. You find no statesman there talk of abandoning a territory,—no general or admiral advocate the resignation of a fortress. The historian who in after-times shall write on the decline and fall of British greatness, may possibly question the policy with which we have from year to year been separating ourselves from possessions that we might, with the advantages of steam and telegraph, have more closely connected with our central power. There is, in fact, already rising a new school of economists who, without disputing as a general axiom the advantage of buying at the cheapest markets and selling at the dearest, are still disposed to consider that under our peculiar circumstances a system of colonial commerce combined with a system of emigration—relieving the mother-country from a superfluous population on the one hand, and creating new and certain customers for her on the other—maintaining the feeling of Englishmen for Englishmen in every quarter of the globe, by giving to our distant countrymen a regular market for their produce, and to our people at home a regular market for their manufactures—might on the whole have been more adapted to our safe and steady prosperity as well as to our imperial majesty than a system which destroys the sentiment of national affection by referring everything to individual interest, and sends us into the world on a speculation for customers whose demands must be regulated by laws over which we have no control, and who in a free struggle for competition must force us, if we mean to surpass them, to produce better articles at cheaper labor—a necessity already resisted by trades-unions and limitations on working-hours, as well as by a poor law which deranges the first movements of the machinery by which the principles of free trade are to be worked out. But without dwelling further on theories which the present is not disposed to accept, and which the future—already compromised—could only, looking to the condition of things now established, achieve by such arrangements with the colonial legislatures as it may be possible to imagine but hardly possible to realize, I pass on to observe that the defense of our colonies, though jealously provided for at the time of which I have been speaking, was not the only reason for maintaining the standing army which was asked for on their behalf. It is strange to us, who can judge the past dispassionately, to read in contemporary memoirs of the panic which existed even among thinking persons during the five or six years which succeeded the war, as to the probability of a general rising against law, order, and government. There were no leaders of any authority in favor of such rising; there were no funds or arms to aid it; there was nothing but the pamphlets of a few seditious writers and the speeches of a few mob orators to threaten the peace of the country. Still, the administration and the friends of the administration had persuaded themselves, and contrived to persuade many others, that we were on the eve of a terrible catastrophe, from which nothing but a few thousand men, each of whom was furnished with a musket and a bayonet and paid a shilling a day for his patriotism, could protect us. He, then, who was for maintaining the army was the friend of the throne and the altar, of the king, and of the Archbishop of Canterbury, as he who was for reducing it was in atheistic league with Cobbett, Carlile, and all the other democrats and demons who were menacing us with irreligion and a republic. A good speech on the army estimates was thus a good speech on the question which most excited public interest, and collected that interest round the speaker. But it is to be observed that, though Lord Palmerston advocated officially the maintenance of a force which was thought necessary to preserve public tranquillity, he never spoke in favor of any of those measures that were adopted to suppress public liberty. One of his biographers, in an able sketch, says, "The sole link by which, in the researches of the careful student of his life, Palmerston is brought into connection with the successive suspensions of old-established liberties which distinguish this gloomy epoch of our history, is the series of speeches delivered from year to year in defense of the magnitude of those military establishments, which, as some would say, the dangerous spirit of the country, or, as others would have it, the oppressive policy of the administration, rendered necessary. He spoke no word in favor of any of the 'Six Acts.' He took no public share in the attempts to cramp the liberty of the press. His name was never identified with the attempts—by many alleged to be unconstitutional—to increase the severity of the laws against so-called sedition and libel. The yeomanry, who sabered their poor, starving fellow-countrymen at Peterloo, found in the War Secretary no apologist. Nor was his voice ever heard in justification of the odious inhumanity which employed spies to lure and incite such pitiable wretches as Thistlewood and Brandreth to the crimes which resulted in their deaths as traitors."

The most notable event of Lord Palmerston's life at this period was his escape from being killed, when a madman, Lieutenant Davies, shot at and slightly wounded him above the hip, on the 8th April, 1818, as he was going up the stairs at the War Office. A happy and accidental turn of his body, it is said, prevented the ball taking a fatal direction, and to this he owed the last forty-seven years of his existence, and the right to be considered one of the most distinguished of England's statesmen. In other respects he pursued undisturbed the smooth and even road of his rising career; and in referring to this period I find abundant proof of a belief I have always entertained, that but a small part of the merits of an able public man is ever seen by the public; I say this, for, after reading through the private correspondence of Lord Palmerston as Secretary at War, I feel bound to state that I have never found in any compositions of the same kind so clear, straightforward, and simple a style, such attention to details, such comprehensive views, such regard for private and public interests, such independence of thought—for the highest authority only weighs with him where the arguments are authoritative; and I only regret that extracts from this correspondence would be of too special a kind to justify me in introducing them to the general reader.

Meanwhile the Secretary at War had become perfectly at his ease in debate, and at times indulged in a certain flippant and overbearing manner, which, with the view of at once discountenancing an opponent, he was occasionally tempted to employ, but never inopportunely to persist in. Thus he says on one occasion, when defending the government from the accusation of having unconstitutionally called out the veterans:

"He could only repeat now what he had said before, that the reasons for this increase of force were so notorious to every person in the country that he should consider any attempt on his part to argue the necessity, *not only a waste of the time of the House, but as trifling with the public understanding.* If the justification of this measure was not sufficiently established by the events that had taken place since August last [the month of the Manchester tragedy], he was certain that no argument he could use, and no eloquence ever heard within these walls, would carry conviction with it." But when this way of waiving the question at issue was found insufficient, and it was again brought forward, he came clearly and boldly to the direct justification of the course which the government had thought fit to pursue.

"With respect to calling out the veterans, the noble lord [Nugent] considered it to be a violation of the Constitution. If, however, he looked back to the Constitution of this country, he would find many instances in which an augmentation of our forces had been made in time of peace, under an apprehension of approaching war or of internal commotion. . . . . . Many instances had occurred in time of peace, where an augmentation of the military force had been effected without any bill of indemnity, or any measure of the kind mentioned by the noble lord, being deemed necessary. He admitted the argument of the noble lord, that no force could be constitutionally embodied without the consent of Parliament; but that consent, he contended, had been obtained. In the speech from the throne, the intention of calling out this additional force was mentioned, and both Houses of Parliament, in their answer to the speech, plainly adverted to the circumstance. If, therefore, gentlemen conceived this proceeding to be unconstitutional, they would find it difficult to answer their country satisfactorily for having allowed so many months to elapse without having agitated the question. But not only was the circumstance mentioned in the speech from the throne, and in the address in answer to it, but a specific vote of money was agreed to for the subsistence of those troops."

The following sentences, rapidly strung together, are rather in the style of Mr. Canning: "The noble lord would ask, 'Is it necessary now to keep up this additional force?' In answer to that, he would only ask gentlemen to turn their attention to the events which had passed since the period to which he had referred. He would forbear from adverting to the conspiracy that was discovered in London. A conspiracy to destroy some hundreds of individuals, to burn different parts of the metropolis, and to create a provisional government, was, it appeared, a matter of no importance to the gentlemen opposite. Did not the noble lord know that special commissions were issued for the North of England, and for Scotland, to bring persons to trial for the highest crime the law of this country contemplated—the crime of high treason? Did he not know that the scenes which gave rise to these commissions took place in February and March last? Did not the noble lord know that meetings of armed men had taken place in Scotland? Was he not aware that, in one instance, a body of these men had acted in hostility to the regular troops? Had he not seen the proclamation that was posted up in the town of Glasgow, purporting to be issued by a provisional government—the object of those signing it being, as they stated, 'to obtain their rights by force of arms'?"

As a specimen of his lighter manner, I quote a few words by which he defends the establishment of a riding-school: "During the recent war a foreign officer had praised in the highest degree the *British cavalry*, regretting only that *they did not know how to ride!*" Nor is it amiss to cite the argument, so pregnant with British preferences, by which he advocates British education for British officers. "The effect of discontinuing this establishment" (the recently founded Military College) "would be to drive these young men to other quarters; and as they would have no means of defraying the expenses of a private education, they would probably be compelled to seek for instruction in German or French establishments, at that critical period when the impressions they received were calculated to decide the character of the future man. He regretted he did not observe a gallant officer in his place, who seldom omitted an opportunity of deprecating the introduction of foreign officers, and every assimilation to foreign customs in our troops; for he was persuaded he would have concurred with him in the propriety of giving to our military youth the advantages of a military education. For his own part, he wished to see the British soldier with a British character, with British habits, with a British education, and with as little as possible of anything foreign."

Tormented as all ministers were by Mr. Joseph Hume, after that gentleman had entered the House of Commons and assumed the character of financial economist, he replies much in the strain which those who saw him in his later days will remember. He says, "He recollected that he had heard of an ancient sage who said that there were two things over which even the immortal gods themselves had no power—namely, past events and arithmetic. The honorable gentleman, however, seemed to have power over both."

This is a pleasant remark; but the merits of the speaker did not lie in making pleasant remarks, but in coming to right conclusions; and the principles which he lays down as those that ought to guide us in times of peace as to our military establishment, are no doubt those which a wise government should still follow. "Let such establishment," he says, "be economical; let it be efficient; let its organization be so framed as to enable us, in the event of war, to recruit the different regiments rapidly and cheaply."

Yet although Lord Palmerston's ability was fully acknowledged, and his public position a good one, it was an isolated one.

His private friends were never such as could be called political friends. Mr. Sulivan, his brother-in law, and Sir George Shee, whom he made afterward Under-Secretary of State, were the only men with whom he could be said to be intimate. Neither did he belong to any of the particular sections which divided the House of Commons and the Tory party. He was not then an adherent of Canning, never having followed that statesman out of office; nor was he an adherent of Lord Eldon, nor even of Lord Liverpool, for he had voted since 1812 in favor of concessions to the Catholics. He certainly was not a Whig, and yet he lived chiefly with Whig society, which, since the time of Mr. Fox, was the society most in fashion. George IV. always disliked him. No one, therefore, had a very lively interest in him, or felt a strong desire to make his parliamentary position more important. Thus, he was offered by Lord Liverpool on one occasion the Governor-Generalship of India, and on another the Post-Office, with a seat in the House of Lords,—it being intended, if he accepted, to satisfy Mr. Huskisson with his place. He stuck, however, steadily to the House of Commons, as if foreseeing his future destiny; and circumstances now gave his fortunes a direction which they ever afterward followed.

I have observed elsewhere,* but I repeat here, that in the war which we had waged on the Continent against Napoleon we had marched with the various nations who finally subdued him, not merely against the tyrant, but against the tyranny which he had everywhere established. The people of Germany were rallied under the cry of "liberty;" all who joined the standard of the allies thought that if victory crowned their efforts they were to live hereafter under the shelter of free institutions. The sovereigns, however, who were liberal in making promises during the contest, shrunk from fulfilling them when the battle was

* Historical Characters.

over. Out of the disappointment which fear or duplicity created grew up a general feeling of distrust and anger. Long smouldering, it at last burst forth. In Spain and Italy there were revolutions; in the North of Germany revolutions seemed impending. In this crisis the military monarchies united in order to overthrow the constitutions that had been established, and to prevent any others from being formed. The doctrines of the sovereigns thus leagued together, and who honestly believed that their power was divine, shocked the feelings most common with the English people. We ceased for a moment to think of reform in England: our minds were fixed with disgust on despotism abroad. Lord Castlereagh, who was thought, in some degree unjustly, to sympathize with crowns and courts rather than with popular rights, was accused of lackeying the heels of a confederacy of which almost every Englishman would have grasped the throat; nevertheless he was about to proceed to Verona to take part in the congress which was to decide the fate of Spain, when his sudden death* brought Mr. Canning to the Foreign Office; and Mr. Canning at once, seeing the means by which he could acquire a popularity which he had always coveted and never yet been able to attain, undertook a task by no means easy—that of satisfying the predominant feeling in England, which was for resisting the despotic pretensions of the great continental Powers, without going to war for constitutional opinions. The extraordinary tact and skill with which he did this, appearing at times rash, but never really being so,—inspiring Englishmen with the conviction of their power, and satisfying them with regard to the principles for which it was to be exerted,—rallied by degrees public opinion around him, and led most men whose gen-

* On August 12, 1822.

eral tendencies were liberal to look up to him as their leader. This was more especially the case with those who advocated the Catholic claims. On the other hand, the anti-Catholic party, as they saw Mr. Canning rising in power, became more jealous of those who were, or who seemed likely to be, his partisans. Under these circumstances, Lord Palmerston, who had been returned for Cambridge University as a friend to Catholic Emancipation in 1812, 1818, 1820, again came forward with the same colors in 1825.

This is what he himself says of this election :*

"Smyth, though beat by me in 1811, had afterward been elected on the death of Gibbs; and on the death of Smyth, in 1822, William Bankes was elected.†

"In November, 1825, it being generally understood that Parliament would be dissolved the next summer, Sir J. Copley, then Attorney-General, wrote to me to say that he was going to begin to canvass the University, with a view of turning out Bankes; and shortly afterward Goulburn, who was Chief Secretary for Ireland, announced himself as a fourth candidate. Bankes, Copley, and Goulburn were all anti-Catholics. I was the only one of the four who voted for Emancipation.

"The canvass lasted from the end of November, 1825, till the dissolution in June, 1826, and a most laborious task for myself and my friends it became. It was soon manifest that the object of certain parties was to eject me

---

* Autobiography.

† After a contest with Lord Hervey (the late Marquis of Bristol) and Mr. Scarlett (the late Lord Abinger, Lord Chief Baron of the Exchequer). The numbers who actually polled were as follows:

For Mr. Banks	419
Lord Hervey	281
Mr. Scarlett	219

as well as Bankes, and the active influence of the anti-Catholic members of the government was exerted in favor of Copley and Goulburn, and therefore—as there were but two to be returned—against me.*

"The Church, the Treasury, and the Army were in anti-Catholic hands; and, though the Duke of Wellington and Peel condemned the cabal, Eldon, Bathurst, the Duke of York, the Secretaries to the Treasury, and many others, did all they could against me.

"I stood on my personal interest in the University, and threw myself on my political enemies the Whigs, for support against my political friends the Tories.

"This support, which I asked on the ground of our accordance upon Catholic Emancipation, was handsomely granted, and enabled me to triumph; Copley, indeed, headed the poll, but I beat Bankes by 122, and Goulburn by 192.

"I had complained to Lord Liverpool, and the Duke of Wellington, and Canning, of being attacked, in violation of the understanding upon which the government was formed, and by which the Catholic question was to be an open one; and I told Lord Liverpool that if I was beat I should quit the government. *This was the first decided step toward a breach between me and the Tories, and they were the aggressors.*"†

---

* Extract from letter from the Right Hon. Charles W. Wynn, President of the Board of Control, to the Duke of Buckingham:

"12 May, 1825.

"I have heard nothing lately about Lord Palmerston, but, from all accounts, his re-election for Cambridge is so doubtful (to say the best of it) that I fully expect him to withdraw from it into the Upper House."—Duke of Buckingham's "*Court and Times of George IV.*"

† The destruction of every party begins by its more violent members driving the more moderate into union with their opponents.

The letters that follow relate in part to this election, but are mingled with others, singularly illustrative of the man of the world—gossiping, racing, and looking after his property. I make no apology for giving them; for, apart from the interest which they possess as affecting the private life of a man so well known to the public, I think that every occupation or amusement which has brought a statesman in contact with his fellow-men, and which has not softened the manly character of his mind or alienated him from graver pursuits, has been useful in awakening for him sympathies and giving to him knowledge which, at the proper time, melt advantageously into his main career.

To the Hon. Wm. Temple, British Legation, Berlin.

"Stanhope Street, July 19, 1825.

"My dear William,—

"I send you the inclosed, which I fancy by the hand relates to some of our joint concerns.

"Canning has had a very dangerous attack of inflammation of the bowels, but is now out of danger, though for forty-eight hours he was in a very alarming state. The Duke of St. Albans is dead, and the bets are that Mrs. Coutts will soon be duchess. Poor Bradshaw goes about the picture of misery and despair. I fancy Miss Tree will be off at last, and if she is wise no doubt she will, as they say she does not like him, and as a speculation the stage is a better thing. Embley is sold for £125,000 to a Mr. Nightingale, some connection by marriage of King-killing Smith of Norwich. George Dawson marries Miss Seymour.* Three objections in my opinion insuperable. He

* The parties referred to are the Right Hon. G. Dawson Damer, M.P., brother of the late Earl of Portarlington, and the lady he

has no money, and she not more than she has been accustomed to spend entirely upon her own dress and amusements. He is four inches shorter than her, and two stone lighter. The Duke of York and Duchess of —— are a pattern of juvenile sentiment; it is delightful to see unsophisticated minds meeting in the mysterious luxury of a first and refined affection. Young ——, who has been in attendance for the last two years, was sent staring and gaping into the country. Lady Emmeline makes no hand of Leopold.

"As to weather, we are fried alive: thermometer above 80° every day for the last week; on the leads out of my study window it stood yesterday at 93°, hanging on the wall, and completely shaded from the sun, though somewhat raised by the reflected heat from the opposite walls. Watson says that two days ago the thermometer on one of the walls in the kitchen-garden stood at 130° in the sun, and at 100° in the shade on the other side of the same wall; of course the heat had got through the wall; but they say it has been 92° fairly in the shade. The wind, too, is to the eastward, and the weather likely to last. We shall have plenty of birds, but not a turnip-leaf to cover them.

" Yours affectionately,

" PALMERSTON."

To the Hon. Wm. Temple, Berlin.

" STANHOPE STREET, August 5, 1825.

" MY DEAR WILLIAM,—

" I have paid for you two hundred pounds, being your second instalment of ten pounds a share upon twenty shares

---

married in August, 1825—Miss Seymour, daughter of Admiral Lord Hugh Seymour, and sister of the recently deceased Admiral Sir George F. Seymour.

13*

in the Cornwall and Devon Mining Company; and I have got your shares made out in your name, and deposited in my iron chest in this room. The two hundred pounds you may pay me whenever it is convenient, and at your leisure. I also send you a power of attorney, to be executed by you, in order to enable the solicitors of the company to sign the deed of settlement for you. I am inclined to think that both this and the Welsh Slate Company will turn out profitable concerns. I have been unlucky in my racing this year as yet, my horses having been ill and lame at the moment when they were to run for stakes which, if well, they would probably have won, and which would have been worth winning. As yet I have just won within two pounds of the amount I have had to pay for stakes and forfeits, so that I have all my training-bills to boot; but I hope to bring myself home yet before the end of the season.

"Fanny is gone to Powis Castle, and goes on Tuesday to Bangor, to meet Bowles, and from thence they go to Sir Watkin's shooting-box on Bala. The Sulivans are gone for a few days to the Flemings. They are, I think, better this year than they have been for some time, especially Sulivan, who is not nearly so much pulled and harassed as he was last year, though he has had fully as much to do; and the children are all remarkably well and evidently much benefited by living at Broom House. I am going in a fortnight to Sligo again, to see the progress of my harbor, and to settle some further improvements with Mr. Nimmo, the civil engineer whom I have employed to survey my bogs. He recommends me to lay down an iron railroad of about six miles in length, by means of which I should be enabled to bring up a shelly sand from the sea-beach to reclaim the bogs, and to carry down in return to my new harbor turf from the bogs, prepared as fuel; and he thinks that a very considerable export trade of this turf could be carried on with the town of Sligo and the coast beyond it. This would require a capital of between five and six thousand pounds to be immediately laid out; but I am inclined to think it will answer, and I could get the money advanced by the commissioners in Ireland, who are authorized by Parliament to issue Exchequer bills in aid of public works of this kind for the internal improvement of Ireland, taking repayment by annual instalments of so much per cent. added to the interest. But this matter I shall settle when on the spot. I expect to be back at Broadlands about the middle of September, and I think it possible I may take a trip to Paris later in the year.

"Yours affectionately,

"PALMERSTON."

To the Hon. Wm. Temple, Berlin.

"STANHOPE STREET, August 8, 1825.

"MY DEAR WILLIAM,—

"As you take an interest about my racing concerns, I send you the list of the Salisbury races last week, by which you will see that I won five races out of eight; and the cup is, luckily, an exact match to that which I won the other day at Southampton. The result of Salisbury is, however, greater in glory than in profit, as it amounts to a cup and £170, as I only got £15 for Biondetta's walking over. Conquest is a three-year-old filly by Waterloo, dam by Rubens, which I took in the early part of the year from Tattersall, in exchange for my brood-mare Mignonet. Day thought ill of her; but she has turned out tolerably well, as she beat 'Black and all black' in a canter; but she had, according to the conditions of the race, a great advantage in weight, in consequence of her age and of her competitor having won this year, of which she had been guiltless till that day. Grey Leg turns out very well.

He won the Coronation Stakes at Stockbridge, value £39, the cup at Southampton, and a £25 stake, and the cup at Salisbury. He would have done more if he had not had the distemper just as he was to have run at Bath and Cheltenham for good stakes; but in a trial with Lugberough, giving weight for age, he was found to be as good as Lugberough. Our weather has been finer than yours, for, till last week, we have had an uninterrupted course of hot and dry weather for a long time. For the last week it has been windy and rainy, but still not cold.

"Yours affectionately,

"PALMERSTON."

To the Hon. Wm. Temple, Berlin.

"STANHOPE STREET, Dec. 2, 1825.

"MY DEAR WILLIAM,—

"It is so long since I have written to you that I really almost forget when it was, and you have been so excellent a correspondent that my silence is the more unpardonable. I received the other day the very pretty little bronzes you sent me, which do credit to the Prussian artists. They have really contrived to give a sharpness and fineness of execution to their iron of which one hardly supposed that metal to be susceptible. I safely delivered all your other packets, which were greatly approved by their respective receivers.

"*I am just setting off for Cambridge, where I am obliged to begin a canvass, as the Attorney-General and Goulburn have both declared themselves candidates for the general election.* It is rather a bore to have to go through the labor of a canvass so long before the time; but this is just a time of year when I have more leisure to attend to it, and I shall not be sorry to get the matter over.

I do not feel much apprehension as to the result, because I think I am sure of a great many Protestants, from a coincidence of opinion on other questions; and of many Whigs, from an agreement on the Catholic question. Indeed, if there is no Whig candidate, I should expect to have all the Whig interest at Cambridge. I believe I gave you a report of my Irish journey, which was very prosperous and satisfactory. I found the general aspect of affairs in that country rapidly improving. I had Nimmo, the engineer, with me for ten days in Sligo; and we made arrangements for carrying into effect divers operations, which I trust will materially improve my property in the course of a few years. From Ireland, after passing a day at Powis Castle, I struck across to Yorkshire, where I also was well satisfied with the state of my Fairburn property. I shall soon bring my lime-works into play, and have some chance of finding coal. I have lately been for a week at Brighton, which is really increasing in the most extraordinary manner. There literally are as many lodging-houses in different stages of progress as there are completed and occupied. Where they are to find inhabitants for them all I do not understand; but it may fairly be said that by next summer the accommodation of the place will be nearly twice what it was last summer, and all the new houses are upon a grand style of architectural decoration.

"What a sad thing the death of the poor Duchess of Rutland is! It was caused by an internal inflammation. She had an attack of the same kind two years ago, and it was subdued only by the most energetic means immediately resorted to. Probably in this case the country practitioners were afraid of doing as much as a London one would have done; but Halford, who was sent for, stated himself to have very little hopes from the moment he first heard of the attack.

"There is a call for ten pounds a share upon the Welsh Slate Company. I shall pay the instalment upon your twenty shares, and you can repay me afterward. I saw our quarry as I returned from Ireland, and found it a remarkably fine one, and I think the undertaking likely to answer well.* All we want is a railroad to the sea, as at present the slates are sent twelve miles along an infamously bad road; but some other slate-owners, whose quarries are near ours, are equally interested in this, and a survey has been made of a line for a railway, and in the course of this next year it is probable that such a road will be made.

"I have just agreed with Breton for the purchase of his estate at Ashfield. I give him £12,000 for it, which is fully £1000 more than it can by possibility be worth to anybody else; but from local contiguity it is so desirable to me that I think the money well laid out. I trust it will enable me to turn the road, and extend the park to the canal, unless I find greater difficulties in dealing with Fletcher than I expect; but as Fletcher's estate is tied up by entail, and cannot be sold during his lifetime, he cannot have much interest in making unnecessary objections. If it was a salable estate, he would refuse every accommodation in order to compel me to give him a large price for it.

"We have had quantities of partridges this year; but, as I returned late from Ireland, they were wild as hawks. I hear a good account of the pheasants, but have not as yet broke cover.

---

* These slate-mines proved a happy speculation. In a moment of panic, many of the shareholders withdrew. Lord Palmerston, as a director of the company that conducted them, felt bound to remain, and he took the shares of all his friends who wished to retire. The ultimate success of the undertaking was complete, and his foresight and perseverance were rewarded.

"Adieu! my dear William. I will let you know the result of my canvass.

"Ever yours affectionately,

"PALMERSTON."

To Laurence Sulivan, Esq., War Office.

"STANHOPE STREET, Dec. 2, 1825.

"MY DEAR SULIVAN,—

"Read the inclosed,* and send it me down to Cambridge by the post, with any remarks that occur to you. I feel that I must make some allusion to the Catholic question, or I should appear to shrink from it, and that I must avow my conviction that I am right, without putting it forward in a manner that would be offensive to those who disagree with me; and that while I ought to state that I do not fear an examination of my public conduct, I must not place my expectation of support upon the result of that examination being with every voter a perfect concurrence of sentiment.

"Yours affectionately,

"PALMERSTON."

To Laurence Sulivan, Esq., War Office.

"CAMBRIDGE, Dec. 4, 1825.

"MY DEAR SULIVAN,—

"Thank you for your amendments. I am going on as well as I could expect—in fact, as well as possible; I think I shall have all the Johnians and most of the Trinity men. The Protestants will support me as a Tory, and the Whigs as a Catholic. That is, if no Whig candidate starts, for that was the qualification with which Smyth of Peterhouse tendered me his vote before I could ask it. The small colleges I have not yet gone into, for I attacked St. John's

* His address to his constituents.

and Trinity first; and I do not hurry, but let every man talk his fill, and many have much to say about the Catholic question, and I encourage them to open their minds and state all their objections, because it gives me an opportunity of explaining my views, which are more rational than some of them fancy; and of suggesting answers to some of their arguments, which may give them matter for reflection; and a man who has been used to hear certain positions echoed about as self-evident among a small knot of his friends, is sometimes surprised to find how much may be said on the other side. The greatest number of those I have spoken to do not promise, saying they wish to keep themselves disengaged, but generally accompanying this with expressions of personal good will, and an admission of a certain degree of claim on the part of an old member. Bankes has certainly lost ground very much, and I doubt his being returned. Copley is unpopular with the Whigs, and there is a general feeling that his canvass is premature—some think it especially so, considering that he would probably succeed to the Chief-Justiceship if vacant. Goulburn has not been much talked of; but the Master of Trinity told me to-day he had heard from him, and that he means to stand. He and Copley cannot both go to a poll, as they would clash in all points, college, politics, and Protestantism. Copley is coming down immediately, and is to form a committee. I am collecting a nominal one, in order to have people engaged; but it is useless to go through all the manual exercise of a contest now, unless, at least, one is driven to it by the measures of one's competitors. Bankes has not yet appeared, but will probably soon be here. The Trinity men are likely to throw him over. People are all extremely civil, and I have not yet had one refusal, though I expect one from Webb of Clare, who is the Dragon of Wantley of the Protestants. I cannot yet say how long I shall stay here, but I shall not leave this till I have seen every man. Bankes, I have just heard, will be here to-night. Wood says he thinks I am secure.

"Yours affectionately,

"PALMERSTON."

To the Hon. Wm. Temple, Berlin.

"STANHOPE STREET, June 5, 1826.

"MY DEAR WILLIAM,—

"I have been a horrid bad correspondent for some time past; but I have been overwhelmed with business, including my canvass, which for the last six months has hung upon me like a nightmare, filling up every interval which anything else allowed to exist. Next week will decide the matter. The election begins on Tuesday 13th, and lasts till Thursday 15th, inclusive. I think I shall succeed if I can prevail upon people to come up, which I hope to do. My own opinion is that Copley will be first, I next, Bankes third, and Goulburn fourth.* The latter certainly goes to the poll, which is a great advantage to me. If I was to guess numbers, I should say it would be Copley and I something about 650 each, Bankes from 600 to a few more, and Goulburn about 500; but I know nothing about their numbers, and may overstate them. The Whigs have behaved most handsomely to me; they have given me cordial and hearty support, and, in fact, bring me in. Liverpool has acted as he always does to a friend in personal questions,—shabbily, timidly, and ill. If I am beat, I have told him he must find another Secretary at War, for I certainly will not continue in office.

"I send you the Foreign Enlistment Act, by which you

* This opinion proved correct.

will see that your friend would be guilty of a misdemeanor if he entered a foreign service without leave from the King of England.

"My dear William,

"Yours affectionately,

"PALMERSTON."

To the Hon. Wm. Temple, Berlin.

"STANHOPE STREET, July 17, 1826.

"MY DEAR WILLIAM,—

"Many thanks for your letters and congratulations, and many apologies for my apparent remissness as to writing, but I really have been so much occupied for the last six months by my Cambridge canvass, that it threw me into an arrear of every other business, public and private, which I am only now beginning to work down. I have within the last five minutes finished working up my War Office arrears, and am even with the papers of this very day, and I turn accordingly to write you a few lines.*

"The result of my contest was most gratifying, and beyond my expectations; I knew my own strength, but not that of my opponents. I had obtained, just before the poll began, about 700 promises; the total number of voters was 1800, of whom perhaps 1300 might be expected to vote. This would give 2600 votes, supposing each man voted for two candidates; and supposing that 200 people gave plumpers, it would leave 2400 votes, which, between four candidates, would be 600 apiece. It was clear, therefore, that the winning candidates must have more than 600 each at the poll; I knew that out of my 700 promises a great number would, from various causes, not be pres-

---

* N.B.—Every one must be struck with the kind and affectionate feeling which this correspondence manifests.

ent. I reckoned my casualties at 100; this would leave me 600 polled votes, and this would barely do. I knew, however, that Copley was strong, and would probably poll more than his 600, and that would leave the numbers to be divided among the other three candidates less; so that it would not give 600 each; and if, therefore, I polled 600 I might win. But then Bankes' friends were most confident in their boasting, and I did not know what their real numbers were. Again, Goulburn's friends might leave him, even though he should not resign— and, in fact, some did—in order to go into Bankes' scale, and to turn me out.

"All these various possibilities and contingencies made me feel the result might be extremely doubtful; and on the day of the dissolution I wrote to Liverpool to tell him that I thought it fair to give him notice then, that if I should fail at Cambridge I should be unable to continue my connection with a government under which and by which such a result would have been brought about. Liverpool wrote me a civil answer, begging me not to come to any decision in the event of failure without communication with him, and so the matter rested; but if I had been beat I should most indubitably have immediately quitted the government. In fact, as it is I feel that I have been dealt with by them in a way in which, probably, no official man ever was before. The first two days of our polling I kept back everybody who had not some particular reason for wishing to vote early—such as wanting to go away, or wishing to give me a plumper and to avoid being plagued by other candidates. Bankes, on the other hand, was urging his friends up as fast as he could, in order to get ahead of Goulburn, in order that the anti-Catholics might think him the most likely of the two to beat me, and might throw their weight into his scale.

When I found on Wednesday evening that, running this sort of race, I was still ahead of him, I began to think myself pretty sure of victory; but even to the last I did not venture to hope for so large a majority. The number of my majority is most satisfactory, because it makes me feel pretty secure as to the future, and because, also, many of the anti-Catholics who voted for me from personal regard or college feeling, and who would perhaps have regretted their sacrifice of opinion if we had been beat or had won by a small number, are now carried away by the pride of triumph by becoming parties in so decided a success. One advantage at Cambridge will be that party feeling on the Catholic question must abate; for all the Johnians who supported me cannot hold now on this subject the violent language which they formerly did. The Whigs supported me most handsomely, and were indeed my chief and most active friends; and to them and the Johnians I owe my triumph over the No Popery faction behind the government, if not in it. I think the question has gained by the general election. In the first place, in numerical strength I am inclined to believe that it will be found that we have rather increased upon the anti-Catholics; but the grand point is, that the No Popery cry has been tried in many places and has everywhere failed; and we may now appeal to the experience of facts to show that there does *not* exist among the people of England that bigoted prejudice on this point which the anti-Catholics accused them of entertaining. The breaking loose of the Irish tenantry from their landlords, too, is a very important advantage. In the first place, it will make the representation of Ireland almost entirely *for* the question; and then it will teach the landlords the folly of splitting their estates into forty-shilling freeholds, and lead them to adopt a system of management more advantageous to themselves and to the progress of society in Ireland.

"I am delighted to see this insurrection of the serfs. As to the commonplace balance between opposition and government, the election will have little effect upon it. The government are as strong as any government can wish to be, as far as regards those who sit facing them; but in truth the real opposition of the present day sit behind the Treasury Bench; and it is by the stupid old Tory party, who bawl out the memory and praises of Pitt while they are opposing all the measures and principles which he held most important,—it is by these that the progress of the government in every improvement which they are attempting is thwarted and impeded. On the Catholic question; on the principles of commerce; on the corn laws; on the settlement of the currency; on the laws regulating the trade in money; on colonial slavery; on the game laws, which are intimately connected with the moral habits of the people: on all these questions, and everything like them, the government find support from the Whigs, and resistance from their self-denominated friends. However, the young squires are more liberal than the old ones, and we must hope that Heaven will protect us from our friends, as it has done from our enemies. The next session will be interesting. All these questions will come under a new Parliament, in which there are about 150 new members.

"I have started most prosperously with my racing concerns. I have four horses this year—Lugberough, Grey Leg, and a mare now four-year-old, which I got last year, and call Conquest, as she is by Waterloo out of a mare by Rubens, and my fourth is a three-year-old colt I call Foxbury, bred by myself, got by Whalebone out of Mignonet, the large Sorcerer mare, which you must remember, and which I bred also, and have had some time. Last year my horses were ill a great part of the season; and, though I won several races, I had to pay forfeits for many which were the best worth having, because my horses could not start.

"I ran for the first time this year the other day, at Bath. Lugberough won the Bath Stakes—a very good stake—beating several good horses. Conquest won a race also, value £110, beating also some tolerable nags; and Foxbury won one race, and lost a second only because he swerved from the course—the boy, probably, not knowing just how to manage him. I thus won three out of four. Foxbury is to run to-day at Wells, and I think may win; and Lugberough is to run at Cheltenham next week for a race which will be worth £700, probably, and is favorite for it among the bettors, his most formidable rival being Shakespear, who was second for the Derby, but with respect to whom, age considered, Lugberough has the advantage.* I shall let you know how I go on, but I hope to make a brilliant campaign of it. I have just been to Broadlands for a couple of days, chiefly to settle to buy the Methodist chapel in Banning Street for a national school. We had raised a subscription to build a school, and had laid the foundations, but this chapel will answer our purpose excellently, and save us some money.

"Adieu, my dear William.

"Yours affectionately,

"PALMERSTON.

"The Bowles set off this morning on their tour of inspection round the southern and western coasts.

"Clanwilliam departed suddenly for Paris."

---

* N.B.—There is no betting in all this,—nothing but the love of horses and sport, and the idea that his expenses might probably be repaid him by his stables.

To the Hon. Wm. Temple, Berlin.

"LONDONDERRY, Oct. 21, 1826.

"MY DEAR WILLIAM,—

"It is a long time since I last wrote to you; I have been busily employed or actively moving about in Ireland. I left London just this day month, the 21st of Sept., stayed only a few hours in Dublin, and went on to Shee's at Dunmore, in Galway, where I remained two days. I found him very busy, very comfortable, and very happy; getting his estate into order, increasing his income, and improving the system of his tenantry. From thence I went on to Sligo, where I remained eighteen days, the greater part of the time at Cliffoney, with Nimmo the engineer, looking over the progress of my improvements and planning arrangements for the future. My harbor is nearly completed, and will be an excellent one for my purposes: it will be about one and a quarter English acres in extent, and will have fourteen feet water at high spring tides—enough depth to admit vessels of 300 tons, and as much as any harbor on the west coast of Ireland, and it has an excellent anchorage in front of it, where ships may wait the tide to enter. I have no doubt that in a short time it will be much frequented by the coasting trade; and if I can get people—which Nimmo thinks probable—to lay down a railroad to it from the end of Loch Erne, a distance of fourteen English miles, it would become the exporting and importing harbor for a large tract of very fertile country lying on the banks of that lake, and would communicate with an inland navigation of nearly forty miles in extent. This speculation, however, I shall leave to others, and only profit by it if they undertake it; in the mean time it will give much scope to the industry of my tenants.

"I have begun cultivating my bogs, of which I have about two thousand Irish acres: I have got thirty acres now producing potatoes, turnips, and rape, which in March last were wet unwalkable bog. The process was first to drain them slightly, which was begun in April; then to dig up the surface and pile it in heaps and burn it; then to level the ground, and form it into ridges and plant it with potatoes, or sow it with turnips and rape, throwing the ashes on as manure, and adding a top-dressing of sea-sand and clay; as far as I am able to calculate at present, this is likely to answer extremely well. It seems probable that in the fourth year after an acre of bog has been thus taken into cultivation it may be let on lease at a rent of from twenty to thirty shillings; and that, setting on the one hand all the expense incurred upon the acre in the four years, and on the other all the profit made by selling the crops which it will have produced, and which will consist of potatoes, turnips, or rape the first year, oats the second and third, and hay the fourth, the permanent outlay at the time it is so let cannot exceed £8, and may possibly fall short of that sum, so that a proprietor may in this manner make 12 per cent. at least upon his money, while he gives employment to his tenantry, and provides the means of enlarging their holdings and improving their condition. I do not expect to be able to accomplish more than about sixty acres a year, and at that rate I shall have scope enough for a tolerable number of years to come. I have, however, begun upon my worst bog, and that which was the most troublesome to cultivate, so that my future progress will be more rapid and less expensive. I have been planting bent upon a great tract of blowing sand, and, I think, with success. I have about 600 acres of that description on the coast, and this year I planted bent on about 140 acres, which only cost me £50. The bent was taken up from parts where it grows in clusters, and planted closely in rows fourteen feet apart; it is almost all growing, and I see that in another year it will very much stop the sand, and I have no doubt that by extending my plantation I shall succeed in covering the greater part of the six hundred acres with green bent, and when that has stopped the blowing of the sand it soon gives way to grass; but it is itself very good food for cattle. I have established an infant linen-market at Cliffoney, held once a month, and have no doubt of its prospering and increasing. I have just got two schools on foot, but am at war with my priest, who as usual forbids the people to send their children. I know that if I was resident I should beat him in a moment, and I hope to do so, even though an absentee. I am getting the people to build some houses according to a plan of village which Nimmo and I have laid out; and as a proof that my tenants and I are not upon very bad terms, I found when I arrived there the other day that one fellow was building a good house two stories high, and to have a slated roof, and which when finished will not cost him less than £150, upon a piece of ground of which he has no lease, and of which he is merely tenant at will. Of course my friend Timon—not of Athens, but of Cliffoney—will have this building lease, and as an encouragement I have promised to give him the cost of his slates. I have established a limekiln at the foot of a mountain, where I can make lime at 6*d.* a barrel, which sells in the neighborhood for 1*s.* a barrel, and by contenting myself with a profit of 4*d.* I can undersell the others and supply the people with an article of great importance to them both for the improvement of their land and the cleanliness of their houses. In the whole, I find a considerable improvement going on in the country, and I trust its progress will be accelerated by the operations I am carrying on. But I have a great mind when I go to Cambridge at Christmas to see if I cannot find some zealous Simeonite who would curb the ardent enthusiasm which would impel him to the banks of the Ganges, and might content himself with winning his Jerusalem spurs by a campaign in the parish of Ahamlish. My own opinion is that a very great deal might be effected by a well-informed man who would talk to the people, and especially by an Englishman, and that even if he did not make Protestants of them he might make them Christians. They really are a good and simple-minded people, though they quarrel among each other without end or reason, and get most joyously drunk whenever they lose a relation or friend.

"I went from Sligo to Lord Belmore's, near Enniskillen, a palace called Castle Coole, built by Wyatt, and faced with Portland stone, very large and handsome. I am going from hence by the Giant's Causeway and Belfast to Dublin, and from thence back to London for the meeting of Parliament. Ireland has been much better off than England as to its crops. The potatoes are beyond example abundant, the wheat very fine, and the oats and barley not nearly so bad as in England, and the hay a fair crop on the western coast, though scanty on the eastern.

"The Catholic and anti-Catholic war is, however, carried on more vigorously than ever, and the whole people are by the ears, like an undisciplined pack of hounds. It is most marvelous, to be sure, that sensible statesmen should be frightened by the bugbear of foreign interference clashing with domestic allegiance, and should see with calmness and apathy a civil war raging throughout Ireland, engrossing all the thoughts and passions of the people, diverting them from the pursuits of industry, and retarding the progress of national prosperity, and menacing, in the event of foreign hostilities, inconveniences of the most formidable and embarrassing description. I can forgive old women like the Chancellor, spoonies like Liverpool, ignoramuses like Westmoreland, old stumped-up Tories like Bathurst; but how such a man as Peel, liberal, enlightened, and fresh-minded, should find himself running in such a pack is hardly intelligible. I think he must in his heart regret those early pledges and youthful prejudices which have committed him to opinions so different from the comprehensive and statesmanlike views which he takes of public affairs. *But the day is fast approaching, as it seems to me, when this matter will be settled as it must be;* and in spite of the orgies in this town and Armagh, the eloquence of Sir George Hill and Lord G. Beresford, and the bumpers pledged to the ''Prentice Boys'' motto of '*No surrender*,' the days of Protestant ascendency I think are numbered. It is strange that in this enlightened age and enlightened country people should be still debating whether it is wise to convert four or five millions of men from enemies to friends, and whether it is *safe* to give peace to Ireland.

"Adieu, my dear William.

"Yours affectionately,

"PALMERSTON."

BOOK IV

Mr. Canning Prime Minister, and Palmerston offered the Chancellorship of the Exchequer—Enters the Cabinet finally as Minister of War—Canning dies—Lord Goderich Prime Minister—Palmerston again offered the Chancellorship of the Exchequer, which the king, however, secures for Herries—Saying of Lord Anglesey—Lord Goderich succeeded by the Duke of Wellington.

IT will be seen from preceding quotations that the partisans of Mr. Canning and those of Lord Eldon were become two factions in Lord Liverpool's government; that Lord Palmerston had taken his place with the former, and that only an event was necessary to range under hostile standards persons who were already of opposite opinions.

That event came on the death of Lord Liverpool and the necessity of choosing his successor. The successor, as we know, was Mr. Canning. His ascent to the Premiership is, no doubt, one of the great events of our later history. It broke down forever the "resistant"—or, as it was then termed, "Protestant"—party which, under the protection of George III , had held the greatest share of political power since the deaths of Mr. Fox and Mr. Pitt, and brought forward a Liberal party of various colors, in which, after the change in our constitution which took place in 1832, the democratic hue has become gradually more and more predominant.

Lord Palmerston naturally became elevated in this new change. Mr. Canning had, in the first instance, to form his administration within a very small circle. A large division of the Tories had deserted him. It was necessary that some little time should elapse before he could form an open coalition with the Whigs. The Secretary at War was therefore at once summoned to the Cabinet, and his reputation as a man of business suggested the idea of making him Chancellor of the Exchequer. But, on the other hand, Mr. Canning shrewdly foresaw that his present condition could not last long, and that before the ensuing session he must join those as friends whom he had so long faced as opponents. He was not indisposed, therefore, as the necessity of this junction became more and more apparent from the bitterness of his former associates becoming more and more increased, to have as many high offices as possible to dispose of, and he made, though in a very friendly way, two or three offers to Lord Palmerston, which, if accepted, would have removed him from England.

Lord Palmerston thus records these offers :*

"In February, 1827, Lord Liverpool was taken ill; and in April of that year Mr. Canning was declared Minister, and commanded to form a government. Upon this the Tories retired in a body. Lord Eldon, the Duke of Wellington, Peel, Lord Bathurst, Lord Westmoreland, Lord Melville, Lord Bexley (who, however, retracted), Wallace, Beckett, Wetherell, Duke of Dorset, Duke of Montrose, Lord Londonderry, all sent in their resignations, leaving Canning 'alone in his glory.' Canning had, some little time before, desired me not to leave town for Easter without letting him know; and upon this break-up he sent for me, to offer me a seat in the Cabinet and the office of Chancellor of the Exchequer. He said he wished to keep the Foreign Office as Prime Minister, instead of being

* Autobiography.

First Lord of the Treasury; but he found that there were official attributes attached to the First Lord of the Treasury which rendered it necessary that the Prime Minister should be First Lord; that he wished, however, to have a separate Chancellor of the Exchequer, to relieve him both in the Treasury Office and in the House of Commons, and to leave him more leisure for general matters, and should be glad to have my assistance.

"I accepted both offers.

"Canning gave a great dinner at his house at the Foreign Office just before the recess; and after dinner he proposed to me to take immediately the office of Chancellor of the Exchequer, in order that I might be re-elected during the holidays, and be ready to start again as soon as the House met. Croker, who had *not* resigned, but who remained in office, and who was standing by, artfully suggested that there was going to be a contest at Cambridge between Goulburn and Bankes for the seat vacated by Copley—made Chancellor and created Lord Lyndhurst—and strongly advised me to wait, in order that I might not incur the danger of being mixed up with that contest; saying that, by the usual courtesy of the University, I should have no contest if I vacated upon changing office, but might be in danger if I ran my head into a battle begun by other people. Canning said that I must take the Exchequer *then*, or else wait till the end of the session, as it would not be convenient that I should be out of Parliament for a fortnight during the session. It was then agreed that I should remain Secretary at War till the end of the session, when I should go to the Exchequer.

"In the mean while intrigues were set on foot. George IV., who personally hated me, did not fancy me as Chancellor of the Exchequer. He wanted to have Herries in that office. There were questions coming on about palaces and crown lands which the king was very anxious about, and he wished either to have a creature of his own at the Exchequer, or to have the office of Chancellor of the Exchequer held by the First Lord, whose numerous occupations would compel him to leave details very much to George Harrison, the Secretary, and to Herries, Auditor of the Civil List.*

"Toward the end, or rather about the middle, of the session, Canning sent for me, and, evidently much embarrassed, said that he wished to speak to me about the Chancellorship of the Exchequer. That it had been arranged that I was to have it, and he had at that time much wished that I should; but that since then it had been strongly pressed upon him by all the financial department that it was extremely important that the First Lord should also be Chancellor of the Exchequer; and that the union of the two offices in the person of the Prime Minister, when that minister was in the House of Commons, was attended with great official convenience; and the result, he said, was, that he felt himself unable to carry our intended arrangement into effect.

"Having finished his statement, he walked to the other end of the room, like a man who wishes to hide from another the emotions of embarrassment which for a moment were shown upon the countenance. I was a little surprised, and saw that there was something behind which he did not choose to tell. I said that my only wish was to be useful to his government, and that I had no selfish objects in view; that if he thought it better for the public service that I should remain as I was, I was perfectly contented to do so; that, moreover, as the office of Commander-in-Chief had been vacant since the death of the Duke of York

* And also Joint Secretary of the Treasury.

in January, and as I was administering the discipline and patronage of the army by virtue of my office of Secretary at War, I might well, for the present at least, be satisfied with the importance of my functions.

"Canning seemed much relieved by the manner in which I took his communication, admitted the justice of my last remark, and said that he would take care that when my double functions ceased, by the appointment of a Commander-in-Chief, some arrangement should be made that would be satisfactory to me.

"I told him that I thought there ought to be a military man as Commander-in-Chief; but that he should well consider who that man should be, as he had the power of doing much mischief, military and political, as well as good.

"Some weeks after this, Canning sent for me again, to say he had a proposition to make to me which he should not himself have thought of, but that the king had said he knew, and was sure, that it was just the very thing I should like, and that was to go as Governor to Jamaica. I laughed so heartily that I observed Canning looked quite put out, and I was obliged to grow serious again.

"Not long afterward he again sent for me, and said he had an offer to make which might be more worth my consideration, and in making which he had only one difficulty, and that was lest I should think he wanted to get rid of me, which he could very sincerely assure me was far from being the case. The offer was the Governor-Generalship of India.

"I thanked him very kindly for his offer, assured him I was not insensible to the splendor of the post which he was now proposing. That I felt what means it afforded for increasing one's fortune, for gratifying one's love of power, for affording a scope for doing good upon a magnificent theater of action; but my ambition was satisfied with my position at home. I happened not to have a family for whom I should be desirous of providing, and my health would not stand the climate of India. I had already, I said, declined the office when offered me by Lord Liverpool, at a time when I was not in the Cabinet, and the same motives which influenced me then still operated now."

The following letters tend to complete the sketch thus rapidly drawn:

To the Hon. William Temple, Berlin.

"STANHOPE STREET, April 19, 1827.

"MY DEAR WILLIAM,—

"You must have been surprised, like the rest of the world, at all the resignations of last week. Peel's was expected by Canning, as he had all along explained that, from his peculiar connection with Oxford, he should think himself obliged to go out if a Catholic were head of the government;* but the others were unexpected, and generally without a public ground. Westmoreland, indeed, stated fairly that he could not serve under a Catholic chief; the Duke of Wellington gives out that he went because Canning's letters were uncivil; Melville, because the duke persuaded him, and told him that if he did not go now he would be turned out six months hence; Bathurst, because his colleagues went; Bexley, that he might have the pleasure of coming back again. *Peel is a great loss; but he parts with undiminished cordiality, and one understands and respects his motive.* The duke is a great loss in the Cabinet, but in the command of the army an irrep-

* This is not an unimportant fact in judging the conduct of this statesman at the critical period we are treating of.

15*

arable one; and it is the more provoking that he should have resigned this office, because it is not a political office; and he felt this so strongly that when it became a question, three months ago, on what footing he should hold it, he declared himself perfectly ready to quit the Cabinet if it was thought not tenable with that situation. The king is very angry with him, and wrote a short and equivocal answer to his letter of resignation, simply saying he received it 'with the *same* regret with which the duke *appeared* to have sent it.' I take it that this was worked about by Eldon, and no doubt he thought it his masterstroke. In the mean time, however, I am glad to find that nobody else is to be appointed. The situation will be left vacant, and the duties done as in the late interregnum; and when arrangements for the new government have been made, and personal feelings on both sides have cooled, I have no doubt the duke will return to his command. The appointment of Clarence to the navy has given great satisfaction to that service, and is certainly a wise measure. The Heir Presumptive cannot be always quite passive, and it is useful to bring him into action by placing him in official communication with the king, and by giving them, as it were, a community of interest, prevent the Heir from being drawn into cabals and intrigues. The present state of things is, that the king has placed everything at Canning's disposal, stating that he wishes the government to contain as many Protestants as possible, but that if none can be found he will be satisfied with an entirely Catholic list.* Canning is at present First Lord of the Treasury and Chancellor of the Exchequer, and Granville Foreign Affairs, but retaining his embassy,

---

* By "Protestants" are meant, of course, those opposed to Catholic Emancipation; and by "Catholics," those in favor of it.

to which he will ultimately return, as Canning will remain Foreign Secretary, having taken the other situation only for the moment, and till final arrangements are made. Robinson is Colonial Secretary. The Home Office is not filled; the king particularly wishes to have a Protestant there, but it is not easy to find one fit for it. Harrowby remains as he is, and, I believe, Huskisson also. The Privy Seal has, they say, been declined by Dudley, who probably learnt that he was meant to hold it only ad interim. Copley is Chancellor as Lord Ashbourne.* I suspect that Leach will go Chancellor to Ireland, and Plunkett be Master of the Rolls here; but this I know not for certain. I am to be Chancellor of the Exchequer; but as Copley's move makes an immediate vacancy at Cambridge, and a contest will thereupon ensue, it is postponed, in order that my re-election may not involve me in this contest; and as it might be inconvenient to have me out of Parliament during the session, it is probable that I shall not be moved till the session is over; but in the mean time I am to be put immediately into the Cabinet. Among other considerations which make me glad of this, one of the chief is, that I trust it will give me better means than I have hitherto possessed of assisting you in your diplomatic advancement.

"Canning has all along received from the Whigs assurances of their support in the event of his forming a government of which he should be the head, even though he made no stipulation on the Catholic question, because they are wise enough to know that in the present state of the king's opinion, no government can be formed upon the principle of carrying that question as a Cabinet measure, and the next best thing is to secure the influence of gov-

* All these are merely the arrangements first contemplated.

ernment in the hands of men favorable to the question. My own opinion, however, is, that some of them ought to be brought into office—Lansdowne and Holland, perhaps, in the Lords, and Abercromby and Tierney in the Commons—and I should not be surprised if this were to happen. The government would then be very strong; and without some such arrangement its chief reliance must be upon a party upon whom we shall have no hold, and who may throw us over at any moment of caprice or cabal. For as to the Tories, who would hardly vote for our measures before, we must not look for any cordial support from them now. Not but that, by degrees and one by one, they will all by instinct come round to the oat-sieve; I know, however, that Canning means to deal out that sieve very sparingly, and to found his government upon public opinion rather than borough interests, *in which I think he is as right as possible.*

"Adieu! my dear William. I am just going down to Broadlands for a few days, and will write again when I return next week

"Yours affectionately,

"PALMERSTON.

"Do not mention to anybody the assurance of support from the Whigs which Canning has received, nor my intended appointment as Chancellor of Exchequer, unless you hear it from other quarters."

To the Hon. Wm. Temple, Berlin.

"STANHOPE STREET, May 4, 1827.

"MY DEAR WILLIAM,—

"All arrangements are now settled, at least as to general principle. The Whigs join us in a body and with zeal, and some of them will come into office immediately.

Those, namely, who are not to be in the Cabinet—Tierney, I believe, Master of the Mint; Calcraft, Woods and Forests; and Abercromby, Judge Advocate; William Lamb is Secretary for Ireland, not as a Whig, but on his own account as an individual. The provisional members of the Cabinet are the Duke of Portland, Privy Seal; Dudley, Foreign Affairs; and Bourne, Home Office; who is to succeed them I do not know, but at the end of the session Lord Lansdowne will come in, and I suppose some others of his party. I should think Lansdowne would be Home Secretary, and Lord Holland Privy Seal, and then Canning will probably resume the Foreign Office, if arrangements can be made by which all the patronage and influence properly belonging to the situation of First Minister can be attached to that appointment; in that case the First Lordship of the Treasury will also be disposable. I am in the Cabinet, but continue Secretary at War till the end of the session, having in addition to my own duties those of the Commander-in-Chief to perform. This is the natural constitution of my office, that in the absence of a Commander-in-Chief the patronage of the army devolves on the Secretary at War. At the end of the session I shall be Chancellor of the Exchequer, and then, in my opinion, some military man ought to be placed in the command of the army; and if the Duke of Wellington cannot be brought back again, some general officer high up in the list ought to be placed upon the staff. The advantage of the present arrangement is, that it leaves the door open for the Duke of Wellington's return when the other arrangements are made, without dispossessing any individual. You will see by the debates that the Whigs have joined us manfully and in earnest, and have boldly faced all charges of inconsistency, declaring that they know it to be impossible that the Catholic question should be made a

Cabinet measure, and do not join us upon any such expectation, but simply because they see as well as Peel that the having Canning at the head of the government must of itself necessarily give a great advantage to the question; and because they agree with him on almost all other great questions of foreign and domestic policy; and because, if they did not support him, he could not, by reason of the defection of his colleagues, maintain his position. Nothing can be more satisfactory to Canning than the footing on which their accession is placed; he gives up no opinion either on parliamentary reform or any other question, and distinctly said so last night in the House. They make him a compliment of most of the questions on which they differ with him. He, in the first place, makes his government and carries it through the session, and they come in as joining a government already formed, and not as original ingredients in its composition.

"The Tories are furious at this junction, because they see that it puts the government out of their power, and excludes them from a return. Peel parted good friends with Canning, but it is easy to foresee that their lines of march must daily diverge, and yesterday showed a good deal more personal opinion between them than might have been looked for. Indeed, Peel's speech two nights before was rather of a hostile complexion. His reference to Canning's correspondence in 1812 was needless; and such a reference, where not necessary, is always more or less personal. If Canning had blamed Peel for retiring, then Peel would naturally have defended himself by referring to Canning's former course; but as Canning had, on the contrary, gone out of his way to acquit Peel of blame or any want of perfect candor, the reference could only be looked upon as unfriendly.

"The duke is, I think, very sorry now that he gave up

the army, and I am sure he was worked upon to do it by the old Chancellor; the king, however, is very angry with him for it, and return at present is impossible.

"Adieu! yours affectionately,

"PALMERSTON."

Poor Canning enjoyed but a short time, as we know, the brilliant triumph of his genius.

The annexed letters extend over the period which intervened between the rise of Lord Goderich to the premiership—one hardly sees why—and his sliding down from that eminence—one hardly sees how!

The first gives a singular evidence of that nice tact with which Lord Palmerston always discerned the place that suited him, at the time when his own advancement was in question, and put aside at once any idea of a higher one. Some friends had probably been speaking of him as fit to be leader of the House of Commons. He was in the prime of life, and had attained a certain degree of eminence; but he saw instantaneously that the distinguished post suggested to him was above the position he had then acquired. He felt, moreover, that to undertake it would exact a strain on his faculties and a change in his habits that he was indisposed to encounter. Singular destiny! Mr. Fox said that no man after sixty could undertake the leadership of the House of Commons. Lord Palmerston—justifying the proverb that "*everything arrives to the able man who can wait for it*," and owing much, no doubt, to his marvelous constitution—arrived at this proud and laborious situation when age, according to a man well qualified to judge, disqualified him from filling it, and held it with undiminished aptitude many years subsequent to the period when, according to the general rule that fixes the term of human existence, he should have been in his grave.

We shall see in these letters the usual traces of a kind heart and of a busy life, occupied with public affairs, with the management of his paternal property, which he never neglected, and with attention to the interests of those he loved.

To Laurence Sulivan, Esq.

"Stanhope Street, August 14, 1827.

"My dear Sulivan,—

"I write before I go out; but if I hear anything more before post-time, I will let you know.

"I quite agree with you that Huskisson is the man who ought to represent the government in the House of Commons. He has every qualification for it in a great degree, except eloquence; but, without having that, he has quite sufficient faculty of speaking to enable him in these times, and in the present state of the House, to perform his duty with credit. He is fully equal to speaking up to the mark of any opponents he is likely to be pitted against; for even Peel's style of speaking is not so much remarkable for eloquence and brilliancy as for those very qualities which Huskisson shares with him. Brougham is the man whose style of speaking would be the most embarrassing to a man of Huskisson's turn of mind, whose powers lie in argument and statement, rather than in ridicule and exaggeration; but Brougham is with us. The Duke of Portland having succeeded Harrowby, there remain but two gaps to be filled; and it is quite clear that Lord Holland must in some way or other be put into one of them, either by going to the Colonial Office himself, or by taking the office of some other person who may go there. As to myself, I have heard nothing; and though I know Goderich's good will toward me, it may not be easy for him to make any arrangement. As to the lead of the House of Commons, *there are very few things indeed in this world which I should so much dislike; even if I felt that I was fit for it. But in various ways I should be quite unequal to it.* To go no further than one point, the person so placed must be in a perpetual state of canvass; and of all irksome slaveries there is none more difficult to me than that; besides, the character of the government is, as it were, identified with the debating success of the individual. I think it not unlikely that Tierney may risk it, and in some respects he has strong claims. *But he would not do; people think him too sly.* There can be no use whatever in your coming up; for even if I were to change office there really is nothing which we have to do that could not just as well be done by successors. The only things unsettled are the appointment of an assistant estimate clerk, and the selection of two juniors to fill the vacancies in the class above. Our regulations could not be finished in a couple of days, even if you were now in town; and therefore, really happen what will or may, there can be no earthly reason why you should cut short holidays of which you stood so much in need, and which, I trust, will do you essential good.

"Yours affectionately,

"PALMERSTON."

To Laurence Sulivan, Esq.

"August 15, 1827.

"MY DEAR SULIVAN,—

"I am to be Chancellor of Exchequer, and Herries Secretary at War. The first office was offered him by the king's desire; but he did not feel his health equal to it—at least, without going abroad; and Goderich could not wait his return. Huskisson goes to the Colonies; and Charles Grant succeeds him at the Board of Trade, probably not in the Cabinet. I am to be sworn in on Friday.

I do not think you need come to town yet; but I will let you know if it should be necessary when I have talked with Herries, which I have not yet done.

"Do not mention my appointment till it is announced officially, for fear of accidents.

"Yours affectionately,

"Palmerston.

"Goderich sent for me to-day, to propose this to me, saying he had written yesterday to the king about it."

To the Hon. Wm. Temple, Berlin.

"War Office, August 24, 1827.

"My dear William,—

"I have not time to make excuses for not having written to you sooner, since the great loss we have all sustained, and I now only state briefly the present situation of things. The king wants Herries to be Chancellor of the Exchequer; the Whigs object to him pointedly, and Goderich wishes to have me. Neither party will give way; and there is a great possibility of a dissolution of the government. Herries himself is not particularly desirous; but he is a great friend of Knighton, who, it is said, urges the appointment. The Whigs certainly have some cause to complain. The king refuses, for the moment at least, to take in Lord Holland, whom they pressed, and presses Herries, whom they reject. Herries is anti-Catholic and anti-Liberal, and I believe has held some indiscreet language about the Whigs. Still, however, I think they would be very foolish to go out on a personal question of this kind, and to give up the means which office affords them of giving effect to all the great principles of national policy, foreign and domestic, to forward which they avowedly joined Canning's administration.

But, looking back to the conduct of that party in trying moments when personal feeling came into play, I think it too probable that they will go out, if some means cannot be found to parry the question; and I certainly should consider their secession as a great public misfortune. One of two things must follow: either a mixed government would be made by Goderich of some of his present colleagues and the Tories, or the whole Cabinet would march, and the Tories come in bodily. The last, it is obvious, would be most unfortunate in every possible way, and would produce the worst consequences on our foreign relations and domestic policy, including commerce and Ireland. The first event would bring back a government just like Liverpool's, consisting of men differing on all great questions, and perpetually on the verge of a quarrel; the result of which is that nothing is done, each party giving up their views on condition that a corresponding sacrifice is made by the others. Huskisson has arrived at Paris, and is expected here in a few days, and it has been agreed to let the matter stand over till his return. He may probably cut the knot by saying that he will not lead the House of Commons—which he *must* do, unless he is himself Chancellor of Exchequer—or else Sturges Bourne, to whom the king at first proposed it, might be induced, much against his will, to take it for a time, to save the government from dissolution. He is intended for the Colonial Office, and Charles Grant to succeed him at the Board of Trade. Dudley remains at the Foreign Office, where he has done incomparably well, and has surprised all those who only knew him by seeing him abstracted and absent in society, or muttering to himself while chinking his sovereigns.

"Our Portuguese affairs are beginning to clear up, and we are getting Austria to take much the same view of the matter as ourselves, and I trust we shall find her co-operate with us in the ultimate arrangement.

"A'Court writes, in a letter received to-day, that they do not expect Don Pedro; and Austria engages to keep Miguel at Vienna till the negotiations with Brazil shall be brought to a close—that is, at least to the end of the year. If this and the Greek affair can be well settled, the state of Europe will be as satisfactory as it can perhaps ever be expected to be; for when Portugal is put to rights the French *must* quit Spain.

"Fanny and Bowles are in Scotland, Sulivan and Eliz. in Wales.

"The Duke of Wellington will be gazetted Commander-in-Chief to-night. He comes in without any stipulations or conditions whatever.

"Yours affectionately,
"Palmerston."

To the Hon. Wm. Temple, Berlin.

"Stanhope Street, Oct. 19, 1827.

"My dear William,—

"I am off to-morrow for Ireland for three weeks, but must be back again in London by the 12th November, as the Cabinet hold their usual autumnal assembly on the 13th, to make arrangements for the business of the session, etc. Fanny and Bowles are not yet returned from their northern tour, but give a very good account of themselves. European affairs have been arranging themselves in a satisfactory manner. Ferdinand has made his bargain with his ultras, and they have all submitted. What his terms to them are remains to be seen: probably he will keep his promises as much as may be convenient to him. He is no fool and no bigot, but has much to do with people who are both; and he wants energy to resist, and good faith to stick to anything inconvenient at the moment. Miguel will, I hope, come here soon, and if we can send him to Lisbon imbued with proper sentiments as to the necessary dependence of Portugal on England, and can undo a little of Metternich's absolutism in his mind, the affairs of Portugal may yet turn out well. Our troops will probably be withdrawn as soon as Miguel arrives, because then, all danger of invasion from Spain being over, the ground of our occupation will cease.

"France would, I believe, be very glad also to get out of Spain, where the position of her army becomes every day more false and unpleasant; and we have reason to think that when our troops are gone, or actually going, France will publicly proclaim the approaching departure of hers from Spain. Greece is an object of more uncertain interest; but yet I cannot believe that the Turk will hold out when he finds the three allies really in earnest. Austria has, I believe, been playing her usual double game on this point, professing to us her anxiety to assist us, and that her only reason for not being a party to the treaty was an abstract principle, which forbade her to recognize the existence on earth of such a state of things as a continued resistance of subjects to their sovereign; while, on the other hand, she has been urging the Porte not to give way, assuring her that the allies would separate, and the alliance end in nothing. Metternich has even had the face to make to the allies, through the French government, an indirect offer of the mediation of Austria and Prussia between the allies and Turkey, stating that it was now evident that the treaty* was become a dead letter, and never could be executed. Damas gave him a very proper

* See Appendix.

answer, saying that the three Powers humbly thought that they were strong enough to execute their own intentions, and that the treaty, so far from having become a dead letter, happened to be just beginning to become an effective measure; that we needed no assistance in the way of mediation from our obliging friends at Vienna and Berlin, but that if they chose now to become parties to the treaty, they might still be admitted, and their assistance in that shape would be willingly received. Metternich, however, will gradually connect himself a little more with England. There was a personal dislike between him and Canning, which influenced the public policy, perhaps, of both; but Metternich must be an idiot if he does not see that Russia is the windward quarter of the heavens, and that his dirty weather must come from thence, and that he should look for shelter to the westward. Parliament will not meet till February, if we can find money enough to go on with till the end of that month. We know that we can do till the end of January, but if we should not have cash or credit beyond that, Parliament must meet in the early part of January, as it takes near a fortnight to get any vote that can be turned into money. The Duke of Gordon will not go to the Ordnance, but probably to Canada, instead of Lord Dalhousie, who goes Commander-in-Chief to India, instead of Lord Combermere. Sir G. Murray will be Major-General of Ordnance, not in the Cabinet. Clinton, who is Lieutenant-General of Ordnance, will go to the Mauritius instead of Cole, who goes to the Cape; and Sir H. Taylor will be Lieutenant-General of Ordnance. These are very good arrangements, but are not yet public, nor indeed definitively settled. The Whigs are getting into good humor again, and Whig and Tory will soon be erased from our vocabulary. The king has not yet forgiven the seceders. He has had a sharp attack of gout, but had been so long free that it was naturally to be expected.

"Adieu! yours affectionately,

"PALMERSTON."

To the Hon. Wm. Temple, Berlin.

"STANHOPE STREET, Nov. 27, 1827.

"MY DEAR WILLIAM,—

"I returned about a fortnight ago from a three weeks' trip to Sligo, where I found my improvements going on well; and I hope to find my people in a few years somewhat resembling a civilized race. My harbor is just finished, and will be very useful for the fishery, and in the end will be a little commercial port. I made a concordat with my bishop about my schools, and, by agreeing to all he asked—which, after all, was not very unreasonable—I have got him to assist me, and have heard since my return that my girls' school has increased from five scholars to one hundred. The boys' school has not yet got a master; but when I get one it will be equally thriving, I have no doubt. I spoke again to Dudley about you the day before yesterday, and he repeated his assurances of an earnest desire to attend to my wishes as soon as any opportunity enabled him. He asked whether you would have any objection to cross the water. I asked what water he meant. He said he meant whether you would feel any repugnance to go to South America. I said that of course when a man embraces a profession he was prepared to go wherever that profession might call him, and that I was sure that was your feeling; but that certainly I should very much prefer some appointment in Europe for you, if it were possible to find one. He said that in Europe they were terribly crowded, and that it was possible it might be more easy to find an opening in America. I asked what the appointment was which he had in contemplation. He said he had nothing particular in view, and his inquiry was only a general one; and so we left the matter. But I am sure he will do what he can for you. By our last accounts from Constantinople, dated the 5th, the Turks seemed as much puzzled as surprised with the smash at Navarino. My own conjecture is, that it will smooth and not increase our difficulties. It is a display of power and an indication of determination which they will appreciate. It deprives them of all possibility of keeping up their army in the Morea; for as to supplies by land, the march is too long and difficult. The only question then is, how long it will take for the Greeks, and sickness, and fatigue to consume their present force in Greece, and whether there is any chance of the alliance falling to pieces before that time; and, on the other hand, they must calculate that if what has been done should not be effectual, something more may perhaps be done in the shape of those 'ulterior measures' alluded to in the treaty. Metternich has acted a shabby and a foolish part. He thwarted us underhand while a different course might have prevented the collision; and now he is frightened, and really wishes to help us, when his influence is diminished. From what I have seen of him since I came into the Cabinet, I am convinced he prefers the tortuous to the straight course, where the option is before him.

"Adieu! yours affectionately,

"Palmerston."

To the Hon. Wm. Temple.

"Stanhope Street, Dec. 4, 1827.

"My dear William,—

"Clanwilliam has hinted to me that it is probable that the Secretaryship of Embassy at Petersburg will be offered to you, under A'Court,* who, however, will not be formally appointed till he returns to England; and he cannot leave Portugal till Miguel has arrived there, because he must deliver to him his letters of recall; and Lamb must, at the same time, deliver his credentials. Let me know your wishes on this matter. . . .

"We are still in uncertainty about Turkey and Greece. What is most probable is, that the Turk will sit cross-legged, and with his hands before him, and say he will do nothing; or, as the French express it, *qu'il se retranchera dans son inertie.* The question then for us will be, how we shall compel him to move; because the Treaty of London *must* be carried into effect, cost what it may, and oppose it who will. I should think that Metternich must by this time be sick of his double-dealing on this subject, and wish that he had inculcated less obstinacy into the Divan. Cunning men are always foolish actors; and nothing could be more silly for Austria than to throw secret obstacles in the way of the allies, as Metternich has done. The protraction of the discussion between Turkey and the allies can do Austria no good; and if it ends in war† she will heartily repent not having used her best efforts to prevent such a crisis.

"Adieu! yours affectionately,

"PALMERSTON."

To the Hon. Wm. Temple, Berlin.

"WAR OFFICE, Dec. 18, 1827.

"MY DEAR WILLIAM,—

"Dudley called here yesterday, to offer to me for you the Secretaryship of Embassy at Petersburg. I told him that I felt no difficulty in at once accepting it on your behalf, with many thanks for so early and kind an attention to the wishes which I had expressed to him. But I added,

---

* Afterward Lord Heytesbury.

† It did end in war.

that as I wished to have no reserve with him, and was desirous that neither I nor you might hereafter appear to him to be changeable or capricious, I thought it best to tell him that you had been for some time at Stockholm, and that you had found a northern climate not favorable to your health; and consequently, that if any opportunity should occur by-and-by which would enable him to remove you to a more southern station, I should be much obliged to him to do so. He said he would bear it in mind. I then asked him if you could have leave to take England in your way to Petersburg, and he promised to see if there was any reason against, and to give you leave if there was none. A'Court goes to Petersburg,* but cannot leave Lisbon till Lamb and Miguel get there, which will be in the beginning, or rather middle, of January. Miguel will be here about the 27th, and will stay six days, and then embark at Plymouth. Though Petersburg may not be the station you would have chosen, yet it is not without advantages. It is a court of great influence and importance in the affairs of Europe. A'Court is a man of eminence in his profession, and if you obtain—as I have no doubt you will—his good opinion and good word, his testimony would be of more use to you than that of most other ambassadors; and by means of the Woronzows you will probably get better Russian acquaintances than many other people could do.

"Here we are again all aback. Goderich, last Saturday se'nnight, pressed on the king, in a personal interview, the

---

* In the *Gazette* of Dec. 28 are the following appointments: the Right Hon. Sir W. A'Court, Bart., to be Ambassador to the Emperor of Russia; the Right Hon. Sir F. Lamb, G.C.B., to be Envoy Extraordinary at the Court of his Most Faithful Majesty (Portugal); the Hon. Wm. Temple to be Secretary to the Embassy at St. Petersburg.

accession of Lords Holland and Wellesley to the Cabinet, which the king put aside. On Tuesday last (this day week) Goderich wrote the king a letter, again urging the matter, and stating that without such an addition of strength to the government he felt himself unable to make himself responsible for carrying on the king's service; and unless his advice was adopted, he begged leave to retire. To this Lansdowne and Huskisson were parties; and they were also prepared to abide by the same alternative. But then Goderich added to this letter a postscript, which nobody saw, and in which he stated that he felt himself—from domestic circumstances, affecting the health of one most dear to him—totally incapable of continuing to perform the duties of his station. The king dextrously avoided any notice of the first alternative, and fastened upon the postscript, and expressed his regret that Lord Goderich should find himself unfit for his situation by circumstances over which the king had no control; and in a subsequent interview on Thursday, he said he would think of the means of relieving him. He has sent for Lord Harrowby, and yesterday saw Huskisson. I have not heard that any decision has been made, nor can any be expected for some days. Goderich is willing, on reconsideration, to remain, if any satisfactory arrangement could be made as to Holland and Wellesley; but the king, probably, will not let him. I do not expect any considerable change, and certainly not the return of the Tories; but some changes there probably will be—beyond the single office of First Lord of the Treasury. If the accounts from Constantinople are confirmed, and that an armistice has been agreed to, we may consider ourselves out of the main difficulty in that quarter.

"Yours affectionately,

"PALMERSTON."

To the Hon. Wm. Temple, Berlin.

"Stanhope Street, Jan. 8, 1828.

"My dear William,—

"I received yesterday your last letter. I am glad you are satisfied with the steps I have taken in your name. Petersburg may not be an agreeable residence, but it was very important for you to secure the step; and, depend upon it, *it never answers for a professional man to decline advancement when offered him, with the view of waiting for something more agreeable;* it creates an unfavorable impression; and, at all events, when that something more agreeable does offer he is nearer its attainment by the preceding promotion. I have no doubt, however, that you will find Petersburg less disagreeable than you expect; and, at all events, it is just now an important post. I am very sorry to find that we shall not see you in your way, and that you are ordered off straight to your new position; but this will still be attended with professional advantage to you, as you will step at once into the situation of Chargé d'Affaires, which in an embassy, I understand, gives the rank of Minister Plenipotentiary. A'Court will probably stay here some months when he returns from Lisbon; but when he gets to Russia there can, I should think, be no doubt of your obtaining a furlough. Things here are in a very unsettled state as to ministerial arrangements; and the fluctuations and changes of the last few months made me still more anxious to secure you your promotion while it was to be had from friends and colleagues. I am afraid it is very doubtful whether Goderich will continue; his resignation has caused a most unfavorable impression as to the stability of the government, and compels even his best friends to doubt whether, with all his talents, he possesses that firmness and energy necessary for his situation. I believe, from private information, that the king means to make some fresh arrangement before Parliament meets, and is only waiting for Miguel's departure to take the matter up. A general change I do not expect, but I think it likely that a new chief may be appointed. . . . The Don goes on Thursday to Strathfieldsaye, shoots and hunts Friday and Saturday, goes on to Morley's on Sunday, and then, I suppose, embarks as soon as the wind is fair. He has taken here very well, but has been unfortunate in weather, having been drenched to the skin three times, hunting, shooting, and reviewing. His manners and appearance are pleasing. Billy of Gloucester cross-questioned him as usual; and as Miguel did not know who he was speaking to, and only viewed him as a prince of the blood, he answered his questions; and the result was, that he meant to consummate his marriage when his wife is twelve, to have a son when she is thirteen, and then to declare himself king, which the old law of Portugal warrants, and on which the Charter is silent; and he means to follow the old law on all points on which the Charter says nothing. The Portuguese ambassador at Petersburg is to be his Minister for Foreign Affairs, and Palmella remains here.

"Yours affectionately,

"PALMERSTON."

The cause of Lord Goderich's resignation was a quarrel between Huskisson and Herries, "whom the king," says Lord Palmerston (in a short portion of his biography, which I have not quoted here in extenso, because its substance is repeated in the letters I have given), "had thrown like a live shell into the Cabinet to explode and blow us all up."

"Instead of going to the king," continues the auto biographer, "and saying, 'Sire, Mr. Huskisson and Mr. Herries have differed, and cannot serve together, and therefore I propose to you to appoint A B, instead of one or the other,' Goderich stated the quarrel, the impossibility of the two going on as colleagues, and gave the king to understand that he had no advice to give, and did not know what to do. But the king knew very well what he had to do; he bid Goderich go home, *and take care of himself*, and keep himself quiet; and he immediately sent for the Duke of Wellington to form a government.

"One of the first acts of Goderich's administration had been to ask the Duke of Wellington to be Commander-in-Chief; Lord Anglesey had been sent to make the offer. He traveled without stopping, arrived at some country-house in the west where the duke was staying, about three in the morning, found the duke in full uniform, just come home from a fancy ball, obtained his immediate acceptance, and arrived with it at Windsor while we were sitting in council on the memorable day in August at which Lord William Bentinck also was present to be sworn in Governor-General of India.

"Lord Anglesey said to us, 'Well, gentlemen, I have done what you sent me to do. I have brought you the Duke of Wellington's acceptance as Commander-in-Chief; and, by God, mark my words, as sure as you are alive he will trip up all your heels before six months are over your heads.'

"Before the six months were well over the duke was in, and our heels were up; but the king was the great plotter, and Holmes and Planta worked upon Goderich, and persuaded him he could never overcome the difficulties he would have to encounter."

The projected arrangements ended, as we know, by the Duke of Wellington being named Premier instead of Lord Goderich, though the post of Premier was one for which he had declared himself a short time previous wholly unfit.

I have been told by a gentleman yet alive, and likely to be well informed on the subject, that Lord Wellesley expected this appointment, and had been encouraged by his brother to do so. That when the duke was summoned by the king, it was understood that he should recommend the marquess as more fit to take the lead in civil affairs than himself; that the marquess expected the duke's return with much anxiety, anticipating his own elevation, and that the disappointment that ensued occasioned a coolness between these two eminent men. Whatever may be the precise truth of this story—and such stories are rarely told with perfect accuracy—I venture to express an opinion that it would have been, upon the whole, fortunate for the duke's reputation, great as that reputation is, if he had followed the course which I have heard he at one time intended to pursue. I have been told by many of his contemporaries that no man of his time was endowed with so many of the highest attributes of a statesman as Lord Wellesley. With great eloquence, large and liberal views, free from impracticable theories, unbiased by obsolete prejudices, he was the man peculiarly fitted to bridge the abyss on which the past had to run into the future, and could have done with credit and consistency what the duke could not do without making concessions which, not being the result of conviction, would assuredly appear the result of fear and necessity; thus commencing a policy which has had too many imitators—a policy carrying bitterness into the hearts of those who have been vanquished, and contempt into the hearts of those who have triumphed; for to give what you dare not deny is a humiliation to one party, and no satisfaction to the other.

BOOK V.

What happened to Lord Palmerston on the formation of the new administration—Extract from autobiography—Private letters to Mr. Temple on foreign and home politics—Extracts from journal beginning March 9, 1828, and including a long, detailed, and interesting account of the events which led to the withdrawal of Mr. Huskisson from the Duke of Wellington's government.

LORD PALMERSTON thus relates what occurred to himself at the formation of the new administration :*

"When the duke came in, he sent for Huskisson to Apsley House, as head of the Canningite party, and asked him to join his government. The inducements held out were these :

"The Catholic question to be, as before, an open question; and to have, therefore, the benefit of the influence belonging to a portion of the Cabinet being in its favor.

"The Greek treaty to be faithfully executed; and Dudley to be left, as Foreign Secretary, to watch over its execution. Huskisson's principles of trade to be acted upon, and Charles Grant to be left at the Board of Trade, as a pledge and security on that point. Huskisson, Grant, Dudley, and myself to have seats in the Cabinet; Lamb to remain as Irish Secretary, as a guarantee that an impartial system would be pursued toward the Catholics. Eldon and Westmoreland to be excluded from the Cabinet, they being the representatives of the most illiberal opinions.

---

* From biographical memoir.

"Dudley, Lamb, Binning, Grant, and myself met at Huskisson's house in Somerset Place, which he still occupied—being very unwell—in order to take these proposals into consideration. We discussed the matter fully, with reference both to the personal question between Herries and Huskisson, and to the public interests and political questions involved; and our determination was that the offer ought to be accepted.

"We did accept it, therefore, not as individuals, but as a party representing the principles and consisting of the friends of Mr. Canning.

"We joined the new government in January. We left it in May. We joined as a party; as a party we retired. The only one who hesitated was Dudley; and he would willingly have given six thousand a year out of his own pocket, instead of receiving that sum from the public, for the pleasure of continuing to be Secretary of State for Foreign Affairs."

The feebleness of the Wellington Cabinet is sufficiently explained by the fact here stated, viz., that the Canningites joined it as a party mistrusting its chief.

The following letter—going back to the formation of that Cabinet—states the feelings with which Lord Palmerston saw himself now transferred from a union with the moderate Whigs to a union with the liberal Tories, whom he distinguishes from the Tories of a more antiquated cast, or, as he styles them, the "pig-tails."

To the Hon. Wm. Temple, Berlin.

"STANHOPE STREET, Jan. 18, 1828.

"MY DEAR WILLIAM,—

"I received yesterday your last letter, stating that you had received the Gazette and official notice of appointment, and had written to Dudley. This is certainly not the most agreeable time of year for a journey to Petersburg; but, under all the circumstances of the case, I think you have no reason to regret the arrangement which has been made, as you might have waited longer and fared worse. The Duke of Wellington has been employed since Wednesday, the 9th, in taking steps to reorganize the government; but he found it so much longer an operation than he expected, that he has been obliged to prorogue Parliament for another week, and put it off to the 29th. He has made propositions to Huskisson, Dudley, Grant, and myself. He first proposed to Huskisson, who said that he could not at all events come in without us three and William Lamb; and we three determined not to come in without Huskisson, considering him as representing in Parliament certain political principles which we profess, and for which his presence in office would be a security and guarantee.

"There has been some difficulty about Herries, with whom Huskisson felt a reluctance to serve, but he referred that point to Dudley, Grant, and myself; and, after two days' anxious consideration, we could not find any sufficient public grounds upon which Huskisson could rest his objection to serve with Herries, provided Herries were not Chancellor of Exchequer, and provided the government and its arrangements were in other respects satisfactory.

"This result was yesterday communicated to the duke, and he was then enabled to go on with his communications with other persons. He wishes to form a strong government, and a liberal one. Eldon and Westmoreland will not be in it, though I fear Bathurst is inevitable, but he will be President of the Council, or hold some other office which gives no departmental influence. But Canning's principles of policy will be preserved, which is a great tribute of homage to his memory; Dudley will carry them on in our foreign relations; Huskisson and Grant in our colonial and commercial. Peel will probably return to his Home Office, where he will prosecute his system of reform. All this, instead of a pig-tail Tory government, shows the great strides which public opinion has made in the last few years. Such a government as Liverpool's even cannot now be established; and such a one as Perceval's could not be for a moment thought of. The Cabinet will probably consist, in the Lords—of Wellington, Lyndhurst, Bathurst, Melville, Dudley, Ellenborough, Aberdeen, and perhaps Roslyn as Master-General of Ordnance; in the Commons—of Peel, Huskisson, Herries, Grant, Goulburn —probably Chancellor of Exchequer—and myself, and possibly Vesey Fitzgerald, who has hooked himself on to Peel, and whom Peel may think it necessary to bring into the Cabinet with him. This list gives a majority of Catholics; and the duke agrees that the Lord-Lieutenant shall not be an anti-Catholic. All these things, however, are still merely guesses and sketches; for the duke has not communicated to us the name of any one individual besides ourselves, except Peel and Herries, whom he proposes to be in the Cabinet. Herries would be Master of the Mint, an office which has no direct connection with Windsor, and no departmental influence.

"The duke has read the detailed explanations about Navarino, sent by Codrington through Sir John Gore, and is satisfied, and also declares that '*the king's treaties must be observed.*' So that there will be no change of policy about Greece; indeed, Dudley's continuance would be a security on this point. However, difficulties of detail may still arise to change the whole of this arrangement, though it is not probable; and I think that Huskisson is so necessary in the Commons, that any reasonable sacrifice will be made to retain him.

"The Whigs of course will be furious and violent, and

lay about them to the right and left. *I very sincerely regret their loss, as I like them much better than the Tories, and agree with them much more; but still we, the Canningites, if we may be so termed, did not join their government, but they came and joined ours;* and whatever regard we may feel for them, we have not enlisted with them, so as to be bound to follow their fate and fortunes, or to make their retention a condition of our remaining; and, indeed, if we had all gone out, I should certainly not have sat with them in the House of Commons, but should have taken an independent and separate position.

"Yours affectionately,

"PALMERSTON."

We see from this letter that a Canningite at that time was not a Whig—was not a Tory. What was a Canningite?

It may not be the fashion at this moment to defend the Canningite party. A democratic current has set in within the last few years, which carries away all merit from those who are not favorable to making democracy the basis of political institutions. But this is a confined view to take of statesmanship, and one which the enlightened people of a great country never do take permanently.

There are doubtless great and powerful virtues that expand in democratic institutions; and perhaps no government is so capable of doing great things as a well-educated democracy with noble-minded leaders as there is no government so capable of committing great errors and great crimes as an ill-educated democracy with low-minded, vicious, or fanatical chiefs.

The form of every government is a means to an end, according to times and circumstances. So also the character of a party has to be judged according to times and circumstances. It should be adapted to the state of existing society; it should aim at carrying on society to further improvement; it should nourish in a nation noble and generous inspirations; it should encourage a spirit of general humanity and national independence, and has a right to our praise if it is the object of imitation, of admiration, and affection among the intelligent and patriotic men of its epoch.

The party of Mr. Canning was in a great degree a party of this kind, and will live in our history, and the history of the world, as the party of the generous, brave, and intellectual Englishmen of the early part of the nineteenth century.

It was not in favor of an extensive suffrage. It favored the existence of a powerful and wealthy landed aristocracy; it was not opposed to that system of so-called rotten boroughs, which was certainly an absurd anomaly in the theory of popular representation. Still, it tolerated universal suffrage as an exhibition of popular feeling in certain localities; it opposed the pretensions of aristocratic pride to exclusive power; and it defended its adherence to the existing parliamentary constitution on the plea that that constitution brought practically the best men, poor and rich, and of almost every station, into the House of Commons.

It had, moreover, for its characteristics, principles which elevated it high above the political adventurers who consider politics as nothing more than a struggle for place. Those principles were in part manifested in the patronage of constitutional opinions abroad, and in the adoption, though not without reservations, of the doctrines of free trade at home; and in the withdrawal of religious qualifications for political functions both at home and abroad. Such, on the one hand, was the Canningite party; on the other hand, that section of Lord Liverpool's Cabinet which had quitted Mr. Canning had a leaning toward the absolute governments on the Continent, was disposed to a protective policy in regard to trade, and was for maintaining unimpaired the maxim of Protestant ascendency throughout the United Kingdom.

Mr. Peel stood in a certain degree alone, agreeing with the Duke of Wellington on the Catholic question, and with Mr. Huskisson and his friends on almost every other.

At first the differences that thus naturally and incessantly occurred were got over without any painful jar between the two parties in the Cabinet; but by degrees these differences became painful and irritating to both.

Some letters and some extracts from Lord Palmerston's journal at this time will show the subacute state of an impending quarrel, which was certain ere long to assume an inflammatory character.

I first quote the letters, though their contents are here and there repeated in the journal which I shall subsequently make use of.

To the Hon. Wm. Temple, St. Petersburg.

"March 25, 1828.

"My dear William,—

"I received your letter from some place near Riga, but have not yet heard of your arrival at Petersburg, which I hope to do soon. Affairs are becoming embroiled at home and abroad. Our government consists of some discordant elements; but still I think it will go on. *Peel is so right-headed and liberal, and so up to the opinions and feelings of the times, that he smooths difficulties which might otherwise be insurmountable.* The announcement which we have received of the intention of Russia to declare war against Turkey creates great embarrassments in the execution of the Treaty of London. We do not mean to go to war with Turkey; and how, therefore, can we co-operate with Russia if she does go to war? We are, however, determined not to throw the treaty overboard on account of this difficulty, but to persevere with France to execute it in our own way.

"France seems equally disposed to maintain her engagements, and anxious for a speedy settlement of the question. We must do our best to get the Turks and Egyptians out of the country, and, that accomplished, the rest will be comparatively easy. Russia has bound herself by so many obligations and declarations not to look to territorial aggrandizement that one must believe her sincere; but successful war offers great temptations to depart from the moderation which may have been felt at its commencement; and the sooner the cause of contest is over, the less likely is it that that temptation will be presented. Europe has a clear right, however, upon general principles, and independently of any engagements by Russia, to see that the war between her and Turkey shall not derange the balance of power, and alter the state of possession as fixed by the last general peace.

"Portugal is in a state approaching to revolution. The actual overt acts of Miguel are few. He has indeed mumbled an oath which he ought to have pronounced loudly. He has omitted to issue a proclamation which he promised to make on his arrival. He has dissolved the Chambers, which he had a right to do, but has made a commission to arrange resolutions, which he had no right to do, and all the members of which are creatures of the queen; and he has been changing the officers of regiments. This, to be sure, is as much as he could perhaps have done in so short a time since his landing. But the panic in Lisbon is universal. Both parties, says Lamb, are running away from each other; but the Constitutionalists are the most active in the race. Lamb detained three thousand of our troops till he could hear again from hence. We have, however, told him, that though we entirely approve his having done so, yet that we went to repel foreign invasion, not to interfere by force in domestic affairs, and that we cannot stay to do that which was no ingredient in the cause of our going. But we shall keep a line-of-battle ship in the Tagus, and seven hundred marines in Fort St. Julian, for the protection of English subjects and property, and to give means of escape to any persecuted Portuguese; we have also sent three sloops to Oporto for similar purposes, there not being depth of water for larger ships to get in there. Adieu! All well.

"Yours affectionately,
"PALMERSTON."

To the Hon. Wm. Temple, St. Petersburg.

"STANHOPE STREET, May 8, 1828.

"MY DEAR WILLIAM,—

"I take the opportunity of a Captain Campbell, to whom I have given a letter of introduction to you, to write a few lines that will not be opened by the Russian and other post officers. We are not going on as I like; but it will depend upon Russia and France whether we break with them or not: if they wish to break with us they may easily find an excuse; if they wish to keep with us they will not give us a pretense for breaking. The duke has the strongest dislike to Russia—more, I think, from personal feeling than from political. Ellenborough is even more adverse than the duke: Aberdeen is Austrian, and Bathurst anti-Russian and Austrian; all these would give anything to get out of the Greek treaty, which they hate, and they set about it dextrously. The duke I believe to be in correspondence with Metternich, and tries to play his game of delay and procrastination—a system so unlike his natural temper about anything which he wishes really to accomplish. Advantage was taken of an objectionable expression in a note from Nesselrode to Lieven, 26th February, in which he said that if the allies did not adopt the Russian proposition of invading, or rather of occupying, the principalities, '*La Russie abandonnée par ses alliés n'exécuterait pas moins le traité de Londres ; mais dans le mode d'exécution elle ne consulterait que ses intérêts et ses convenances.*' This was announcing that she meant to violate the conditions to which she had bound herself by treaty, and required remonstrance and a demand of explanation from us. We, however, took advantage of this to leave off the conferences and lay upon our oars, and do nothing but propose to France a long string of propositions for defining those ultimate arrangements left indefinite in the treaty. The Russian answer to our remonstrance must, however, soon arrive ; and if, as I expect, it shall state that Russia does not mean to depart from the treaty, and if it confirms the explanation given to France that the *indemnities* announced as wanted from Turkey are indemnities to individuals, and not to the state, I think we shall be forced to renew the conferences, and shall not have a pretense for declining to do so.

"The Chambers in France are becoming all-powerful, and are impelling the government to more active measures about Greece. The French government say they must send money, and wish to send troops, and propose that six thousand English and an equal number of French should go; that was always my plan, and I proposed it to Goderich in November, when it was determined to evacuate Portugal; but nobody else approved it, and it is not more in favor now, and will not be done. Money we cannot give without a vote of Parliament; and I doubt whether that could at present be obtained for such an object. Huskisson, Dudley, Grant, and I try to keep things together, and have done so; and if Russia and France are *civil* to us, we shall manage it still; but if they send us uncivil papers, we shall not be able to prevent a separation of the alliance. I shall be sorry for this; not that it will prevent the liberation of Greece, for Russia and France will then do that work without us; but it would be unfitting for England to back out of such a treaty, and abandon the position she has taken in Europe. In the mean time France is urging us to resume the conferences, as a means of keeping a hold upon Russia; and there is much good sense in this. The government is very strong, and there is in fact no opposition. The Corn Bill will satisfy all parties tolerably well. The Finance Committee will not do much harm, and, if so, it will do much good. There is a general disposition to give us rope, and see what we shall do with it. You will probably hear it alleged that our government wishes to break with Russia and abandon the Greek cause; you may with truth say that this is not the feeling of some of the most influential members of the Cabinet; and that if Russia shows a disposition to abide by the treaty we shall not depart from it.

"Adieu! my dear William.

"Yours affectionately,

"Palmerston."

EXTRACTS FROM JOURNAL.

Sunday, March 9, 1828.

CABINET at four on Greek affairs. Huskisson proposed that Austria should be formally requested to prohibit all commercial intercourse between her subjects and the Turks in the Morea, in order to give effect to our blockade of Ibrahim Pasha; and that they should be told that they must be answerable for any consequences which her refusal may lead to, by its rendering our blockade abortive, and inducing Russia therefore to invade Turkey. This seemed to be agreed to.

The Duke of Wellington brought his memorandum of the arrangements which he proposed, in order to define the details of the treaty:

1. That the Greeks should pay Turkey an annual tribute of £200,000.

2. That they should pay £1,500,000 as compensation for Turkish property in the Morea.

3. That their territory should be confined to the Morea and certain islands to be named.

4. That they should be governed by persons to be appointed in one of three ways: either that a list should be sent to the Porte, out of which the Porte should select; or several lists, which the Porte might reject in succession till an agreeable one was presented; or else that the Porte should actually name, provided they named Greeks.

5. That the Greek state should be bound to follow Turkey in peace and war.

To this arrangement many objections were urged.

Everybody thought the tribute much too high, and the duke admitted it; and Aberdeen said he knew the whole tribute of the Morea was carried on about twelve mules.

Peel strongly objected to placing the new government in such dependence on Turkey.

If he had been to frame the treaty, he should have preferred independence to suzerainty.

He thought the relations between Greece and Turkey must in future be unpleasant, and no good could come of a right of interference on the part of Turkey. Ought we, too, not to pause before we admitted that war between us and Turkey must necessarily be followed by war between the Ionian Islands and Greece? He thought, too, we had no data upon which to fix tribute and compensation.

I expressed a strong objection to the proposed limit* of the Morea, as at variance with the spirit and principles both of protocol and treaty, because permanent pacification could not be looked for when large districts, long in revolt, were excluded from the settlement. Dudley stated strongly his full concurrence in this view. Grant had already read a memorandum on a former day to the same effect. Ellenborough and Bathurst, as usual, were for cutting down the Greeks in every way.

It was settled that, instead of making any specific proposal on these points, Dudley should, in a conference he is to have to-morrow with Lieven and Polignac, sound them as to the views of their courts on these topics. Peel threw out that the tribute might be fixed by reference to the sum actually paid by the Greeks during the last seven

* Afterward, as it will be seen, enlarged.

years preceding the revolt, and that the commissioners might determine the compensation.

It was proposed to recall Codrington, or at least to send out a superior officer to supersede him, on pretense of some negotiations with Egypt. It was, however, determined first to call upon Codrington to account for his having allowed 45 sail of ships, with 20,000 people on board, including 5500 captive Greek women and children, to sail quietly in December from Navarino to Alexandria, without his knowing anything about it till he heard of their arrival at the latter place.

Monday, March 10.

Examined by Finance Committee upon Army Estimates. Cabinet at half-past three on proposed Corn Bill. Duke of Wellington wanted to have the 20s. duty begin when the average price was 65s., instead of when it was 60s., and to bring in his last year's clause about warehousing. Huskisson declared he could not face the House of Commons to support such a bill, but proposed, as a modification of Liverpool's bill, that when in any consecutive twelve weeks more than 200,000 quarters should have been imported, the duty should be increased one-fourth, and that increase should continue till the average taken upon six successive weeks should have amounted to 66s. Grant objected to this, but the agricultural part of the Cabinet seemed to like it. Peel and Melville were for Lord Liverpool's bill, with such changes only as might be necessary to make it palatable to the House of Lords.

Tuesday, March 11.

Cabinet on the proposed Corn Bill. The duke strongly pressed his duty on warehoused corn according to his amendment of last year, or a higher scale of duty. Huskisson could not agree to either. Peel took much the same view as Huskisson, and so did Melville. After a great deal of discussion, the Cabinet separated without any formal decision, but with an apparent understanding that the bill of last year should be again brought in, only with the addition suggested yesterday by Huskisson. The duke was evidently ill pleased to find so large a majority of his Cabinet against him on a point on which individually he committed himself last year, and he left the room without saying whether he agreed or not to Huskisson's proposal.

Don Miguel took the oath to the Constitution at Lisbon on the 20th, a few days after his landing.

Wednesday, March 12.

Cabinet again on the Corn Bill, the duke clinging to his clause of last year, imposing an additional duty of 2*s.* 6*d.* a quarter on all corn taken out of warehouse.

Huskisson showed very ably that the Act of 1791, from which the duke took his idea, never was in operation as to warehousing, and that no corn ever was warehoused under its provisions. Peel stated his decided preference for Huskisson's plan, and urged that if the government were to break up at this moment, just on the eve of a war between Russia and Turkey, no man would believe that it was upon a clause in a Corn Bill, but that general opinion would impute deeper differences, more important to the general policy of the country. Bathurst and Ellenborough, not at all wishing to go out again, after having so recently come in, professed themselves entirely satisfied with Huskisson's clause, which they had not fully understood in all its bearings yesterday. Melville was entirely for it. Aberdeen was satisfied; and the only unyielding party was the duke, who feels that he shall be in an awkward situation in the House of Lords if he does not propose something about warehouses. He wants to make a difference between corn imported direct and corn taken out of warehouse. Huskisson's principle is, that both must stand on the same grounds. The Cabinet separated at five, without having come to any decision.

Last night Lieven communicated to Dudley a note from Nesselrode of 26th February, announcing that the Emperor of Russia meant to declare war against Turkey, upon Russian grounds: the violation of the Treaty of Akermann, the interruption of Russian commerce, and the interference of Turkey to prevent the conclusion of peace between Russia and Persia.

The Cabinet dined at Ellenborough's. After dinner we discussed what should be done about the proposed disfranchisement of Penryn—to be transferred to Manchester, and Retford to Birmingham.

Peel proposed to transfer Penryn, and throw Retford into the hundreds; Huskisson the reserve. Both wished to prevent establishing the rule that in all such cases the right should be transferred. *Dudley was strongly for seizing the golden opportunity of giving members to great towns, and thus getting rid of the great scandal of the present state of our representation.* I was clearly of opinion that we should be beat if we proposed to throw Penryn into the hundreds. The House of Commons had twice beat the government upon a similar proposal as to Cornish boroughs, Grampound and Penryn; would it be wise to risk a third defeat as to Retford? The difficulty would be that it was a worse case than Penryn, and therefore seemed to call for a course at least as severe; and there was also a general impression that to throw it into the hundreds would give it to the Duke of Newcastle. The result seemed to be, that we should transfer Penryn, and try to throw Retford into the hundreds, taking away altogether the burgesses, and making the right entirely in freeholders; or at least that Retford should be given to the agricultural interest in some way or other.

Saturday, March 15.

Cabinet on Corn Bill; further discussion. All the Cabinet except the duke had come round to Huskisson's proposition, and even the duke had given up his warehouse clause. Peel suggested, as a modification of Huskisson's arrangement, that when 200,000 quarters should have been imported in twelve weeks, the average being above sixty shillings, the duty should be raised a fifth,* and that the addition should continue till the average should have reached sixty-six shillings imperial taken on six weeks, or until some given day, say the 1st January then next ensuing. This seemed generally acquiesced in, except by Grant. He was to take time to consider.

Sunday, March 16.

Cabinet at four on Nesselrode's note to Liverpool of 26th, announcing that Nicholas meant to declare war against Turkey upon his own grievances, namely, the interruption of his commerce by the closing of the Bosphorus, the expulsion of some Russian subjects, and compulsion upon others to register themselves under Turkish authorities, and the interference in the Russian dispute with Persia, to make the Persians refuse to conclude peace. That he should still persevere in executing the Treaty of London, and look for no conquests. That if England and France would agree to his last proposal of December, 1827, he would finish the great question in conjunction with them. But that if they refused to co-operate with him on

* Mr. Huskisson had proposed a fourth.

that arrangement he should nevertheless execute the treaty, but in the mode of execution consult *only his own intérêts et convenances.* It seemed the general sense of the Cabinet that this latter declaration was announcing an intention to depart from the treaty, because the treaty binds the allies to concert measures, and this amounts to prescribing them. The mere fact of his being at war with Turkey does not dissolve the treaty, because the protocol contemplated the case of a separate war between Russia and Turkey.

Monday, March 17.

Cabinet at four upon Corn, and at ten at night upon the Russian note.

Tuesday, March 18.

Cabinet at ten at night on Portuguese affairs. Letters from Sir F. Lamb, of the 12th, received to-day by steamboat. The greatest alarm in Lisbon; everybody expecting a convulsion the moment our troops should embark; the Queen Mother had got entire possession of Don Miguel; had persuaded him that the Freemasons threatened his life. He never goes out, walks from room to room with two guards, lest he should be assassinated, and eats nothing but what has been prepared by a particular person (an old nurse), for fear of being poisoned. Every symptom of an approaching convulsion. Miguel pretends he did not swear to the Constitution, though he pretended to do so; Constitutional officers had been removed from four out of six Portuguese regiments in Lisbon; the other two would not part with their officers. The mob had been encouraged to insult everybody supposed friendly to the Charter; all the Liberals feared immediate proscription, and the English were preparing to escape. Two thousand English troops had gone off to the Mediterranean; Lamb had taken upon himself to detain the other

3000 till he could hear from us by return of the steamboat, to give the government an option as to the course they would pursue. Some means of protection for English persons and property had become absolutely necessary, in case of a convulsion both at Lisbon and Oporto.

Wednesday, March 19.

Cabinet at three at St. James's before Recorder's report. Settled dispatches to Lamb and Clinton according to determination taken at Cabinet at ten last night. We approved Lamb having detained the troops, but stated that it had never been our intention to interfere in the internal affairs of Portugal. That we had sent our troops to protect her against external attack, when requested by her government to do so; and that danger being over we had determined to withdraw our troops. The recent aspect of affairs did not alter our view, and the troops should come away as before settled; but to afford security and refuge to British subjects or persecuted Constitutionalists, one line-of-battle ship and a frigate or brig should remain in the Tagus, and marines should continue to occupy Fort St. Julian till further orders from hence, and a second frigate, the *Briton*, would be sent there from hence, and two brigs to Oporto, to protect the English there. Lamb was directed to ask for an interview with Miguel, and expostulate with him in the strongest terms upon the conduct he is pursuing, and to declare that we never can sanction or recognize an usurpation which would be founded upon hypocrisy, injustice, and perjury. If Miguel should already have declared himself king, Lamb's credentials being to the regent, he should consider his functions suspended. If the thing is not yet done, he is to remind Miguel of his oath at Vienna, and the engagement there made to proclaim amnesty and the Charter, of his renewed assurances in England, and his oath at Lisbon, and to say that we cannot advise Pedro to complete his abdication while Miguel pursues such a course as his present one. He is also to remonstrate against the choice of the present ministers. This dispatch, and a corresponding one to Clinton, were to go by the steamboat which brought Lamb's; copies of Lamb's to be sent to Paris, to be communicated in substance to the French government by Lord Granville, who should urge the French to use their influence at Madrid to prevent the Princess of Beira from being allowed to go to Portugal.

Monday, March 24.

Cabinet at three; Duke of Wellington read letter from Charles Grant, resigning, as no arrangement satisfactory to him could be made about the Corn Bill. Letter from Granville, stating that La Ferronaye had said that, as we object so decidedly to being parties to the Russian plan of invading Northern Turkey, France will not further press that measure; but that she thinks it of the utmost importance to drive the Turks quickly out of Greece, and seems determined to send troops there, whether we consent or no. Accounts from Portugal that Miguel had dissolved the Chambers and appointed an apostolical commission to arrange fresh elections; but in all probability he does not mean to call the Chambers again. Lamb says that both parties are running away from each other, but the Constitutionalists seem the most persevering in this intention. A strong letter prepared by Dudley for Lamb to remonstrate with Miguel.

Friday, March 28.

Grant not having made up his mind this morning to move the Corn Resolutions, Dudley, Lamb, and I met at Huskisson's, to consider what was to be done if Grant should resign upon this question. We had all used every persuasion in our power during the last week to induce him to overcome his objections, and I had spent two hours with him yesterday morning before the levée; but, though he seemed shaken, he had written to Huskisson last night late, to say that he could not bring himself to agree.

He objects to the scale of duty proposed, as being too high and too great a departure from sound principles. I urged that we were not considering what was abstractly right, or what we should ourselves prefer, but what, in the divided state of opinion on this question, would be most likely to be acquiesced in by the two contending parties; that the whole arrangement was in its nature a compromise, and therefore it was wisest to make such a compromise as would be successful; that the prejudices in the Lords were strong, and must be met by some concessions, or the bill would not pass their House.

The Duke of Wellington had conceded a principle by giving up his warehousing clause, and this was a great sacrifice, and was deeply felt by him. If we were prepared to contend that the particular scale of last year involved a principle, we might consistently refuse to depart from it. But that scale was by necessity fixed arbitrarily and by guess as an approximation, and not as a scale which could be demonstrated to be right. There was, then, no broad public ground of principle upon which he could put his resignation; and in point of etiquette the duke had conceded infinitely more than Grant was called upon to concede.*

---

* The Corn Law of 1815, proposed by Mr. Robinson (Lord Goderich), was based on the two extremes of complete prohibition up to a certain price of corn in the home market (eighty shillings), and complete freedom as to the introduction of corn above that price. The bill brought in by Mr. Canning (March 1, 1827) toward the end of Lord Liverpool's administration, and to which

The duke was the head of the government, and could not be discredited without some portion of his discredit reflecting on the government.

He could not, however, abandon his warehousing clause with any credit, unless he was able to say that the measure afforded in another and better way that protection to agriculture which the warehouse clause was intended to give; and unless there was some increase of duty that could not be pretended. We ought to make him a decent bridge to retreat over. If the Lords threw out the bill we should remain under the law of 1815. The great object was to get established the principle of protection by duty,

---

Lord Palmerston alludes, was conceived on the directly opposite principle, viz., that of avoiding extremes. Taking an average of twelve years, sixty shillings a quarter was fixed as the fair price of wheat—neither ruinous to the farmer, nor hard on the consumer. At this price, according to weekly averages, corn was to be introduced. This bill, carried in the Commons (April 12), was lost in the Lords, the Duke of Wellington proposing in committee and carrying an amendment—"that no foreign corn in bond should be taken out of bond until the average price of corn should have reached sixty-six shillings." The difficulty now was how to satisfy the duke, whose amendment had thrown out the former bill, and the Canningites, who had rejected his amendment. Mr. Grant, who, as Vice-President of the Board of Trade, had particularly distinguished himself by supporting the preceding bill in the House of Commons, and advocating the general principles of free trade, was the most compromised. The various modifications proposed were for bringing about some arrangement to which two parties, who a few months before had essentially differed, could now agree. Lord Palmerston treated the difference as one of detail, on which each party might give way in a certain degree to the other; and it must be said that this is the way in which Mr. Huskisson had previously treated it, inasmuch as that he had written to the duke, saying he would accept any change that could satisfy the Lords and not dissatisfy the Commons.

instead of prohibition, and that once done the particular scale might afterward be varied according to experience of circumstances and fluctuations in the value of currency. If he went out Huskisson must go too, although prepared to support the measure either in or out of office. His character and reputation were staked upon the principles of free trade, and especially on the Corn Law. He had been accused of coming into office with the enemies of Canning's person and principles, of sacrificing his principles to place, and of having prepared all the measures to which he had been previously committed. He had at Liverpool denied the charge, had alleged that Grant and Dudley and Lamb were his guarantees that sound measures would be pursued in the departments in which they were continued. But if upon the first measure that was to be brought forward in Grant's department, Grant were to resign a good office and a seat in the Cabinet rather than propose the intended measure to Parliament, and if Huskisson remained in, it would be said that he, an older man, hackneyed in office, corrupted by place, clinging to power, and sacrificing principles, had consented to that which Grant, a younger man, independent and high-minded and respecting principles, had rejected with disdain, and no explanation that could be given could ever remove the impression which this would create. If Huskisson went out I must do so too, for similar reasons, and because if his influence were withdrawn from the Cabinet the arbitrary party would soon predominate, and I could no longer co-operate with my colleagues. We should then all of us make ourselves highly ridiculous; we had said, when the government was first formed, that before we joined it we had explanations and understandings with the duke on all important points of policy, and now it would appear that on one most important point, which we must have felt from the beginning could not fail to come under consideration the moment Grant was re-elected, we had had no understanding at all. I also represented to him that if we all went out there must be formed a purely Tory government, that would speedily throw over all those measures on which Canning had founded his fame. We should break immediately with Russia, probably also with France, back out of the Greek treaty, and unite ourselves again with Metternich, and adopt the apostolical party in Spain and Portugal. For even if the king were to send for Lansdowne, Huskisson and we could not join him without exposing ourselves to the imputation of treachery to our present colleagues, by having broken up the government upon a mere pretense, for the secret purpose of getting rid of the Tories and joining again with the Whigs. But a purely Whig government could not be formed, and therefore the king would have no choice but the Tories. In any case, too, Huskisson would be abused; it would be said that, having broken up the last government by a quarrel upon an unimportant point with Herries, he had now broken up this government upon a question still more trifling, and that either he was an intriguer upon whom no party could rely, or a captious quarreler with whom no government could agree.

Huskisson to-day read us some letters which had passed between him and Grant last night, by which it appeared that up to that time no change had taken place in Grant's intentions, and he had heard nothing from him this morning. He was going at three to the king to state to him the whole affair, of which the king had heard for the first time the day before yesterday. Huskisson strongly urged Dudley and Lamb and myself to remain in. I said at once that I had very fully made up my mind on this matter, and that viewing the composition of the Cabinet, and my own situation in the House of Commons, I could not remain in if he retired, and, thinking as I did that his retirement was inevitable, I should go with him. Dudley, who had at first put as a question—whether it was absolutely necessary for Huskisson to retire, acquiesced in the reason which Huskisson gave in detail for doing so, and said that if I deemed it necessary to go, it was still more impossible for him to remain. I had certainly joined Canning's Cabinet, but had not been, like him, personally connected with Canning by long habits of private intimacy and political co-operation—he must therefore go also.

Lamb did not say what he should do. Huskisson went at three to the king to tender his resignation, and explained to the king the course of the transaction, and his reasons for retiring. The king urged him to stay by all the arguments he might have been expected to use, complaining that he was abandoning his king; and Huskisson said that the king was a man of the world, and would therefore understand his feelings by an illustration. It might often happen to a man in society to be obliged to fight a duel when he knew he was in the wrong, but could not avoid being shot to prove that he was not a coward.* He was now obliged to go out without wishing to do so, and without any public reason, merely that he might not be accused of corruptly clinging to office. The king admitted the force of the illustration, but asked if he could not go out provisionally, and return again. This Huskisson said would only be a juggle, which would at once be detected, and only be worse than staying in.

While they (the king and Huskisson) were talking, Huskisson received a box from Peel, with a note, dated

---

* This argument, urged in such a quarter, shows the great change in social feelings that has taken place since it was used.

four o'clock, to say that Goulburn had called on Grant at Somerset Place at a quarter before four, to tell him that the notice for his motion stood for to-day, and that he must decide whether he would make it or not; and that Grant had at last said he would make it,* but begged it might be put off till Monday. The king was delighted, told Huskisson to kiss his hand, as a token that he was to remain in, and they parted.

Wednesday, April 2.

Esterhazy communicated a dispatch from Metternich, inclosing one from Ottenfels, at Constantinople, dated 23d February, by which it appeared that the Porte had granted to the Greeks an armistice for three months.

The Russian preparations on the Pruth have probably begun to alarm them. It is always said that the Turks are obstinate in November, and tractable in March.

Cabinet this evening after dinner at Apsley House, to settle draft of a dispatch to France, stating our proposals for defining more clearly the objects of the Treaty of London. *As usual, much discussion and entire difference of opinion;* the duke, Ellenborough, and Aberdeen being for cutting down the Greeks as much as possible; Huskisson, Dudley, and myself for executing the treaty in the fair spirit of those who made it. The duke, while he professes to maintain it, would execute it in the spirit of one who condemns it. The limits were proposed to be the Morea and islands. I again urged that Livadia, or at least Attica, should be added; but nobody else supported this opinion. The tribute was to be fixed upon a reference to what has been actually paid to the Porte during the seven years subsequent to 1814. Commissioners to be

* It is amusing to see how this instance of firmness in the amiable, clever, and irresolute Charles Grant terminated.

appointed by both sides to value the private Turkish property to be surrendered to the Greeks. The Greeks to conduct their own internal government and commercial concerns. The Porte to have a negative upon the nomination of their chief; but this negative not to go beyond a second choice. The Greeks to be allowed to have commercial relations with other countries. Much discussion upon a proposal by the duke, that the Porte should have some officer in Greece to inform it as to what was going on, but rejected as at variance with the treaty. Still more debate and difference of opinion as to the nature of the relations which Greece should be permitted to have with other states, and in what degree she should follow Turkey in peace and war. Peel again repeated his opinion that it would have been best to make Greece wholly independent of Turkey. The duke, on the contrary, wishes to make her as dependent as possible. It was proposed that, according to the nature of suzerainty, the Porte should have a claim for a fixed contingent in men and ships from Greece in the event of war, but that Greece itself should not follow Turkey in her external relations; after much altercation, this was left unsettled. Huskisson then proposed that so much of the Foreign Enlistment Act as prevents our ship-builders from constructing vessels for foreign states should be repealed; the low price of timber, want of employment among shipwrights, and the fact of £500,000 being ready in London to be so laid out, or to be sent for the same purpose to other countries if it could not be employed here, were the reasons on which he founded his proposition.

Ellenborough was against the bill, and the duke would not listen to it; and so we parted at half-past one, Huskisson very angry, and the duke ill pleased. Melville and Bathurst were absent.

Good Friday, April 4.

Cabinet at three, to settle draft of Dudley's letter to Lord Granville about Greek affairs, containing our project for defining those points which were left vague in the Treaty of London ; renewed discussion whether Greece should follow the Porte in peace and war, in consequence of the suzerainty of the Porte. The duke strongly for this; Huskisson, Peel, Dudley, myself, against it. The treaty of 1800 between Russia and Turkey about the Ionian Islands, and the condition of Ragusa, were quoted and adverted to; at last, finding the sense of the Cabinet to be that Greece should *not* follow Turkey in war, the duke proposed that nothing should be said on this point, though it is obviously one that must be determined. His wish, however, was agreed to. It was also agreed that the annual tribute should be in lieu of any contingent of men and ships. The duke ill pleased to find Peel for Greek independence.

Much discussion whether Russia, having announced her intention of going to war with Turkey upon her own grounds on the Pruth, can co-operate with us in the Mediterranean, we being neutrals and she belligerent. It seemed to me that if she consents to place her admiral under the same instructions which we are prepared to give to ours, there can be no difficulty. The duke thought it impossible. He is evidently anxious to break with Russia. He has a strong personal feeling of dislike to Russia. He has had violent quarrels with the Lievens, and thought himself not civilly received at Petersburg. A great many little things have contributed to set him against the Lievens. Mrs. Arbuthnot and Lady Jersey, who have both influence over him, both hate Madame de Lieven. Madame de Lieven was foolish last year when Canning came in, and too openly expressed her joy at the duke's retirement, and was to a certain degree personally uncivil to him.

Peel again started the proposal which I had made some weeks ago, that we should make some effort to get back from captivity the Greek women and children carried off as slaves from the Morea by Ibrahim Pasha and sent to Egypt.

Cabinet adjourned to Sunday se'nnight. The duke said that Polignac, with whom he had conversed, thought we might hold that there were two Russias—one at war on the Pruth and Danube, and the other acting with us as a neutral in Greece. Accounts from Lamb from Lisbon, of 22d, that the attempt to have Miguel proclaimed king had totally failed, but that severe proscriptions were expected the moment our troops depart; that no class cares anything for the Charter, but the general wish seems to be for tranquillity, and to avoid convulsions; that Miguel has irretrievably lost the confidence of the nation; and that the most constitutional party look now to Pedro as their only hope.

May 22.

The Cabinet has gone on for some time past as it had done before, differing upon almost every question of any importance that has been brought under consideration:—meeting to debate and dispute, and separating without deciding.

Without pursuing for the moment these quotations further, I cannot help observing, in reference to the sentence last quoted, that the father of the late Lord Holland, who had lived all his life in intimate acquaintance with Cabinet ministers, once said to me that he had never known a Cabinet in which its members did not dispute more among themselves during their councils than they disputed with their antagonists in the House of Commons. It is probable that Mr. Pitt's Cabinet and Lord Derby's were exceptions to this rule; but I fancy that a peep behind the scenes would pretty generally demonstrate that a Cabinet is more often held together by the same interests than by the same opinions. At all events, the squabbles which in Lord Palmerston's language I have been relating, are a natural prelude to the great quarrel which finally took place; a quarrel of which history may well desire to learn the particulars from biography—inasmuch as it is the starting-point of modern events.

I speak of the quarrel between the Duke of Wellington and Mr. Huskisson, which led to Mr. Grant being succeeded by Mr. Fitzgerald at the Board of Trade,—which led to the election for Clare,—which led to Catholic emancipation, —which led, by a new defection in the Tory party, to the Reform Bill,—which led to a complete social and political revolution in our country.

Mr. Huskisson had come into the mixed Cabinet recently formed very much in the character of Mr. Canning's representative, which made him in some degree the duke's rival. But Mr. Huskisson was not Mr. Canning. He had not the claims to distinction of a great orator; he had not trodden the public stage as one of the principal actors on it for many years of his life. He had never until lately (though considered for his knowledge of finance and trade) played more than a subaltern's part. He expressed himself with difficulty, and in a style that neither inspired fear nor pleasure. He did not belong to any great aristocratic family. He had little of dignity in his bearing or disposition, and was thought to be at once too anxious for place and too boastful of independence.

This was not the sort of man to be accepted as an equal by the conqueror of Waterloo, who had been listened to with respectful attention by the great sovereigns of the earth.

Already, and at the very commencement of their connection, the difficulty of keeping them united had become apparent, for Mr. Huskisson had declared on the hustings at Liverpool that he had only consented to accept office on receiving pledges that Mr. Canning's views would be followed out; a declaration which the duke took the first opportunity in the Lords of indignantly denying, and from which Mr. Huskisson was obliged, with some discredit, to shuffle out.

The subsequent disputes—each day, as it will have been observed, more or less renewed—had completely irritated the nerves of one party and worn out the patience of the other; and it was certain that the first occasion for getting rid of a disagreeable colleague would be seized by a Prime Minister accustomed to keep his temper under control, but not accustomed to have his will disobeyed.

That occasion came; and the facts relating to it are given, minutely and vividly, in the journal, to which I now return.

EXTRACTS FROM JOURNAL.

A SUBJECT on which we had differed from the beginning of the session was the mode of dealing with the franchise of Penryn and East Retford, both of which the House of Commons had pronounced corrupt and deserving disfranchisement. The duke, Bathurst, etc. were for throwing them both into the hundreds; Huskisson, Dudley, and I for transferring the right to some large towns. Peel rather favored the latter opinion, but proposed to take one and one, so as to give one to the manufacturing and the other to the agricultural interest. This course it was determined to pursue. Huskisson wanted Penryn to go to the hundred and Retford to a town. Peel would send Penryn to a town and Retford to the hundred. Huskisson maintained that Retford was the worst case, and should therefore have the strongest measure. Peel, on the other hand, thought that taking the two previous delinquencies of Penryn, that case became accumulatively strong, and that Cornwall was so thickly studded with boroughs that the House of Commons would be unwilling to throw any corrupt place there into the hundreds; while, on the other hand, Retford, though more extensively corrupt on this occasion, had never been proved so before, and was in the hundred of Bassetlaw, which contains 2000 freeholders. I inclined to Peel's opinion, especially as I thought it hopeless to expect to get the House to put

Penryn into the hundreds after Canning had been beat upon it on the 28th May, 1827. Peel accordingly proposed his arrangement to the House, saying he had waited to see whether we had two places or one to dispose of, and finding we had two, he would give one to manufactures, one to agriculture. Huskisson went further, and on the 21st March said that if there were but one place he would give it to a great town. On the faith of this arrangement we carried an instruction to the committee on the Retford Bill to alter it by substituting the hundred of Bassetlaw for Birmingham, and Penryn was sent to the Lords, and Retford lay to, to wait the result of Penryn. The Cornish men, however, regained courage, and swore so stoutly at the bar of the Lords that even Lord Carnarvon, who had charge of the Disfranchisement Bill, gave up the case as far as sending the right to a town, and said he should propose the hundred instead. In this state of things Tennyson gave notice that he should, on Monday the 19th of May, go on with Retford; and Nicholson Calvert was to move in the committee his alteration substituting the hundred for Birmingham.

On Monday, 19th May, at three o'clock, we had a Cabinet to consider a variety of things, and among others what should be done about East Retford, which it was said Tennyson was determined now to press on. Peel said he considered himself free to vote as he liked on the motion which Nicholson Calvert was to make in the committee to strike out Birmingham, to which, as the bill was originally drawn, the franchise was to go, and to insert the hundred of Bassetlaw. Huskisson stated, and his statement was admitted, that on the 21st March he had pledged himself that if there were but one place to be disfranchised he would vote for sending that place to a town; and it seemed that the case had occurred, inasmuch as it was known that Penryn would go to the hundred or remain as it is. I reminded Peel that if Penryn went to the hundred he would be bound by his own pledge to send Retford to Birmingham. Bathurst objected to voting in any case for a town, and proposed that it should be an open question, like the Catholic question. This proposition seemed to be agreed to, and Melville showed, by reference to the parliamentary debates, that in the case of Grampound all the Cabinet ministers in the House of Lords had taken their own view and voted different ways.* Neither the duke nor Peel expressed any dissent, nor did they say that any inconvenience would arise to the government from the Cabinet ministers voting different ways upon this question. It was thought, however, that for the purpose of that night's debate it might be maintained that the Lords had not yet actually decided against sending Penryn to Manchester, and that consequently in the present stage we might adhere to the original arrangement. I said I thought this ground scarcely tenable, but it was agreed to try it. In the course of debate, however, Peel was charged with inconsistency in not sending Retford to a town, now that it was known to every man that Penryn would not go to one. He vindicated himself by asserting, what was true, that he had never pledged himself as to what he should do if there were but one place; but it was admitted on all hands that Huskisson had, and this pledge was claimed from him in the most direct terms by Lord Sandon, and the claim was received with the most taunting cheers from the Opposition. The plea that Penryn was not formally decided was quite knocked over, and indeed was abandoned by Peel himself, who begged

* Lord Eldon and Lord Bathurst had opposed the Bill for the disfranchisement of Grampound; Lord Liverpool had supported it.

the House to take warning from the fate of the Penryn Bill in the House of Lords, to be more cautious as to the evidence upon which they dealt with the franchise of towns. Huskisson was in great perplexity what to do,—repeatedly said to me he could not possibly vote for Calvert's motion. I told him I thought he could not, and that I would vote against it if he did, because his vote would make it no longer a government question, and then my vote would become an expression of my own personal opinion, which was directly at variance with Calvert's. Huskisson suggested to the House an adjournment of the question, to give time to ascertain the formal decision of the Lords on Penryn; and he pressed this the more because Nicholson Calvert's proposition was altogether a new measure, and not in conformity with the instruction to the committee which had been previously agreed to. That instruction directed the Committee of the whole House upon the bill to make provision to extend the right of voting to the hundred of Bassetlaw; but Calvert's proposition went to extinguish the present right of voting as it stands in Retford, and to create an entirely new right, to be vested in freeholders of Bassetlaw, and thus not to throw Retford into the hundred, but to annihilate Retford and create a separate little county of Bassetlaw. Peel, however, would not support Huskisson's proposal, though when Huskisson got up to speak he had desired him not to forget to point out the difference between what he had said on the former night and what Huskisson had said Huskisson was in a state of great hesitation and uneasiness during the latter part of the debate; and he was in that state of anxious doubt that any strong advice would have led him either way. I then pressed him to sit still on the Treasury bench, on which side those who voted like us, "that the words proposed by Calvert to be left out should stand part of the question," were to be counted, and we accordingly voted against Peel. I observed during the division that Peel looked much discomposed, and that he turned his face aside and seemed to avoid looking at us across the table. He had been a good deal nettled by Stanley's attack in the debate, and in fact must have felt that he was sailing as near the wind as possible, since, though he was free to any pledge, yet the course of his argument certainly led to a conclusion different from his vote. For my part, after the manner in which at the Cabinet in the morning it had been proposed to leave the question open, it did not strike me that we were doing anything that was a material breach of official allegiance. I walked home by myself, and heard nothing from any one on the subject.

The next morning, Tuesday the 20th, I was detained at home by some business that required attention free from the interruption unavoidable at an office, and I did not get down to the War Office till half-past three. At four, while with Sulivan, I received a note from Huskisson, saying he wished to see me as soon as I could go over to him. I went over immediately, and found Dudley with him, to whom Huskisson said that I knew nothing of what had been passing that morning, and that he would tell me all, and then I would go over to Dudley and talk the matter over with him. Huskisson then showed me a copy of the letter which he had written the night before to the Duke of Wellington on his return to the House of Commons, tendering his resignation, and the duke's answer, informing him that he had laid that letter before the king. I immediately said that it was a pity he had not put into his first letter an explanatory sentence stating that he tendered his resignation, IF the duke thought that his continuance in office would be inconvenient to the public service;

that there was evidently a misunderstanding, but something must be done without loss of time to clear it up; as the duke's letter was a dry announcement that he had laid Huskisson's before the king, it gave him no opening for any further explanation nor for a personal interview. But as I had been a party to the vote, and as this matter arose out of the vote, it became proper for me to go to the duke and explain my conduct to him, and in so doing I could also explain to him the sense in which Huskisson's letter had been written. Huskisson acquiesced in this proceeding. I went then over to Dudley at the Foreign Office, and he told me that, having seen Huskisson in the morning on some of the Russian questions, he had incidentally mentioned what had happened the night before, not as a matter of importance, but as one of those little rubs which created difficulties at the moment, but which we should ultimately get over. Dudley had afterward seen the duke, with whom he had a conversation of some length, but who did not mention the subject till Dudley spoke of it, which Dudley said was somewhat strange, as the duke could not but feel that if Huskisson really had resigned, his resignation must be a matter of some interest and importance to Dudley. Dudley had assured the duke that Huskisson did not mean what he, the duke, supposed; but the duke did not conceive that there could be any mistake in the matter. Upon leaving Dudley I called at the duke's door in Downing Street; but he was gone to the House of Lords, it being then about five, and in turning to follow him there I met Peel, and took him in the Cabinet-room to talk with him on the subject. I explained to him the circumstances which had led to Huskisson's vote and mine, and reminded him of Bathurst having proposed that the question should be an open one, of Melville having seconded that proposal, and that neither he nor the duke had objected to it.* He admitted this, but said that he considered that arrangement as applying to a subsequent stage of the bill, and was firmly impressed with the expectation that everybody was that night to have voted the same way; that Huskisson, going out of the room, had said, "Well, to-night, at all events, we may stand upon the ground that the Lords have not disposed of Penryn;" and that the vote which was given seemed to imply a charge of breach of faith on his part toward the House. He seemed evidently hurt and angry, though his manner to me was perfectly kind and conciliatory. I told him that I was going to the duke, that I felt I ought to apologize to both for not having come to them the first thing in the morning to explain my conduct; but though I saw now that I had not attached sufficient importance to the matter, it really did not occur to me, under all the circumstances, that it was an affair of such moment as Huskisson had considered it to be.

* *Note by Lord Palmerston.*—In the following year, 1829, when the Catholic Relief Bill was pending, Lord Lowther, then Chief Commissioner of Woods and Forests, Sir John Beckett, Judge-Advocate-General, Mr. George Bankes, Secretary to the Board of Control, Mr. Holmes, Treasurer to the Ordnance, all sent in to the duke their resignations; that is to say, wrote word that they could not support the bill, upon the fate of which the existence of the government was staked; and that if their voting against it would be inconvenient to the government, they were ready to resign their offices. Of these letters no notice was taken, and to them no reply was sent. The individuals in question voted against the government in every stage of the proceeding, and remained undisturbed in their offices; a pretty good commentary upon the eagerness with which Huskisson's resignation was acted upon in a case where the bill out of which it arose was not a government measure, nor a proceeding upon the issue of which the existence of the government in any degree depended.

I then went down to the House of Lords, and sent a note in to the duke, requesting a few minutes' conversation with him. He came out to me, and, finding no committee-room vacant, we went to the long gallery made for the king's entrance, and walked up and down there for half an hour. I stated to him very much what I had said to Peel, that, speaking as a man of honor, I must honestly say that I thought Huskisson had no option as to his vote after the course which the debate had taken; that he would have been discredited had he not given it; and that, how ever inconvenient to a government an appearance of disunion might be, it would be still less for its advantage that one of its leading members should be discredited in the face of Parliament; and I then explained that he seemed to have mistaken the meaning of Huskisson's letter; that all he intended to say was, that if the duke objected to his remaining in office after giving that vote, he declared beforehand that he should have no just cause of complaint if the duke chose to remove him; but that he had no wish or desire to quit the government. The duke said that he had received Huskisson's letter with the greatest surprise; that, as it alluded to circumstances which had taken place in the debate, he had concluded that some personal discussions must have occurred between him and Peel; that he looked to the newspapers, but could see nothing of the sort or which accounted for the letter; that he could only understand the letter as a positive resignation; that he had shown it immediately to Peel, who had also so understood it (he did not tell me that which was much more important, namely, that he had shown it also to Lord Bathurst, who had strongly exhorted him so, and in no other way, to understand it); that such an event having taken place as a division among the Cabinet ministers in the House of Commons, and the king being in town, it was his duty to lose no time in stating the matter to the king, and having received such a letter from Huskisson, he could not avoid, at the same time, laying that letter before the king. That he had heard nothing from all quarters but the shocking scene of the night before; that the Chancellor told him people were talking of nothing else; that we had been coming to this for some time; that no government could go on without a party; that our friends were leaving us, and the government would very soon fall into as much weakness and contempt as Goderich's.* I said to this that I did not think that we had experienced any difficulties in Parliament. He said, No, because we have had no questions; but we must not expect that this would last; questions would soon come on, and then our difficulties would begin. He said that if he had had any doubt what Huskisson's letter meant, he should have applied to Huskisson for explanation; but neither he nor Peel, to whom he had shown it, had any doubt upon the subject; and the king, to whom he had shown it, had no doubt either, but had expressed great regret at receiving it, but had said, Well, we must do the best we can; that he, the duke, would stand by the king to the last, I might depend upon it; that, having no doubt whatever that Huskisson's was a positive resignation, he could not go

* *Note by Lord Palmerston.*—Here came out the Duke of Cumberland's cloven foot. He had been telling the king that the Duke of Wellington had no energy or decision, and was as weak as Goderich. The king repeated this to those about him as his own opinion; and from them it got round to the duke, and nettled and goaded him on to acts of violence. The king had more than once said to Huskisson that he was much disappointed in the duke; that he was no doubt a man of energy and decision in the field, but that in the Cabinet he was as weak and undecided as Goderich.

upon all fours to Mr. Huskisson to ask him to withdraw it, and lay the government at his feet by requesting him to stay in. I said no man could wish him, the duke, to take any step inconsistent with his personal or official character, or to make submission to any man; but it did not appear to me that there was any submission or anything derogatory in receiving an explanation of that which had been misconceived; that so far from Huskisson's letter being a demand for submission on his part, it was an act of submission to him, that it was like a soldier who has been guilty of indiscipline and insubordination, and who, instead of waiting to be apprehended, comes of his own accord to his general to say that he is conscious he has done that which may be objected to, and that he is ready to submit himself to the discretion and judgment of his chief. I said that I felt in this matter as much personally involved as Huskisson; that, in fact, whatever blame might attach to Huskisson, more blame must attach to me; he was bound by a pledge given in a former debate, and which left him no choice; I was bound by no such pledge, but had voted because Huskisson's vote, which I had myself told him I thought him bound to give, would have divested the division of the character of a government question, and then my vote would have been an expression of individual opinion; and as my opinion was, as he well knew, for the town, I could not vote for the hundred; but that, as I had been mixed up in the vote out of which this discussion arose, if the end of the matter should be that he were to find himself under the necessity of recommending to the king a successor to Huskisson, I should be obliged to ask him to do the same for me; that I should feel the greatest regret at separating myself from the government, and that nobody who knew me would for a moment doubt my strong personal feelings of respect and regard for him; but that under all the circumstances of the case, and mixed up as I had been with the vote, I could have no choice in this matter. I remarked that while I said this he raised his eyes, which had been fixed on the ground as we were walking up and down, and looked sharply and earnestly at me, as if to see whether this was meant as a sort of menace or a party measure; but he could not fail to see by my manner that I was merely stating to him my own feelings beforehand, that I might stand acquitted afterward of having used toward him any concealment or reserve. He said that as to the vote, it was certainly an unfortunate vote, but that did not signify so much, and might be remedied; it was the letter he objected to, and upon that he laid the main stress. At last I said I wished to know how he considered the matter to stand, and whether he looked upon it as a complete transaction, or still as an incomplete transaction. He said the state of the matter was this, that he had received from Huskisson a letter which he understood as being a positive resignation; that he had laid it as such before the king, who as such had received it; that he had informed Huskisson he had done so, and had heard nothing from him since. I said, When you say that you have heard nothing since, do you mean from Huskisson, or from the king? He said, From Huskisson. Upon this we parted, and I returned to Huskisson, and told him that though I thought he could not ask a personal interview with the duke, yet it seemed to me that he had a fair opening for a written communication without compromising in any degree his own character. Dudley and I had both had personal communications with the duke; we had both of us informed him what was the duke's understanding of his letter; and he might fairly make that the groundwork upon which to rest a voluntary explanation in writing of what his meaning really was. He said, Well, let us try, took up his pen, and between us we wrote the letter which he read afterward as his second letter in the House of Commons.* I confess I thought that this letter would set everything right, that the duke was merely standing upon a point of etiquette, and that when that was conceded to him, as it would be by this letter, he would be satisfied, and the affair would end. Huskisson sent the letter to the duke at a little after seven, and the duke received it in Downing Street while he was dressing for dinner. Huskisson told me that he had, immediately on receiving the duke's first letter, written to the king to beg an audience, but supposed he should not have an answer till next day. We debated whether we should go down to the House, but in the end we did so, and he spoke on a matter concerning the Civil List which was before the House that night, by way of showing that he did not consider himself as having resigned. He expressed through Planta a wish to communicate with Peel; but Peel tossed up his head, and said, It is now too late. The next day, Wednesday the 21st, he received the duke's second letter, and wrote in answer a very long explanation, and one so clear and explicit that it seemed to me impossible that anybody could mistake the matter after receiving it. The duke's reply to his letter of Tuesday evening appeared, however, to throw a new light upon the matter, and evinced a disposition by no means easily to accommodate the affair, and led us to think that deeper motives were at work than a mere misunderstanding of the first letter, or a simple feeling of etiquette.

"On Wednesday evening I went to Almack's, and there

---

* See Appendix, page 370.

found everybody full of the report that Huskisson and I had resigned. I of course contradicted that report as far as I was concerned, for obvious reasons.

On Thursday the 22d I went to Huskisson as soon as I got down to the Horse Guards, and he said, It is now quite clear this was a settled thing from the first—here is a letter I have this morning received from the duke. When I read that letter I found that the duke passed by entirely all the explanations, verbal and written, which Huskisson had given, and pinned him down to the meaning which the duke himself had put upon the first letter when first he read it, and before he had received any explanations, and then arguing upon that meaning concluded by saying, "Your resignation, therefore, is your own act, and not mine" (as if a *resignation* could be the act of anybody but the resigner). I saw plainly that the matter was at an end; that letter closed the door upon any further explanation from Huskisson, because it left wholly unnoticed all he had previously given, and did not leave him a peg on which to hang any further communication. If it had argued his explanation and pointed out deficiencies in it, he might have answered the arguments or supplied the deficiencies; but when all he had said was treated as if it had not existed, there was nothing further left to be done but to wait to hear who was to succeed him.

I returned to the War Office and wrote to Peel to say I wished to see him before he went to the House, and he appointed me at his own house at Whitehall at three. I went, and told him that I called in consequence of having seen the duke's letter of that morning; that that letter appeared to me to close the door to all possibility of accommodation, as it left Huskisson nothing upon which to found any further step. That under these circumstances I could have, as I had told him on Tuesday, no choice as to what

I must myself do; and therefore, as I could not in this state of things go down to the House as a Minister, I wished he would put off till after the holidays the notice for the Army Estimates, which stood in my name for the next day, Friday the 23d. I said that we could not question, and did not mean to question, the full and perfect right of the duke to remove us if he chose in consequence of our Retford vote; but I did not think it fair by Huskisson to put his removal, not upon the vote, but upon a letter which he had repeatedly and fully explained was not written in the meaning which had been put upon it, and was intended as an act of courtesy, not as an offense. Peel said that resignations given and not acted upon gave the minister making them a great advantage afterward over his colleagues. I said, Yes, if the resignation is founded upon a difference of opinion upon prospective measures, because then, when the resigner is asked to withdraw it, there must be implied at least an acquiescence in the measures upon which the difference of opinion arose: but here the case is totally different; the resignation, if such it is to be called, was not given with reference to any measure to come, but as an *amende* for an act done and performed; and, instead of requiring future acquiescence, it simply meant to say that Huskisson forewent any pretense of complaint if the duke chose to remove him, but had no desire to leave the government unless the duke wished him to do so. I admitted that it would have been better if the letter had been more explanatory, and had not been written at all; but it seemed to me that its original defects, whatever they might be, must be considered as cured by the subsequent explanations. I then shook him by the hand, and we mutually expressed our regret at parting with each other.

From this time Dudley took the matter in hand, and

endeavored to negotiate between the duke and Huskisson; and if there had been the slightest desire whatever on the part of the former to retain the latter, that negotiation must have been successful.

He proposed, what certainly did not seem unreasonable, that the letters should all be withdrawn on both sides, and considered as *non avenues*, stating that he was not indeed authorized by Huskisson to make this proposition, but had no doubt that it would be acceded to. The duke said he did not feel himself called upon to give an opinion upon a hypothetical case, but, said he, Huskisson is a sensible man, and a man of the world, and he must know what it is right for him to do under any given circumstances. When Dudley reported this conversation to Huskisson and to me, I observed that it was very oracular, but did not advance us much; but I wished to know how Dudley understood it, and what he supposed the duke to mean. He was not very clear on this point, but seemed to think the duke wished Huskisson to say that he withdrew his *resignation*, and that he had not suggested this step in order not to appear to dictate it. It was manifestly impossible that Huskisson could say he withdrew his resignation,* because he had all along contended that his first letter was not meant as a resignation; he could not therefore falsify his own deliberate statements, and those he had made through Dudley and me. Dudley said that he had opened his communication by laying down two propositions as a basis on which it could not be difficult to come to an understanding: the first, that Huskisson had no wish to go; the second, that the duke had no wish that he *should*

* He might have withdrawn the letter without saying whether it was a resignation or not.

go. The second proposition, however, seemed to me much more doubtful than the first.

On Saturday morning Huskisson made his mind up to stand upon his right as Secretary of State to demand an audience of the king, and to say that having ineffectually endeavored to explain himself to the duke, and having been informed that his first letter had been laid before the king, but not having been told whether his subsequent letters had also been shown, and having asked for an audience on Tuesday, but having as yet had no answer, he could not go into any further explanations with anybody else till he had seen the king, but then he should be ready and willing to give to the duke any explanation he wished. Dudley was to dine with the king that day, Saturday, to meet the duke and some of the foreign ministers, and was to say this to the duke, and ask the king again for an audience.

Dudley, however, next day informed Huskisson that the king wished not to see him till he had settled the matter with the duke, but that the duke still declined pointing out what was to be done, and that Peel also declined making any suggestion, saying that if he suggested anything as a step which ought to be satisfactory, and the duke should think it not so, he should thereby be unpleasantly committed as against the duke.

I was going across the parade toward Downing Street at about two, when Dudley and Lamb called to me from the balcony of Melbourne House. I went up, and Dudley said he imagined the matter at an end, and that the duke, conceiving that sufficient time had now elapsed without any arrangement effected, was gone, as he, Dudley, believed, to the king, to recommend a successor to Huskisson. He said it was now necessary for us to consider what we should do. I said that, as far as I was concerned, there was no further consideration necessary; that I had, as early as Tuesday, informed both the duke and Peel what I must do in a certain contingency, and, that case having now arisen, my course was perfectly plain.

Lamb also said that he thought we had no choice as to what we were to do.* The whole thing evinced such a thorough determination to get rid of Huskisson that it was quite time for all of us to retire also.

Dudley stroked his chin, counted the squares of the carpet three times up and three times down, and then went off in the agony of doubt and hesitation.

I went over to Huskisson, and found him finishing a long letter to the duke, which he requested the duke to lay before the king, as the only mode left to him, now that he was debarred from access to the king, to make known to his Majesty the statements and explanations which he wished to have submitted to him in an audience if he had had one. This letter he sent about five o'clock.

I dined at Sir Thomas Farquhar's in St. James's Street, and met Dudley there. After dinner, when the ladies were gone, Dudley came round to me, and told me he was doubtful whether he had done right or not. The duke had told him that morning that unless he heard something satisfactory from Huskisson by half-past two, he was to go at that time to the king to submit the name of a successor; that he had not told this to Huskisson, for fear of

* George IV. was very anxious that Mr. Lamb should remain. At least the Duke of Cumberland, whose acquaintance I had made as attaché at Berlin, sent to me (I was then in London), knowing that Mr. Lamb had procured me my appointment and was very kind to me, and requested that I would go to him, and mention as the king's particular desire that he would not quit the government. I gave the message, and carried back a civil answer, but one that left no doubt of Mr. Lamb's determination.

doing mischief; that Huskisson's letter had arrived after that time, and had been returned by the duke to him (Dudley) unopened, with a request that it might be so sent to Huskisson, as the duke did not think it fair to him to open it after he had named his successor. Dudley said he was going to Huskisson at eleven o'clock that evening, and I said I would meet him there.

On arriving I found Dudley and Lamb. Huskisson said he had sent his letter back again to the duke, with a note to say that it had no reference to the appointment of his successor, and that he begged the duke to open it, therefore, and lay it before the king. We all left Huskisson together,* and Dudley proposed we should walk up a little way, our cabriolets following. He was in the middle, and said, Well, now we are by ourselves in the street, and nobody but the sentry to hear us, let me know, right and left, what is meant to be done—"in" or "out." I said "out," and Lamb echoed "out." "Well," said Dudley, "I am under some embarrassment as to what I shall do. The king has been pleased to take a great fancy to me, and will, I am sure, be much offended if I go out. He and the duke have both taken for granted that I mean to stay at all events, and told me so, and I have neither affirmed nor denied their assumption, and they certainly are under an impression that I mean to stay. On the other hand, if you, Palmerston, who have all your life been in office with the Tories, feel it impossible to stay, how much more difficult must it be for me, who never belonged to that party, and who came in as the personal friend of Canning!" He asked our opinion, and I said that I thought he would do best for his own credit and

* Huskisson was living in the house belonging to the Foreign Office in Downing Street.

comfort by going out. That it would be felt that he, having come in as the personal friend of Canning, was staying in when all the other personal friends of Canning were going out, and that nobody would think that he, singly, could have power and influence enough to secure the maintenance of those principles and that course of policy to which he was pledged.

He said that as to that there was great vagueness in talking of the policy of particular men. I said there might be, but still people fancied they knew what the expression meant.

He said the Colonial Office would be filled by a moderate Tory, a man of promise, a member of a noble Tory family. Lamb then said that for his part he did not happen to know any young member of a Tory family who was a man of promise; but that upon Dudley's own showing the character and complexion of the government were to be altered first by withdrawing Huskisson, and then by putting in his place a decided Tory. That this would decide him, at all events; that not being in the Cabinet, and having no deliberative voice, his confidence in the government must depend upon those who composed the Cabinet, and so great a change as was about to take place must make him withdraw from his office.

Dudley said that there was something in attaching one's self to so great a man as the duke. "For my part," said Lamb, "I do not happen to think that he is so very great a man; but that's a matter of opinion." I left them, and on my return home wrote to the duke a letter of resignation, which was to be sent to him early the next morning.

On Monday, the 26th, we heard that Sir George Murray was to succeed Huskisson as Colonial Secretary; and in the course of the week it appeared Sir Henry Hardinge was to succeed me as Secretary at War; that Aberdeen was to be Foreign Secretary, Arbuthnot, Chancellor of the Duchy of Lancaster instead of Aberdeen, and Lowther was to succeed Arbuthnot in the Woods and Forests.

Thursday, the 29th, there was a council to receive the seals from Huskisson and from Dudley, who on the Tuesday had made up his mind to resign, everybody having told him he ought to do so, and even Baron Bulow, the Prussian minister, having said that if he did not do so he would be in a month's time entirely "*perdu de réputation.*"

On Wednesday, the 28th, the Pitt dinner was held, at which Lord Eldon begged for "one cheer more" for the toast of Protestant ascendency.

The king had a long interview with Huskisson upon receiving the seals; and when Huskisson was beginning to express his regret at quitting his service, he said, "I cannot bear to enter upon that subject; my heart is too full—pray spare me. I am going to-morrow to the country, to get out of the way of all these horrid discussions."

He affected to regret that he had not seen Huskisson's last letter before the arrangements had been submitted to him, stating that if he had, he never would have agreed to them, and intimated that it was by his desire that no step had been taken between the Tuesday and the Sunday.

Saturday, June 7.

There has been great violence among all the Tories, and after abusing Huskisson for resigning, they now abuse him for proving too clearly by his speech on Monday that he was deliberately turned out. They do not find fault with my speech, but, on the contrary, affect to praise it, in some sort as contrasting it with Huskisson's. At all events, my statement succeeded, because on the one hand it gave the most perfect satisfaction to Huskisson and his friends, who thanked me very sincerely for what I had said, and on the other hand, all the friends of the government praised it for being temperate, though, as they said, manly and gentleman-like.

The king had a large party at the Lodge during Ascot Races last week, and was much puzzled to know upon what footing to place the recent changes. He did not like to admit that the duke had ill-used Huskisson, because all had of course been done in his name and by his authority. He therefore tried to maintain that Huskisson had determined to go, and the duke had tried all he could to keep him. Some persons, however, who had his ear, and ventured to speak out to him, denied this to him in a manner which left him nothing to say, except, "Well, I hate politics, and do not wish to quarrel with you about them, so let us leave this topic." The Duke of Cumberland abused me for a democrat, saying it was all my fault, and that I had urged Huskisson to go out. To be well abused by H.R.H. is no mean praise to any man. It is quite clear that the king is very much dissatisfied with the turn which affairs have taken. He says he wanted the duke to have recourse to Lord Lansdowne, but he would not. Cumberland says also that the duke must have lost his head not to have taken in Eldon.* Grey, they say, is angry that he had no proposition made to him.

---

* *Note by Lord Palmerston.*—The king told Madame de Lieven that he had urged the duke to apply to Lansdowne to join him, but the duke would not hear of it. Madame de Lieven dextrously expressed to the Duke of Cumberland her surprise that Wellington should not have attempted to get into office so able a man as Eldon. "Oh," said Cumberland, going into the trap, "it is indeed astonishing; but as to the Duke of Wellington, he has lost his head entirely."

Our party, though small, is very respectable, and consists of—

LIBERALS OF JUNE, 1828.

Lords.

Dudley,	Bristol,	Haddington,
Goderich,	Seaford,	Granville,
Stafford,	Howard de Walden,	Carlisle.
Gower,	Morley,	

Commons.

Huskisson,	Denison,
Palmerston,	Lord Spencer Chichester,
Lamb,	Sir Thomas Acland,
Charles Grant,	Lennard,
Sturges Bourne,	Lock,
Wilmot Horton,	John Fitzgerald,
Frankland Lewis,	Sir G. Warrender,
Lord F. Leveson Gower,	Aug. Ellis,
Lord Sandon,	Stratford Canning,
Lord Jermyn,	Lord Geo. Bentinck (Pub.),
E. Littleton,	Liddell (Pub.),
Spencer Perceval,	Morpeth (Pub.),
John Worsley,	Normanby (Pub.),
William Lascelles,	

besides several others who have a great leaning toward us. Goderich has been very anxious to organize some immediate arrangements, and that we should meet at Pembroke House, where he now lives; but this has not been relished. Besides other objections, it would have the appearance of putting ourselves under his lead, which, considering what an unfortunate display he made last December as head of a party, it would by no means be expedient for us to do.

BOOK VI.

The Canningites not sympathized with in their quarrel with the duke—The duke's mistake—Forced to become more liberal, and to quarrel with extreme Tories as well as Canningites—Quotations from journal as to affairs under his Administration during 1829—Letters in the same year from Paris and London—Speeches on Portugal and Greece—Goes to Paris at the end of the year—Interesting letters in December describing the state of affairs—Events in England and France—Quotation from Biography—Offers from the Duke of Wellington—Retirement of the duke from office—Lord Grey's Administration—Lord Palmerston's appointment as Secretary of State for Foreign Affairs.

THE Canningites, whether right or wrong in their differences with the head of the Cabinet they had seceded from, were not sympathized with. It was thought that they had too hastily coalesced with the enemies of their old leader. The reproaches which it was said that Lady Canning addressed to Mr. Huskisson found a pretty general echo. The Whigs, moreover, whom the Canningites had quitted when enlisting with Peel and the Duke of Wellington, chuckled over the treatment their late confederates had received. The vote also which both Mr. Huskisson and Lord Palmerston gave, on Feb. 26, 1828, against Lord John Russell's bill for removing the Dissenters' disabilities—though that vote was not intended to be hostile to religious equality, but rather to the religious inequality that would be established by removing Protestant and not Catholic disabilities—was highly unpopular; whilst Mr. Huskisson's conduct in letting a resignation slip out of his hands, and then trying to pick it up again, was considered shuffling and undignified. Thus the great public, which always likes character, clapped its hands at the stern soldier's determined phrase, "It is no mistake, it can be no mistake, and shall be no mistake." But the duke himself made a mistake when he would not acknowledge that Mr. Huskisson had made one. He not only gave powerful auxiliaries to the Whigs, but led to a state of things which dissatisfied and finally alienated a large portion of the Tories. For the loss of liberal coadjutors made it necessary to adopt liberal measures, and liberal measures disgusted his illiberal supporters.

There is an entry in Lord Palmerston's journal which applies to these remarks, and they are sustained by those that follow. I return, then, again to this journal.

CONTINUATION OF JOURNAL.

HUSKISSON says the government are becoming mucn more liberal than they were when we were among them. This is not unnatural, and I always expected it might happen. They may be disposed to do things, when they have the credit of doing them spontaneously, which they refused to do when it would have been supposed that we were urging them to do them. Thus, they are going to send Lord Heytesbury to the head-quarters of the Russian army, and Stratford Canning to Corfu, and mean to resume the conferences with Lieven and Polignac; though when I proposed these things in one of the last Cabinets I attended, they scouted them as inadmissible propositions. The fact is, that Metternich is changing entirely his line; and, having found that he could not prevent the Russian war and the liberation of Greece by virtue of the Treaty of London, he is now turning round, and by endeavoring to outstrip the allies in the career of liberality, to appear in this way to lead Europe, which is his great ambition. Thus he now maintains that Greece ought to be made quite independent of Turkey. It remains to be seen whether the duke will agree to this—which, at a Cabinet dinner at his house, he declared he never would consent to.

Sunday, June 8.

Aberdeen called to-day on Madame de Lieven. She said, "I am always glad to see you, but I am very sorry to see you Minister for Foreign Affairs, because I consider you Austrian, and an enemy to Russia."* Aberdeen said he had called on purpose to explain himself, as he had heard that she had expressed strong opinions about him, which were entirely mistaken. He assured her he was not at all in the interests of Metternich or of Austria; that, as an English minister, he was English, and in no foreign interest; that he could not be Austrian, as he had not been at Vienna for many years, etc. She said that as he gave her his word of honor that he was not adverse to Russian interests, she could not say she did not believe him; but she knew well the duke's sentiments about Russia, and she would tell him what she had heard about himself only two days ago: a countryman of hers had met Esterhazy in the street, and Esterhazy, slapping him on the back, exclaimed, "Eh bien, mon cher, chacun à son tour, vous avez eu votre ministre, à présent j'ai le mien." Aberdeen was very angry at this, and defended himself, but said nothing in defense of the duke.

Thursday, June 12.

The debate in the Lords on the Catholic question, which lasted two nights, was much more conciliatory in its tone than any former discussion, and has been considered as indicating a disposition on the part of the duke to give the question consideration—with a view to an adjustment. I much doubt, however, his having any real intention to take it up; though he must be sensible what an obstacle it is to

* When the Crimean war was under consideration, Lord Aberdeen was accused of being over-Russian. The fact is that he was, as he said, neither Austrian nor Russian, but honestly and entirely English, and only Austrian inasmuch as that Austria was, like himself, inclined to moderate courses. No man was a safer steersman on a calm sea; but neither nature nor habit fitted him for the daring pilot in extremities.

the formation of any government upon a basis satisfactory to the country or to the minister. When Canning came in last year, that question deprived him of the support of Peel, and afterward created difficulties at every step in the formation of his government. When the duke came in, every man to whom he proposed office answered him by talking about the Catholic question. If Lord Anglesey had resigned Ireland, that question would have limited his choice of a successor, as he feels that the Lord-Lieutenant ought to be a *moderate Catholic.** That question now limits his choice of a Chief Secretary for Ireland, who must be of the same *shade* of opinion. But how Bathurst is to agree to *any* settlement of that question it is not easy to see; and Peel has declared in private to Lamb, that he could not remain in office while the arrangement was making; *though he takes the most sensible view of the matter*, and would simply repeal the disabling laws, and wait to see if any inconvenience arose, and then legislate according to the occasion.

The king had a concert last night; he was particularly civil and attentive to Dudley, very cold to Aberdeen and Peel, and did not invite Ellenborough.

Lieven told me to-day that the conferences had been resumed, and were attended by the duke as well as by Aberdeen; but that the duke's feelings of dislike to Russia have in no degree abated, and that he is just as impracticable as ever. He said that the last note received from our government was in an unfriendly tone, and not well reasoned.

December, 1828.

Various circumstances have led me to neglect keeping up this journal for some months.

---

* *i.e.* A moderate man, in favor of Catholic Emancipation.

The session of Parliament went off languidly, and without any events of particular interest. Lord Francis Leveson Gower,* about ten days after he had resigned the office of Colonial Under-Secretary, accepted that of Secretary for Ireland, vacant by Lamb's resignation. Reasons for this apparently inconsistent course he assigned little or none, but chiefly rested it upon the vague expressions in the Duke of Wellington's speech, indicating, if not favorable sentiments toward the Catholics, at least the absence of any unfavorable ones. His family put it more upon the ground of the higher importance of the new office. His acceptance, however, made Wilmot Horton a little, and Frankland Lewis very much, I believe, repent that they had refused the appointment, which had been previously offered to them.

In the Commons we made a battle upon the further stage of the East Retford Bill. The government made a great whip, and gave out that upon the result would depend its character for strength; and we were certainly beat by a very large majority. The bill was then put off till next session by Peel. There was also a little splash about a Silk Importation Bill, in the course of which Courtenay, the new Vice-President of the Board of Trade, in the absence of Vesey Fitzgerald at his Clare contest, made an unguarded promise to the English silk manufacturers that he would continue the existing duties of importation for a year longer, although there had been a pledge by the government that they should cease sooner. In the course of this debate Grant made a good speech, and Courtenay declared that his mind and that of Fitzgerald were, upon all questions of trade and commerce, like sheets of blank paper, free from all preconceived opinions.

---

* Afterward Earl of Ellesmere.

Somebody said that, considering the military character of the present government, Courtenay should have likened their minds to *cartridge paper*, at least. Huskisson went abroad for his health before the session was quite over.

The Whigs would do nothing, professing that they had great hopes the duke would take up the Catholic question, and being very angry with Huskisson for not having made common cause with Lansdowne in January.

The only important matter in the king's speech was the announcement that Russia had declared war against Turkey upon grounds of her own, and that the emperor had nevertheless *consented* that his fleet in the Mediterranean should act under the same instructions as the French and English squadrons, and that he had, therefore, in that sea consented to waive his belligerent rights.* The natural impression from this would be, that we had asked him to do all this, and that *he had* (reluctantly, perhaps) *consented;* the truth being that *he had offered all this long ago*, and that the duke and his party in the Cabinet never could be prevailed upon, as long as we were there, to give their consent.

---

* "His Imperial Majesty has fouud himself under the necessity of declaring war against the Ottoman Porte upon grounds concerning exclusively the interests of his own dominions, and unconnected with the stipulations of the treaty of 6th July, 1827. . . . His Imperial Majesty has consented to waive the exercise in the Mediterranean Sea of any rights appertaining to his Imperial Majesty in the character of a belligerent power, and to recall the separate instructions which had been given to the commander of his naval forces in that sea, directing hostile operations against the Ottoman Porte. His Majesty will therefore continue to combine his efforts with those of the King of France and his Imperial Majesty for the purpose of carrying into complete execution the stipulations of the Treaty of London."—*Extract from King's Speech.*

A great and decided change took place about this time in the measures of the government as to the Greek question; and many of the things which we had in vain been urging day after day, and which had been pronounced either improper or impossible, were now found possible and right.

1. The co-operation of the Russian fleet with ours in the Mediterranean was accepted.

2. Lord Heytesbury was sent to the Russian head-quarters.

3. Stratford Canning was sent back to Corfu.

4. The conferences were resumed.

5. A land-force expedition to the Morea was determined upon.

I had always thought that this was the true and only way of accomplishing the Treaty of London; all the other methods of coercion which were proposed were sure to prove ineffectual. The occupation of the provinces could not produce a settlement of the Greek question except through the prostration of Turkey. The blockade of the Dardanelles must be ineffectual unless we became actually at war with Turkey; since, till we obtained belligerent rights, we should not be able to stop the only material supplies, namely, corn and other provisions, which would be brought by neutrals. But to land a sufficient army, and sweep the Turks from Greece, would execute the treaty practically; and then the formal acquiescence of Turkey became less important.

I proposed this in December, 1827, to Goderich; but neither he, nor Huskisson, nor Lansdowne, nor Tierney relished the plan, still less did the duke give in to it when I proposed it afterward to his Cabinet. His objections, as he stated them, were these: less than fifteen thousand men would be too little; we could not send so many without inconvenience. To let the French go alone would be objectionable; to let the Russians, or Russians and French, go alone, equally so; and a combined force would not do by land, however it might answer by sea.

The French, in the spring, became very urgent, and said their Chambers pressed them so much that they must send ten thousand men; and they actually collected troops near Toulon for the purpose. But at the duke's urgent remonstrance they abandoned the plan, and dispersed their troops again. In July, however, the duke all of a sudden changed his views, and urged the French to go, and to send eighteen thousand men. They did so: our ships escorted and helped to transport their troops; and the result was the prompt clearance of the Morea. The change came from Metternich, who, frightened at the commencement of hostilities between Russia and Turkey, and feeling that till the Treaty of London was out of the way it was impossible for France and England to interpose in favor of Turkey, became as anxious, on a sudden, for the speedy fulfillment of the treaty as he had before been desirous and industrious to defeat it. To Metternich is ascribable the sending of Lord Heytesbury to Nicholas' head-quarters. He wrote, in the name of the Emperor of Austria, to Nesselrode, to say that Austria, having tried every means to bring Turkey to reason, and having failed, now determined to throw her moral weight on the side of Russia; and, as a manifest proof to the world of his good understanding with Russia, the emperor begged that Nicholas would allow him to send an ambassador specially to his head-quarters. The answer was that Nicholas "*le permet.*" After this, of course there could be no doubt about sending Lord Heytesbury.

Lord Cowley* wrote in the spring, 1828, that the Aus-

* The ambassador at Vienna, father of the present Earl Cowley, the late ambassador at Paris.

trian army was in the most deplorable state of inefficiency; the whole amount everywhere (Italy included) was not more than 150,000 men, and even upon their then establishment they wanted 60,000 horses to make them effective. They wished much to have put into the field 50,000 men, to observe Wittgenstein's corps, but could not muster so many. Metternich, therefore, finding his maxim of trying to "*gagner du temps*" fail, now became suddenly anxious to precipitate everything, and ran—as men without principle do—from one extreme to the other. The duke, too, now became an advocate for making Greece independent; which, with great emphasis, in March he protested he *never* would consent to.

Sir Pulteney Malcolm was sent out to supersede Codrington; but before he could get out, Codrington had made a treaty* with the Pasha of Egypt for the evacuation of the Morea by the Egyptians and Ibrahim, his son, with an article about the slaves, viz., that those who were still unsold should be returned; and as to those who had been sold, the Pasha should, in conjunction with the consuls of the allies, use *his influence* to restore them to liberty.

I had given Peel notice, on the morning of the last day of the session, that I should ask him in the House a ques-

---

* Dated 6th August, 1827, at Alexandria.—Article 1: "His Highness Mehemet Ali Pasha engages to give up all persons under his control made slaves after the battle of Navarino, who have been sent to Egypt, and will immediately place them at the disposal of Admiral Codrington. His Highness likewise promises that he will, in conjunction with the consuls of different nations, use his utmost endeavors to induce such persons as have purchased any of the slaves to deliver them up. And Admiral Codrington on his part engages to set at liberty all Egyptian soldiers taken prisoners, and to give up the corvettes captured in the waters of Modon by the *Hussar*."

tion about what had been done respecting these slaves. When first the account came that the fleet of forty sail which left Navarino in December, after Codrington's boasted annihilation of the Turkish fleet,* and which consisted of seventeen sail that had actually got into Navarino after the battle, although Codrington was ordered to prevent any sea-movement — when accounts came that this fleet had carried away five or six thousand Greek slaves, I called the attention of the Cabinet to this circumstance, and urged that it would be a stain on our national character if we did not make an effort to recover these wretches. The duke received the proposition coldly; Aberdeen treated the matter as a thing we had no right to interfere with; Bathurst, as the exercise of a legitimate right on the part of the Turks; and Ellenborough, as rather a laudable action. I reminded the Cabinet that, two years before, we were informed by Lieven that Ibrahim meant to carry off into slavery the whole Greek people, and to colonize Greece with Arabians and Egyptians. Canning had then taken up the matter warmly; a dispatch had been written—probably by Canning—and signed by Bathurst, desiring Adam† to send to Ibrahim, to require him to disavow such an intention, and to warn him that we should oppose it by force; and a strong remonstrance was also sent to the Porte. Bathurst said

---

* "The whole Turkish and Egyptian fleets have paid the penalty of their treacherous breach of faith. The boasted Ibrahim Pasha promised not to quit Navarino or oppose the allied fleet, and basely broke his word. . . . . Out of a fleet composed of eighty-one men-of-war, there remain only one frigate and fifteen smaller vessels in a state ever to be again put to sea."—*Extract from general order issued by Vice-Admiral Codrington after the battle.*

† Sir Frederick Adam, G.C.M.G., Lord High Commissioner of the Ionian Islands.

that was a different case; what we then objected to was the carrying off the Greek people and *replacing them by* an Egyptian colony. In the present case there seemed to be no intention of replacing those who were carried off, and the captives seemed to be all women and children! Such was literally and gravely his argument. I met it by reading to him a passage in his own dispatch, stating that the king objected "*particularly to the carrying off of women and children.*" I got a laugh against him, especially from Ellenborough and Aberdeen, but only a laugh. I reminded the Cabinet that the fact of these persons being sold to individuals could be no reason why the Pasha should not give them back, because it was stated in Lord Exmouth's dispatch, giving an account of his attack on Algiers, that when he came away there was not a Christian slave of any sort left in Algiers;* and this proved that sovereigns of that stamp have ways of settling these things with their subjects when they choose to do so. They said, What! do you propose we should do as at Algiers, and go to war for these slaves? I said, No; but we have some hold over the Pasha by the presence of Ibrahim and his army in the Morea; you are going to starve him, and thus compel him to evacuate. The same means that will make him evacuate will also make him give up the slaves; extend the pressure to this point also, and let him and the Pasha know that till the whole of the slaves are given up that army will be starved in pawn.

* "To have been one of the humble instruments in the hands of Divine Providence for bringing to reason a ferocious government, and destroying forever the insufferable and horrid system of Christian slavery, can never cease to be a source of delight and heartfelt comfort to every individual happy enough to be employed in it."—*Dispatch of Admiral Lord Exmouth to Secretary of Admiralty,* dated *Queen Charlotte,* Algiers Bay, August 28th, 1816.

The result was that a dispatch was sent to Adam and Codrington, desiring them to send off Cradock* to ask the Pasha to have the kindness to give up these slaves, and to ascertain how many they were. It was so managed on the last day of the session that there was no possibility of asking any question. The Speaker did not take the chair till after the Black Rod was in the lobby; and as soon as a few writs had been moved—Grant having got up to move for some shipping returns—the well-known tap was heard at the door of the House, and there was an end of speaking. Peel, however, who had not come into the House before the usher tapped, showed me on our return from the House of Lords a dispatch recently received in answer to the inquiries above mentioned. By this it appeared that the practice of the Egyptians had been, from the time they first entered the Morea, to consider the Greek population as a preserve of slaves; in every action or siege every soldier took as his own property all the men, women, and children he could lay hands upon. Sometimes these captives were sent to Alexandria, to be there sold; but latterly slave-merchants used to come over to the Morea to buy them up there, as horse-dealers go down to Horncastle Fair. The total number thus seized, first and last, was from fifteen to twenty thousand; the women were put into harems, the men applied to the most laborious menial employments, and those children who were not kept for worse uses were sent to a great school at Cairo to be brought up as Mohammedans.

---

* The present General Lord Howden, then Lieutenant-Colonel Cradock, who afterward took the name of Caradoc. He distinguished himself at this time, both as an officer serving as aide-de-camp to Admiral Codrington at Navarino, and as a diplomatist in different matters on which he was employed.

As it did not seem to me probable that any effectual steps would be taken on this matter—though I again pressed on Peel my suggestion that Ibrahim and his army should be made hostages for the slaves—I pressed this point strongly on Lieven, whom I met at dinner that day at Falck's ;* and I called the next day on Polignac to do the same thing. Polignac said he had just had orders from his Court to make inquiries as to the number and treatment of these slaves, and to state that, as far as a moderate sum would go, the King of France would willingly buy them up. He was astonished when I told him how many they were. I believe, however, that in the end nothing was done beyond liberating some one hundred and eighty men who were still unsold at Alexandria.†

In August the Duke of Clarence resigned, or rather was turned out of the Admiralty. He had managed to put himself quite in the wrong, and, in fact, was half mad. He did all sorts of strange things, and incurred all kinds of foolish expenses. He insisted upon going aboard every ship that went to sea before she sailed ; he was perpetually going down to Portsmouth and Plymouth to give colors to regiments and dépôts in garrison who wanted none. On these occasions he ordered the general officers commanding to give entertainments which put them to ruinous expenses. Poor Sir James Lyon, at Portsmouth, spent nearly his whole year's staff pay in this manner. The duke also on these occasions reviewed the troops, and on one occasion found great fault with the —th Infantry, and told the commanding officer it was the worst regiment

---

* Then Austrian ambassador in London.

† The interest which Lord Palmerston exhibited unostentatiously in this matter shows the genuine humanity of his character.

he had ever seen. After dinner he renewed the attack, and asked Sir Colin Campbell, who was then Major-General commanding, if it was not so. Campbell fired up, and said, "I do not know what your Royal Highness may think of this regiment, but *we soldiers* consider it as a very fine one." Whenever he went about the yards he was saluted with discharges of artillery; and there was a curious calculation made of how much he cost the country in powder every half-hour during these expeditions. He at last became impatient of the control of his Council, who used naturally to remonstrate against his proceedings, and he took it into his head that when he was at sea he was exempted from their control. Anxious to try the experiment, even before he could get down to Portsmouth he wrote at Bushy Park an order to his Council, dated on board some ship, I forget the name, "*at sea*," and sent it off to the Admiralty by a groom; he then posted off, sailed down the Channel, and sent orders to the admiral at Cork to leave his station and come and join him in the chops of the Channel. The Board were astounded to hear that their Cork admiral was gone without their knowledge or concurrence. Remonstrances ensued; the duke took offense,—protested that if Sir G. Cockburn was not turned out he would resign. The other Lords all made common cause with Cockburn; and at last the king wrote him a letter in his own hand, to say that he must either conform to the provisions of his patent or resign; and his answer was a resignation. This was followed by an immediate fit of jaundice, and afterward by a severe illness in the autumn, during which he was almost childish, in desponding spirits, and often in tears. When they announced to him the death of the Queen of Würtemberg (the Princess Royal of England), he exclaimed, "Ay, she is dead, and I am going to die. We are all of us going to die." He had a bad rupture in the spring, which about this time became worse.

The Admiralty was offered to Melville, who declined it; the Board of Control, which he held, was nearly as good in salary, less expensive in representation, easier in labor, and attended with Indian patronage and connection—agreeable to a Scotchman. He had been twelve years at the Admiralty, and was tired of it, and knew himself unpopular in the navy. The Duke of Wellington, however, wanted the Board of Control for Ellenborough, and at length wrote to Melville to say the public service required that he should go to the Admiralty; but that at all events he could not stay where he was, adding that Croker must in any case remain Secretary to the Admiralty. Croker had grievously offended Melville last year when the latter went out upon Canning coming in. It was supposed he had suggested to Canning the Duke of Clarence's appointment, but he had certainly announced it to Melville at some unusually early hour, and in an offensive manner, and had urged Lady Melville to leave the house, inconveniently to herself. The Duke of Clarence and Croker, however, had not gone on well together, and Croker had been very uncomfortable with him. But when the duke had resigned, he sent for Croker to tell him he had done so, and added, "And now I am going, I must say to you, Mr. Croker, that in all these differences which have led to my retirement, you are the only member of the Board who has behaved to me like a gentleman." Croker, it is said, shed tears of acknowledgment, and hastened, *with his usual tact*, to communicate this flattering compliment to the assembled Board; upon which Lord Brecknock broke the silence, which he is supposed to have held since his first appointment, by an humble opinion that Croker might as well not have accepted a compliment at the expense of all his colleagues.

Melville was furious, and all his friends indignant, at the duke's usage of him; but nevertheless his prudence led him to acquiesce and march according to orders.

The king had a very severe inflammatory attack in October and November, lost one hundred and twenty ounces of blood in two days, was frightened about himself, and had himself felt all over, to see whether water was forming. His natural strength, however, carried him through; but up to Christmas he was still weak and ailing,—not himself till *after dinner*,—and taking great quantities of laudanum and colchicum, to relieve violent pains in the bladder and urethra, which his physicians consider to be gout; but one of the turns of his attack in the autumn was inflammation of the bladder and stoppage of water for twenty-four hours, which became extremely alarming, and only yielded to excessive leeching.

He had a party at Windsor Castle at Christmas—as it were, a house-warming, he having just got into the new apartments of the Castle. He complained that the rooms were too small, and the furniture too large. The party consisted of the Duke of Devonshire, the Lievens, Cowpers, Melbourne, F. Lamb, Agar Ellises, Granvilles. He was in great good humor, extremely civil to them all, praised Melbourne and F. Lamb greatly to Madame de Lieven, was delighted at a variety of snuff-boxes and things of that sort which the Duke of Devonshire produced, and said, "Ah, the last thing he had made in diamonds he cannot now produce, and I am sorry for it." He meant the Chamberlain's key, which the duke had had finished a few days before he went out of office.

The French expedition of about eighteen thousand men completely effected, in a short time and with little trouble, the expulsion of the Egyptians and Turks from the Morea. Ibrahim and his army evacuated under the treaty made by Codrington, leaving small Turkish garrisons in some of the fortresses, Coron, Modon, Patras, and the castle at the mouth of the Gulf of Lepanto; these garrisons, however, surrendered speedily, some of them without resistance, others with little. The French General Maison was then going to march into Attica to complete the expulsion of the Turks; but our government made a strong remonstrance against any operation beyond the Morea till the limits of Greece should be finally settled, and the French government acquiesced and ordered him to stop. The French for some time during the autumn suffered from the fever of the country.

Portuguese affairs went ill. After Miguel had completed his usurpation, all the European sovereigns except Ferdinand* withdrew their ministers and broke off diplomatic intercourse with him. Imprisonments multiplied in Portugal, and the prisons were crammed with victims.† An insurrection broke out at Oporto in favor of Donna Maria da Gloria, and a force of eight or nine thousand men was got together. Miguel's army was inferior in numbers, and if the Oporto people had had any leader of enterprise who could have led them on to Lisbon, the thing would have

---

* Lord Palmerston might have added "and the Pope."

† "In the beginning of October the prison of the Limoeiro alone, in Lisbon, contained 2400 prisoners, of whom 1600 were confined for political delinquencies. The total number of individuals throughout the kingdom incarcerated on similar charges, or who had avoided the scaffold and the dungeon by flying into exile, amounted to upwards of 15,000 men, among whom were forty-two members of the Chamber of Peers, including some of the highest nobility, and seven members of the Chamber of Deputies."—*Annual Register*, vol. lxx. p. 202.

been done. Each party, however, feared the other—neither dared to move; the Constitutionalists waited for Palmella, Saldanha, and Stubbs, and Taipa, who were to join them from England; but these had a long passage. In the mean time the Miguelites took courage and advanced; the others of course retreated. By the time the party arrived from England the Oporto army was in full retreat, and the cause was given up as hopeless Palmella and his friends re-embarked instantly, leaving the army to shift for itself: five thousand men kept together, and the greater part of them made good their retreat into Spain; there they were required to give up their arms, were exposed to the worst usage, the officers separated from the men, and both tempted in every way to go over to Miguel. At last, by the intercession of the French government, the Spanish government allowed these people to go to England, and about three thousand came to Plymouth—not at our expense, but at their own, in vessels which they hired at Corunna.

After a time, and about Christmas, Miguel's government began to grow uneasy at the presence of these three thousand men in one of our seaports, and feared they would return and make a descent on Portugal; indeed, it was known that Palmella had been making arrangements to get a corps of Germans to join them in order to renew hostilities in Portugal. D'Asseca, the unaccredited minister of Miguel in London, made remonstrances; and the duke told Palmella that these people must be separated and scattered about the interior of England, as the prisoners of war formerly were. Palmella protested against this, and denied the duke's right to insist upon it. He consulted Brougham and Denman. Their opinion seemed to be, that as these people were organized, regimented, and equipped as a military body, though not actually armed, they must be considered as foreign troops, and not as a number of individual aliens; that, consequently, the government would have a constitutional right to deal with them differently from what it would with simple strangers. Palmella then said he would send them to Brazil. The duke said he would escort them, to prevent their landing in Portugal or elsewhere on their way. Palmella protested against this. In the mean time arrived an application from the island of Terceira for one thousand men to help them to keep out the Miguelite expedition. Miguel had been permitted by our government to send an expedition to conquer Madeira—a strange straining of the system of neutrality, and a decided indication on our part of partiality for Miguel. It was right enough not to interfere in the internal affairs of Portugal, in order to force any particular form of government upon the majority of the people; but why should we allow the Portuguese to force a particular government on the people of Madeira? We ought to have said to Miguel, If the Portuguese choose to have for their sovereign a man whom we have to his face taxed with treachery, bad faith, perjury, usurpation, well and good. Much happiness may it confer upon them. But we will not permit you to go and conquer Madeira, the territory of Donna Maria, in which she is queen *de facto* as well as *de jure*. Miguel's success at Madeira encouraged him to attempt the same at Terceira; but bad weather drove off his ships and postponed the attempt.* Palmella, on receiving the application from Terceira, told the duke he should comply with it. The duke said he

* In August an attempt was made by the Miguelites to reduce Terceira; but it was defeated by Count Villa-Flor, commanding for the Queen, with a loss to the Miguelites of the commander-in-chief, the second in command, and between 900 and 1000 men of the expedition.

would prevent him by force, and wrote him a violent letter, of three sheets of paper, in which he said, "Monsieur le Marquis, *I have conveyed to you the commands of his Majesty, and I expect you will obey them.*" Somewhat imperative language to be used toward the ambassador of an independent and allied sovereign, but which would have sounded better had it been used toward a stronger Power. However, Palmella was stout, and the expedition sailed in the beginning of January for Terceira, the duke at the same time dispatching two frigates with sealed orders, probably destined for Terceira, to prevent a landing.* If this is done, surely it will rouse the indignation of the public and of Parliament! How well satisfied I am, and have been every day since I went out of office, that I have escaped from the embarrassment of choosing the precise points of difference with the duke at which it would have become absolutely necessary for me to quit his government!

In the mean time the king, toward the end of December, received the little Donna Maria da Gloria at Windsor Castle with all the honors of sovereignty, the duke, Aberdeen, and the other ministers being present. He was charmed with her; thought her like Princess Charlotte, well mannered, and, above all, beautifully dressed in lace and diamonds. When he handed her to her carriage, he

* This was the case. Captain Walpole, of the *Ranger*, who was in command, warned the expedition under Count Saldanha from attempting to land, and fired into the leading ship, killing one man and wounding another. Count Saldanha in consequence proceeded with his squadron to Brest. This affair created a good deal of excitement both at home and abroad. But the severest criticism on the Wellington policy was in the Lisbon Gazette, wherein Miguel announced "that the conduct of England towards Portugal, in such circumstances, had been above all praise."

stopped to make her a farewell speech, in which he expressed his hearty wish to see her restored to her throne. The child was so overcome with his kindness and her own difficulty of expressing herself in French, that, as the readiest reply, she instinctively threw her arms round his neck and kissed him, to thank him. This completely captivated him. He is particularly fond of children, and he said that everything else might have been taught her, but this *must* have been her own. We shall see how this reception is to be reconciled with the line about Terceira and the general moral support given to Miguel.

With Russia our relations have continued cold, but uninterrupted. The duke is anxious to bring about a peace between her and Turkey, but does not set about it in the right way. The campaign has been unfortunate for such a result; the Russians, having partially failed, and lost about sixty thousand men by *feu et fer* and disease, want a second campaign to redeem their honor. The Turks, elated by their unexpected success in resistance, undervalue the dangers of another campaign, and are more than ever obstinate. But yet the Russians *know* what they have lost, understand better than they did the difficulties they have to contend with; and the losses of the Guards, twenty-seven officers of which, all belonging to the first families, fell at Varna, have tended—though they may not acknowledge it—to sicken them of the war. Woronzow is for peace, and so probably are many others. The Russians begin to discover that they have *land* enough, if they were only to cultivate and improve to its utmost what they have; that the possession of Constantinople, even if Europe would permit it—which they know could not be—would indeed create a new empire, but would not strengthen existing Russia. What they indispensably want, is a certainty of a free passage through the Bosphorus and Dardanelles for their commerce, and that they might have secured to them by treaty. I had on the 14th January, 1829, a long conversation with Pozzo di Borgo, at his house in Paris, and this seemed to be the general result of it: that the emperor's honor required some concessions in any treaty of peace; that Russia could not accept a formal mediation, though she could not object to the good offices of her allies if used to promote peace. On the other hand, there is a large party in Turkey who are inclined to peace. In spite of the obstinacy of the Sultan, it is not impossible, therefore, that an accommodation may take place before spring.

Irish affairs have gone on from bad to worse ever since the summer. *The Clare election began a new era, and was an epoch in the history of Ireland.* O'Connell did not at first mean to stand himself, but no eligible Protestant candidate could be found; and as all the landholders, with scarcely an exception, were for Fitzgerald, nothing perhaps but the influence of O'Connell as a candidate could have carried the point. The event was dramatic and somewhat sublime. The Prime Minister of England tells the Catholics, in his speech in the House of Lords, that if they will only be perfectly quiet for a few years, cease to urge their claims, and let people forget the question entirely, then, after a few years, perhaps *something may be done for them.* They reply to this advice, within a few weeks after it is given, by raising the population of a whole province like one man, keeping them within the strictest obedience to the law, and, by strictly legal and constitutional means, hurling from his seat in the representation one of the Cabinet Ministers of the king. There were thirty thousand Irish peasants in and about Ennis in sultry July, and not a drunken man among them, or only *one,* and he an Englishman and a Protestant, and O'Connell's own coachman, whom O'Connell had committed, upon his own deposition, for a breach of the peace. No Irishman ever stirs a mile from his house without a stick; not a stick was to be seen at the election. One hundred and forty priests were brought from other places to harangue the people from morning to night, and to go round to the several parishes to exhort and bring up voters. The government were not idle or unprepared. Lord Anglesey told me he had seven thousand regulars, all out of sight, but within a short distance of Ennis, and capable of being brought to bear upon it, in case of disturbance, in a few hours. All passed off quietly; but the population of the adjoining counties was on the move, and large bodies had actually advanced in échelon as it were, closing in upon Ennis, the people of one village going on to the next, and those of that next advancing to a nearer station, and so on; and thus, had anything produced a collision, the bloodshed would have been great and the consequences extensive. The Association had ordered peace to be made between all the local factions; and after the election the people assembled in large bodies in various parts of the south, without arms, but regimented, and with some outward badges like uniforms, mostly on foot, but sometimes on horseback. Anxious and eager inquiries were made of O'Connell and Shiel to know *when the people were to begin.* They had made peace among each other, as ordered, but surely that could only be to enable them all to join in making war upon somebody else! If they were not to fight each other, whom were they to fight? Of course the Orangemen and the government—and when were they to begin? These inquiries embarrassed and frightened the Association, and they were delighted by a hint which they received from Lord Anglesey, through Parnell and Spring Rice, that these meetings could not be permitted, and that he *must* put a stop to them, and only wished that the Association would themselves anticipate him; and they accordingly issued their proclamation a few days before his came out. The effect of the *two*—and *one* would have been insufficient—was magical; and all popular demonstrations from that time ceased on the part of the Catholics, though not entirely on that of the Orangemen.

I was in Ireland in October and November, and saw Lord Anglesey several times—once on my way to Sligo, and two or three times on my return. He said that neither the duke nor Peel ever wrote to him anything but official letters; that he had no confidential communications from either, and was utterly ignorant what the duke intended to do about the Catholic question; that he wrote to them incessantly to press upon them the indispensable necessity of settling it; that at that moment there would be no great difficulty in the way from the Catholics, *who would agree to any reasonable arrangement with regard to securities, such as the payment of the clergy, an arrangement for the nomination of bishops, and even, he said, a regulation of the forty-shilling freehold. He had also seen a letter from Huskisson, from Rome, stating that no difficulties would be made by the Pope.*

This last was afterward confirmed to me by Huskisson, whom I saw on my return to London. He had had a conversation with the Pope and with Cardinal Bernetti, his Secretary of State, a man about forty, who has seen the world, and has been employed in Russia and Germany. The Pope expressed a great desire to have the matter well settled; and Bernetti said, "We know that we are not what our predecessors were some centuries ago; we are a feeble and decaying Power; it is for our interest to be friends with the great Powers of Europe, and with none more than with England" (probably alluding to our means of protecting the Pope against the hostile designs of Austria, who wants some of the northern districts of the papal territory). "Do not, however," said he, "ask us to rescind the edicts of ancient councils, nor to change the principles and doctrine of our Church: this we cannot do: look forward, and not backward. *Dites-nous ce que vous convient,* and we will do it if it is possible."

Lord Anglesey *begged that when I got back to London, if I was able by any means whatever to pick up what were the intentions of the government, I would write him word.* The Lord-Lieutenant of Ireland begging a private gentleman to let him know, if he could find out, what the Prime Minister meant upon a question deeply affecting the peace and welfare of the country which that Lord-Lieutenant was appointed to govern, and upon which question he was every week stating to the government the opinions he himself entertained!—a strange instance of the withholding of that confidence which, for both their sakes, ought to have existed. He said he had had a good deal of communication with the Catholics, and could answer for keeping them quiet for the present. They were contented with impartiality and justice. The Protestants, on the contrary, required partiality to themselves, and injustice to the Catholics. Still some of those leading Protestants would be very glad to have the question settled for them by an overruling authority; as long as it remained unsettled they are compelled—or, rather, think themselves compelled—to keep their places in their party by heading meetings, etc. This was very much the case, he thought, with Enniskillen, and perhaps with Longford. He said the king was very angry with him because he would not do a great many violent things which the government at home required of him, and proceed against this man and that man who gave them offense. He was determined, however, not to do so, as such measures could only irritate without deterring. He had seen O'Connell, who asked to see him on business, and of course he never refused admittance to anybody. He had availed himself of the opportunity to impress upon O'Connell the inexpediency of personal attacks upon the duke and Peel, and the wisdom of trying to conciliate the duke. With him it rested to determine whether any measure of relief should be proposed, and no good could come of making him their enemy. Lord A. asked me if I had not observed of late a more moderate tone on this point in the Association—which I had, and he attributed it to this communication. I said I did not see how it was possible to go on governing Ireland upon the present system even for another year. He said, Yes, he could engage to keep them quiet for another year, but that every year's delay would bring us worse terms of settlement. He dwelt much upon the difficulties under which he labored from being left in entire ignorance of the duke's intentions, and being obliged to govern according to his own notions, without knowing whether he was thwarting or forwarding the views of the duke. Doherty, the Solicitor-General, said that they could just keep the country together till Parliament met, and hand it over to the table of the House, but could not be answerable for more. He was very shy, however, of entering deeply into the subject with me; but I understood that he was the guiding adviser of Lord Anglesey. Sir John Byng,* the Lieutenant-General commanding, told me, that being asked by Lord Anglesey where he would place

* Afterward created Earl of Strafford, and a Field-Marshal. He was a younger brother of Mr. Byng, M.P. for Middlesex, mentioned at p. 63.

two regiments which were coming over from England, he said at once that he would send them among the Protestants of the north, who were much more violent and likely to disturb the public peace than the Catholics of the south; and they went accordingly to Belfast. He mentioned that the High Sheriff of Clare had lately called out the military upon his own authority, to preserve the public peace from being endangered by a meeting called to form a Brunswick Club, of which meeting the said Sheriff was to be Chairman—a good specimen of Ireland.

It is certain that the duke did not wish to increase the difficulties, because all the friends of the government studiously discountenanced the formation of Brunswick Clubs. Peel too told me, the day after the Repeal of the Test had been carried in the House of Commons, and after a long interview he had with the king at the Lodge at Windsor, where we went to hold a Council, that the king having adverted to the Catholic question, and expressed his hope that this vote would not lead to giving way on that question, and alluding also to his scruples of conscience arising out of the Coronation Oath, he, Peel, entreated the king well to consider before he rested his objections upon a point of conscience: circumstances of necessity might arise to compel him to agree. From objections of state policy he might recede, but from objections of conscience he could not with honor recede, and yet he might be obliged to waive them.

About the end of December came out the duke's letter to Dr. Curtis, Titular Primate of Ireland, a Catholic, with whom the duke had got acquainted in his Peninsular War, Curtis having then been in office in one of the Spanish universities and having made himself useful to the British army.

A little while afterward came out Lord Anglesey's letter

to the same person, in answer to one by which Dr. Curtis had communicated to Lord A. the duke's letter to him ; and at the same time was announced the recall of Lord Anglesey. It seems that on the 31st December, 1828, he informed his household that they were to prepare for his departure from Dublin in a fortnight from that time. The recall had certainly nothing to do with Lord A.'s letter to Curtis, but grew out of differences long existing and a correspondence that had long been going on between the duke and Lord A.* In fact, nobody who is not, like Peel, indispensably necessary to the duke can go on long serving under him, without an entire abandonment of all his own opinions. But on Saturday, the 3d January, the day on which Lord Anglesey's letter to Curtis appeared in the "Courier," Sir George Murray, Secretary of State for the Colonies, being asked about it by Lady MountCharles, his niece, knew nothing of it, and had not heard of its existence, though of course he knew of Lord A.'s recall.

Jan. 10, 1829.

I came to Paris on the 10th, and saw Madame de Flahault, Pozzo di Borgo, and others. La Ferronaye, the Minister for Foreign Affairs, had recently been seized with a paralytic attack, which renders his resumption of official duties quite impossible; but it is hoped he will get well enough to go to Nice, where his health may be somewhat restored. He had long been in bad health, and was very unwilling to take office last year, but the king made a point of it. He will be a great loss to the government, if, indeed,

---

* When M. de Talleyrand heard that Lord Anglesey was recalled, he saw at once that the duke had determined on giving the Irish Catholic Emancipation, and that he did not mean any one else to have the credit of it.

his retirement does not quite break it up. There have been warm debates in the Council on the appointment of a successor. Hyde de Neuville proposed Châteaubriand, but the king's party objected, and it was supposed that he would not have come in without bringing in also Sebastiani, Casimir Périer, and others of the ultra-Liberal party. On the other hand, Martignac wanted to have Pasquier, but to him the Liberals objected; and the Baron Agier, who heads an independent party of forty members, declared to Martignac that if Pasquier was appointed they should oppose. It was offered to the Duc de Mortemart, the ambassador at the Court of Russia, and now at home on temporary leave, but refused by him from a distrust of his own capacity and talent for speaking; and it is said he made a juster estimate of himself than those who made him the offer. For the present it has been settled that Portalis, Minister of Justice, shall carry on the duties, with the assistance of Rayneval, the Under-Secretary of State; and thus matters will remain till the Chambers meet, when it is far from improbable that a considerable change will take place; and if there is change it should be toward the Liberal side.

Constitutional principles have made great advances in France, and public opinion is acquiring considerable force. There remain very many abuses of detail which require correction; and if the government does not of its own accord give the tone upon these points, it will be compelled to do so. The king is quite satisfied with the present state of things, but would wish any change to be toward Toryism. He was uneasy last summer about his disputes with the bishops on the subject of the schools, but was satisfied by the report made by Châteaubriand of his conversation with the Pope, who said, "What a troublesome set of bishops you have in France! they are the most so of any in Christendom. What do they want? They have the most pious and Christian king that ever reigned—indeed, I may say, a very saint; why cannot they be satisfied?" The present administration is very Russian; but there is growing up among public men a *French* feeling, and this is directed for its first object to the recovery of the provinces between the northern frontier and the Rhine—Belgium, in short, and part of the Prussian territory. The ultra-Liberals say they would support any minister who would recover this territory for France; and I am told that Pozzo di Borgo secretly assures France that if in the event of a general war in Europe they will side with Russia, Russia will assist them in obtaining this object. The "Journal des Débats," the other day, denied any intention to send troops to Algiers or Egypt. "France," it said, "has objects nearer home of deeper interest, for which it should reserve its resources." If Châteaubriand and his party come in, the government will probably be looking to the possibility of extension to the north and also to the south. Pozzo di Borgo, with whom I had a long talk, said that the appointment of Châteaubriand would be a great misfortune; that he is a man whose frequent changes of opinion have deprived him of all consideration as a politician, and his wildness would make him dangerous. The happiest thing for France would be a government that would act upon the system of the late Duc de Richelieu (that is, I presume, which would lean on Russian connection); but the difficulties are great, from the dearth of eminent public men. Bonaparte crushed everybody else, both in politics and war; he allowed no one to think and act but himself, and has left, therefore, nothing but generals of division and heads of departments, but no man fit to command an army or govern a country. France, however, is prospering, and wants only peace to become powerful. The interest of her debt is only seven millions sterling, and her sinking fund for redemption of debt is three millions sterling; her taxes are light and her people happy.

With respect to the Russian war, he said peace was difficult; the emperor must yield to public opinion. The nation was mortified at their want of success, and desirous of redeeming their honor,* and on the other hand, the Turk is proportionably more obstinate from his unexpected success. He said the best-informed Russians no longer wished for extension of territory in Europe; they might, indeed, require *quelques bicoques en Asie* (alluding to Anapa and Poti on the Black Sea), and the security for free passage for their commerce through the Bosphorus—which they would require to have assured, not by territorial possession, but by guaranteed treaties.

I threw out to him that the other Powers of Europe might easily put an end to the war, since, without a for-

* *Note by Lord Palmerston.*—Madame de Flahault and Olivier Verac told me that the Duc de Mortemart says that much of the failure of the Russians is owing to the disinclination of Nicholas to sacrifice lives; that after every affair he dwelt more on the loss of men than on the success obtained, and forbade several enterprising attacks at Varna and elsewhere, which perhaps might have been successful, but at the hazard of severe loss. The spirit which led to the conspiracy against Alexander is not extinct; the snake is scotched, but not killed; and the punishment which has been inflicted upon some of the offenders, though meant as a more merciful one than that of death—to which legally they were subject—tends, perhaps more than death would have done, to keep up the irritation. Six or seven nobles, whose wives were among the most fashionable women of Petersburg, have been exiled to Siberia, and work in the mines. The wives went with them. The husbands are under ground six days in the week; the wives are forced to wash and perform all menial offices. Of course they write to their friends, and their letters of course cause great sympathy.

mal mediation, which Russia might object to, they might say to Turkey, You were the aggressor—as she certainly was; such and such terms, including compensation for mercantile losses, but excluding territorial cession, would be just between you. If you will agree to these, we are persuaded the fairness of the emperor will lead him to accept them; but they must be compatible with his honor. If you refuse these terms, take care of yourself; and, mind, you must look nowhere for help. I did not add to Pozzo what, however, would in that case be indispensable, namely, that we should say to Russia, We will leave Turkey to you, or even help you against her; but then, mark you, you must make peace when you have beat her, without taking any of her territory in Europe. Pozzo did not seem to disrelish this notion. I remarked that whatever advantage Russia may have gained by getting Varna, the Turks, if they were not egregiously stupid, would have time, between this and the summer, to fortify Constantinople in a way that would make it no easy capture, especially as it is behind intrenchments the Turks fight so desperately. Touching on the possible extension of the war through Europe, he said that as to Austria, they did not fear her; Hungary might, perhaps, be invulnerable, because they were almost independent, and would hate Russian connection; but Galicia would fall at the first blow, being open to Russia, and having the Carpathian Mountains on the wrong side, namely, to the rear; Austrian Poland would be more likely to be excited by Russia than Russian Poland by Austria. The Austrian army is *mou;* not but that if one hundred thousand Russians and one hundred thousand Austrians were to meet in pitched battle the chances would be even; but war is carried on differently; and in all the difficulties and enterprises of war he thought the Russians would make an example of the Austrians; and so they probably would. And he added that Russia would probably be too happy to get out of the hard bargain she has got of Turkey, and would fall entirely on Austria, and revenge upon her the hard blows she has received from the Turks.

If England and Austria took the field against Russia with Turkey, France would not long remain quiet; she *could* not do so; and her first attempt (as Pozzo said) would be upon Savoy and the Milanese. Austria has certainly been preparing for events. Lieven told me, a fortnight ago, that her army had been augmented from 150,000 to 300,000, Italy included, but still was deficient in horses. I remarked to Pozzo that if England took part with Turkey it would probably be by sending a fleet to the Black Sea, which of course, by cutting off the sea line of communication, would cripple the Russian operations, and that Austria in that case need not stir. This he said was exactly the plan of Metternich, who always boasted that he would throw England at the head of Russia. We, however, both hoped that no such rupture would take place. I then touched upon Greece, and he said that he had sent on to London, a fortnight ago, a very long and labored report by the three ambassadors, upon the state of Greece, its probable resources, its proper limits, and the amount of tribute it could pay to Turkey. As to limits, they unanimously recommended that it should extend to the line drawn from Volo to Arta; the tribute they proposed at £60,000 a year—a large sum as it seems to me, and for the payment of which I should be sorry to be a guarantee. They recommend that the president should be hereditary; but Capo d'Istria had positively refused to be president, and a notion had been broached of getting some little German prince unconnected with any of the great Powers. In the mean time, though the French have been stopped at the

Isthmus of Corinth, the Greeks are still carrying on operations on the continent, and it is to be hoped with success. Pozzo said that 640 Greek slaves had been redeemed by the French government, and he believed (though I do not) that the English government had contributed something toward the expense of this redemption.

Saturday, Jan. 17, 1829.

Dined at Girardin's; met Pasquier and Casimir Périer; went in the evening to Madame de Broglie's; met Benjamin Constant, Royer-Collard, and Pasquier. Royer said, when Pasquier was gone, that the present government could not make a Minister of Foreign Affairs who would not be ridiculous and break up the government, and yet that it was scarcely possible they should be able to go through the session without one.

Lord Stuart has not succeeded since his return here: when he went, people all thought him gone for good, and out came all sorts of stories about him; and those who had made free with his name are shy of his society. He behaved, too, very shabbily about Lord Granville's furniture, which he would not take till compelled by Aberdeen, and then he sold it by auction next door to the Embassy.

Jan. 23, 1829.

Met Baron Louis at Madame de Bourke's; he was Minister of Finance, and seems an intelligent man and well versed in the true principles of commerce. He explained to me the reasons for and against the intended new municipal law. The communes and departments are taxed pretty heavily for local expenses, repair of roads, bridges, public establishments, etc. The funds so raised are applied by officers named by the Crown; there is reason to suppose there is much waste; and when there is any surplus, as there often is, instead of being kept in reserve for the purposes for which it was raised, it is applied to establish convents and schools under the Jesuits. The intention of the law which has been under preparation is to constitute in each department a local assembly to regulate these expenses. The assembly is to consist of persons belonging to the district, and to be elected by those who pay a certain amount of direct taxes; the president is to be appointed by the Crown. This law, which seems so plausible and just, is objected to by two classes of men: first, by the party of the Congregation, as it is called, or the Jesuit or High Church party, because they see it will diminish the number of convents and religious establishments; secondly, by the Tories, because these local councils will be chosen by electors of a lower rate of contribution than those who now choose the deputies; and the Tory party think they shall thus lose part of their influence by the admission of a new class of electors to any kind of election. It is probable, however, that the law will pass, though it will be much debated.

I dined at Flahault's yesterday, and met Sebastiani and Talleyrand: the latter seems sunk and broken, and said but little; the former is a self-sufficient, consequential coxcomb. He maintained, in a loud voice and a declamatory style, that it is of great importance to a country to have a large capital town, as it tends to create a public opinion, and to advance the political freedom of the state; that Paris is not large enough, and ought to be *forced;* that the best mode of doing this would be to exempt from taxation for fifteen or twenty years all houses that should be built from this time for a certain period to come;—he not perceiving that a large capital town may be a good political establishment when it results from the activity of commerce and arises spontaneously, but that an aggregation of stone and mortar is different from an aggregation of thinking beings. After dinner he did me the honor to tell me, *avec franchise*, that it is a thousand pities that all parties and government in England take so mistaken a view of the principle on which we ought to deal with France. It is essential and indispensable to France to get back to the Rhine as a frontier; Landau and Sarre-Louis are particularly necessary to her. So long as the policy of England is opposed to these resumptions, so long will it be impossible for cordial alliance to exist between England and France; and France, whose real interests lie in a connection with England, will be led rather to seek to unite herself with Russia and Prussia, or any Power that will aid her to accomplish these objects. Prussia—though at first sight interested to prevent these resumptions by France—might be bribed to acquiescence by slices from Austria or Saxony, or by Hanover. I expressed great doubts whether any party would be found in England sufficiently enlightened to see this matter in this point of view, and thought it would be very difficult to persuade the people to such an arrangement.

Jan. 24, 1829.

After a week or ten days spent in intrigues and negotiations, Portalis, hitherto Minister of Justice, takes Foreign Affairs.

To the Hon. Wm. Temple, St. Petersburg.

"STANHOPE STREET, Jan. 7, 1829.

"MY DEAR WILLIAM,—

"I am just setting off for Paris, and have neither time nor materials for a long letter; I stay there about three weeks, and mean to be back here a few days before Parliament meets. Matters at home seem to be clearing up; the government is taking its line about Ireland, and people will now know how to steer. No Catholic question, and no liberal treatment of the Catholics, is the tardy decision of the duke; this must lead to warm work in the two Houses. Lord Anglesey's recall seems, as far as one can learn, to have been the consequence of differences of opinion upon several points connected with his government, and which had been the subject of a good deal of previous correspondence with the duke.

"The dismissal of Gorman Mahon from the magistracy —which Anglesey would not do when first ordered, because, upon consulting his Chancellor and law officers, he thought he had not grounds, but which he did do afterward, without orders, when fresh occurrences gave him grounds; the appointment of two or three Liberal barristers to be what are called assistant barristers, or assessors to the quarter sessions; Lord Anglesey's reception at the Phœnix of Lord Cloncurry, and other overt acts of Liberalism and good sense, have been stated to form the subject-matter of the bill of indictment upon which his recall has been placed. His successor is not yet known, nor has anybody been named by public report, except Melville, who has certainly declined. Whoever goes will have a difficult task. I fear this will create unpleasant times in Ireland; nothing but the near approach of the session would keep the Catholics quiet; we shall see what the session will do for them. The duke is pursuing a strange course about Portugal; on one hand the king—partly, I believe, of his own motion, at least as regards the manner of doing the thing—receives 'the little Glory' as queen, and on the other the duke, in the most peremptory manner, tells Palmella that if the Portuguese from Plymouth, whom he has driven out of England by threatening to scatter them like prisoners of war if they remain, shall attempt to land at Terceira, where they have been entreated by the there existing government to go, he—the duke—will prevent it by force; thus maintaining the integrity of Miguel's dominions, even in a place in which he reigns neither *de facto* nor *de jure*. Palmella, however, is very stout, and says they *shall* go, and if the duke stops them by force he will lay the case open to the world.

"Adieu! yours affectionately,

"PALMERSTON."

To Laurence Sulivan, Esq., War Office.

"PARIS, Jan. 13, 1829.

"MY DEAR SULIVAN,—

"I shall be much obliged to you if you would frank the inclosed cargo of letters on Irish affairs for me. La Ferronaye is going to Nice, and continues nominally Secretary of State for Foreign Affairs. Portalis, the Minister of Justice, or Home Department—I forget which—carries on his business for him in the mean time. The fact is that La Ferronaye's illness will break up the government; and a change is confidently looked for as soon as the Chambers meet; and therefore no one likes to take an office out of which they may be ejected in three weeks. . . . This country is, however, making rapid strides in improvements of all kinds; and, as Miss Berry said last night, 'It is a joke to talk of danger to Europe from Prussia;' if any exists, it is from France it is to be feared. However, this is a chapter far on in the volume, and we have a long way to go before we come to it. I dined at Pozzo's yesterday, a small and select party of *fifty*, and the whole thing as well managed and arranged as it could have been for *five*. The frost still continues, and the cold is considerable, for among the improvements that of making doors and windows to shut has not happened: and then such a *country* as the streets of Paris to go across—over hills, and down dales, and across brooks you go; they are like a model of

Switzerland almost, or, rather, like a model of a sea after a storm and before the swell has gone down. All the sewers are still above ground, so that, besides the central river, each house supplies its feeding channels; and bump, bump, bump, you go, all the way. Then, in this weather, the snow is all swept into mid-channel, and left there to await the day of thaw; and the streets being as slippery as ice can make them, *ergo* all the carriages you meet are illustrating the resolution of forces: the horses trotting straight along half-way up the street, between the gutter and the houses, the fire wheels of the carriage a few feet nearer the gutter, and the hind wheels sliding diagonally along said gutter; so that when two meet there must be a stop, and a heavy tug on each side toward the opposite house-doors, to get the wheels out of each other's way.

"Adieu! yours affectionately,

"Palmerston."

To the Hon. Wm. Temple, St. Petersburg.

"Stanhope Street, March 30, 1829.

"My dear William,—

"I am quite ashamed to think how long it is since I last wrote to you. I really believe it is not since I set off for Paris; and we have been so occupied with Catholic affairs since my return, that one has really hardly had time to think of anything else. I send you two copies of a speech which I made the other day;* one for yourself, and the other, with my compliments, for Lord Heytesbury. It had great success, and I have had so many civil things said to me about it by persons whose judgment on these matters is valuable, and who could have no motive for saying much more than they thought, that I have been

* On 18th March.

very much gratified. The bill came on as for a third reading to-day, but the debate will probably last to-night and to-morrow; and the bill will scarcely go up to the Lords till Wednesday. In that case they will probably read it a second time on Monday next; that is, this day week, and it will scarcely get through before Easter. But the duke says there shall be no Easter till the bill *is* through; and there he is right. They will have a decided majority for the bill in the Lords; the Protestants say about thirty, the Catholics hope for sixty or seventy; if they carry it by fifty, that will do perfectly well. Ten bishops, including two Irish ones, will vote for the bill, and that will be sanction enough; it is better, perhaps, for effect, that some of them should remain opposed to it. The Lowthers and Beckett have gone on voting against, and are not turned out, and will not be so; the duke considers them as the last link between the government and the Tory party; and he waited for Wetherell's speech, to found upon that a distinction between his case and that of the Lowthers; a distinction which Nature had made for him, since she had made it out of the question that the said Lowthers or Beckett should speak. Orders have been given to all the government people to redouble their attention to the Tory opposers of the bill, and to be, if possible, more civil to them than to those Tories who have come round; and the duke gave them all a grand dinner the other day, and talked to Knatchbull, and Gooch, and others, of what was to be done after Easter, just as if he were reckoning upon their certain support. What he will do I can hardly guess; some think he will try to strengthen his government; I doubt it; he may, perhaps, take in two or three young men, if they will come, and he will try to get Rosslyn as a hold upon Grey; but Grey himself he will not wish for: in fact, he feels his government sufficiently strong in the Lords, where he himself is; and he does not attach quite importance enough to the Commons, where he is not. But if any question were to arise upon which a strong attack could be made upon the government in the Commons, I think they would be found very weak. Peel is the only man among them who can speak effectively to the House. Fitzgerald is a good speaker, but not an agreeable one, and he has an inbred vulgarity about him which the House does not like. On the other side of the table are a number of men, with Brougham at their head, who can make good fight; and Huskisson, both of the Grants, and myself, would make a troublesome squadron on their flank.

"We must have a turn-out upon foreign politics before the session is over. Portuguese matters cannot be allowed to pass unnoticed; the conduct of the government has been too bad upon that subject. I fear, too, about Greece, they have been sticking to their text of last year, and wanting to confine the new state in all respects as much as it is possible to do. As to Russia and Turkey, that war has lost much of its interest; it seems pretty certain that the two parties are a tolerable match for each other; and although the advantage will most likely be on the side of Russia in this next campaign, yet one's notion that she could eat up Turkey at a mouthful has been utterly dissipated; and, for my part, I heartily wish her success, as the only chance of making a good settlement of the Greek state. The French I found much more liberal on that point than ourselves; but they have, like us, been so engrossed with domestic affairs since the beginning of their session that they have not much noticed foreign relations. I was at Paris at an interesting moment, when La Feronaye was taken ill, and intrigues were going on about his successor. Pasquier seemed most wished for by the

Ultras, Châteaubriand by the Liberals, and Polignac by the Duke of Wellington. The duke wrote a letter to the King of France in December, when Polignac went over for a fortnight, to say that he availed himself of the return to Paris of one of his Majesty's most faithful and devoted subjects to bring himself under his Majesty's notice at the beginning of the new year; and he thought he could not give a stronger proof of the great interest he took in his Majesty's welfare than by entreating him to allow Polignac to lay before him the true nature of his Majesty's situation and the dangers by which he was surrounded. On this hint Polignac spoke, and preached about revolution, and all the nonsense which the spirit of Toryism and Ultraism could suggest. The thing failed, and Polignac returned ; but upon La Ferronaye's illness, a fortnight after, he went back to Paris on a summons from Portalis ; but before his arrival an explanation took place between Portalis and his colleagues, and they all, Portalis included, went to the king, and declared that if Polignac was appointed they would unanimously resign. I see there is again mention of filling up the situation ; the Liberals, including Sebastiani, Royer-Collard, and De Broglie, all want to have Châteaubriand. If he comes in he will make a rumpus; he is violent about the old story of frontiers, and will throw France into any hands that will help her on toward the Rhine.

"You are of course aware of the understanding between Russia and Prussia, entered into about this time last year, to agree, under certain contingencies, that France should move on to the Rhine, at the expense of Prussia and the Netherlands ; that Prussia should be indemnified by taking Saxony, and the King of Saxony be transferred to the Milanese ; and that Holland should get some equivalent on her northern frontier. I heard this the other day at

Paris, and from a quarter which makes me pretty confident that there is some foundation for the statement. France was cognizant of the undertaking, but declined making herself, specifically or formally, a party to the agreement, wishing to leave her hands free to act according to circumstances.

"Sebastiani lectured me one day upon the unfortunate jealousy which all English governments feel about the aggrandizement of France: he said that an accession of territory toward the Rhine was indispensably necessary to her; that her general interests led her to cultivate an alliance with England, and what a pity it was for both that this confounded jealousy of ours should oppose obstacles to a good understanding, or tend to drive France into the arms of Russia, whom it was so much to the real interest of France to watch and control! The general idea was that Mortemart's true reason for refusing Foreign Affairs was his distrust of the stability of the government, and his disinclination to give up a good embassy for a precarious office at home. The Duke of Cumberland has been doing all he possibly could to thwart the government and prevent emancipation; and nothing could have foiled him but the absolute impossibility of making any government that would stand one day upon the principle of resistance. In the Lords they might indeed do with Eldon, Colchester, Mansfield, Sidmouth, and some others; but in the Commons it would be perfectly impossible. The Speaker is the only man in the whole House fit for a Cabinet office who is not pledged the other way.

"Notwithstanding this, however, on Sunday the 1st of March, next before the Thursday on which Peel proposed his measure, I went down to Strathfieldsaye to meet the judges; and at *three* on Monday morning the Chancellor arrived from Windsor to tell the duke that the king had changed his mind, and would not consent to the measure being brought forward. He remained with the duke till six in the morning, when he set off for London, where he was to be in the Court of Chancery at ten. The duke went off at eight for Windsor, and gave in his resignation. The king did not refuse it, but took time to consider of it: the duke, Peel, and Lyndhurst went down to the king again on the Wednesday, and returned to town to dine at Bathurst's, without having been able to bring the king to reason; and they summoned a Cabinet for ten the next morning—that is, for Thursday, the day the measure was to be brought forward—in order to consider how they were to announce to Parliament that they were out, and the whole thing up; but at seven that evening the duke received the king's surrender, which he wrote on Wednesday night before he went to bed. It is quite clear that neither Canning nor any other minister could, *this year*, have done the thing, because nothing has brought the king to agree to it but his being checkmated by having no other move left upon the board. If Canning had now been alive, and the duke and Peel available, the king would have taken them; and in that case they would perhaps have supported him in making a government upon the principles of delay and postponement.

"Adieu! yours affectionately,

"PALMERSTON."

To the Hon. Wm. Temple, St. Petersburg.

"STANHOPE STREET, Sunday,
"June 14, 1829.

"MY DEAR WILLIAM,—

"You have been an excellent correspondent of late, and in return I send you a copy of my speech on foreign affairs,* and one which I wish you to present from me to Lord Heytesbury. I have had many civil things said to me about it; and even the friends of the government, who think it too strong an attack, have spoken well of the speech itself. I thought it would be very unfortunate if the session was allowed to pass away without anybody making any comments upon the course of policy pursued by the government in our foreign relations; and as the Whigs were too coquetting with the Treasury Bench to do so, it fell to my lot to make the move.

"My objects were, first, to put on record my own opinions, both now and when I was in the Cabinet; secondly, to excite public attention to these matters a little; and, thirdly, to let the government see that they were not to suppose that they could have their own way entirely in foreign affairs, and that, however incompetent the individual might be who broached the subject, yet when once the stone was set a rolling, it would acquire a force which did not belong to the first mover. I had taken measures to insure these matters being touched upon also in the French Chambers, because that was the way to stir up the French government to more active feelings about them; and I trust that some good may be the result: at all events, there can be no harm done. What will happen here at home as to ministerial arrangements nobody can guess; some changes seem inevitable. The government is wretchedly weak in the House of Commons, and would be out-debated in a moment if questions were to arise in which the Whigs chose vigorously to attack them Peel is the only good speaker they have, and he has lost much of his weight in the House from the ill will which the anti-Catholics still bear him for changing on the Catholic ques-

* Made on the 1st of June.

tion. Fitzgerald is a clever ready-fighting speaker, but not a favorite with the House; Goulburn is very indifferent. Murray can hardly speak at all in debate, and Herries is entirely mute. The friends of the government feel the necessity of additional strength to it in the Commons, but the difficulty will be to know how to get it. I do not think the duke would like to take us back again as a party; and individually I doubt any of us joining him, because we would then have no security against being obliged to concur in measures which we disapprove. What he would best like himself would be to get in some of the rising Whigs, who would fight for him in debate, and, from their youth, give way to him in Council. But that, again, is not so easy, and every step in advance toward the Whigs widens the breach between him and his old Tories, who are already ill pleased at the appointment of Rosslyn.* In the mean time the king has not forgiven his ministers, and would be glad to throw them over if he could see how to do so. Cumberland does not know what to be at; he wishes for revenge on the duke, but not the accession of Whigs to power. I believe he would like to see a government consisting of our party and the old Tories—a thing impossible for many reasons. The best government that could be made would be one composed by a union of Huskisson and Lansdowne; in short, the government of Goderich, with a better head and some changes, omitting Herries and some subordinates.

"All this, however, is mere moonshine; the duke is fully resolved to remain minister as long as his health will allow him to do so; and, if he only follows the same principles in his foreign policy which he has in his domestic, there is nothing to prevent him from holding on. In home

---

* As Lord Privy Seal.

matters he has yielded up his own opinions and wishes to necessity and public opinion; he found that he could not carry on the government of the country without yielding the Catholic question, and he immediately surrendered that point. Public opinion has not touched foreign affairs, but these have hitherto been left as *carte blanche* to the unscrutinized discretion of the government.

"Whenever public opinion applies itself to foreign affairs—which it will certainly do next session—the duke will give way upon that point also, and, by so doing, will retain his power.

"I am sorry there has been so much abstinence and apathy on these topics this session, because if the screw had been strongly applied this spring, it would have had its effect upon the policy of our government about Russia, Turkey, Greece, and Portugal in the course of this summer; and might have prevented them doing things which when done become irrevocable, and have impelled them to do others which, when the opportunity is gone by, can never afterward be done. I heard by accident the other day a strong proof how entirely the duke's acquiescence in Catholic relief was a bending to necessity, and not a change of opinion; but it was told me in confidence, and do not repeat it: A Catholic gentleman applied to him lately to be placed in the Commission of the Peace, but though the man was perfectly respectable and eligible, and a landed proprietor, the duke refused him because he was a Catholic; not, indeed, assigning that reason to him—to whom he merely said that no appointments could be made—but having stated that reason to another person whom he consulted as to the character and circumstances of the applicant. The session is over, and yet Parliament is not up, and may not be prorogued for a fortnight: we are waiting till the Lords get through a committee about

London Bridge. The making an approach to the bridge has proved more expensive than was expected; means must be provided; the city applied to Parliament to give them means by continuing for twenty-one years longer a tax on coals landed in London, which would expire in 1851; the bill passed the Commons unnoticed and unopposed.

"Londonderry is angry that he did not go to Ireland instead of the Duke of Northumberland. Durham is furious because his income has disappeared, in consequence of a fall in the pit-mouth price of coals. Grey is out of humor because the king refused him and took Rosslyn. These three have set to work to make a violent opposition to the continuance of the tax, and want to throw upon the city the whole expense of the approach. The government fight for the city; and Londonderry and Lambton swear they will keep Parliament sitting till September, by protracting the examination of witnesses before the committee, unless the government give way. This is the only business now for either House, and so the Commons adjourn from Friday to Friday, waiting till Londonderry's coals shall be burnt out.

"There have been strange stories current within the last few days of malpractices of the Chancellor that are said to have come to light—the receipt of money from suitors. I do not believe them, though I doubt his integrity of mind; but he would hardly place his existence so much in the power of any man. He certainly is much embarrassed in his pecuniary affairs, and has borrowed money from friends; but that is another thing. Scarlett would probably be Chancellor if he were to be removed; and a very good Chancellor Scarlett would make, though I suppose he knows next to nothing of Chancery law at present. I shall go to Ireland for a month some time in the autumn, and may perhaps run over to Paris for three weeks before Parliament meets, but have no other plans for this year, reckoning upon your being able to get leave to come over. I shall probably stay here in town till the latter end of August. London is by far the best place to read in; in the country one is tempted to be out all day, and especially so at one's own house.

"Adieu! my dear William.

"Yours affectionately,

"Palmerston.

"I should think that Cavendish will come in for Cambridge;* and I hope he will, as there will then be less chance of a contest at the general election. The University would never sit down contented under a banker."

The two or three letters which I have just given, from January till June, 1829, go naturally over some of the ground which had been previously traversed in the "Journal." But they are not the less interesting. We see from that of the 7th of January, how little even so close an observer of events as Lord Palmerston foresaw the Duke of Wellington's real intentions as to the Catholic claims within a few weeks of the meeting of Parliament. It is curious also to read an account of the city of Paris forty years ago—with its streets like the model of a sea after a storm; nor is the Duke of Wellington's letter to Charles X., recommending Prince Polignac, if the story as related is correct, an unimportant fact in the duke's biography. The allusions in March and June to the two speeches—one on Catholic Emancipation and the other on Portuguese affairs—convey a right impression of the effect they pro-

* The present Duke of Devonshire; he did come in, and was also returned next year.

duced. I was under the gallery when that on Portuguese affairs—which also touched toward the conclusion on foreign affairs generally—was spoken: it was not only composed with great care, both as to style and argument, but singularly well delivered, and in a tone which happily combined conversation with declamation. Lord Palmerston, in fact, never stood so high as an orator, until his famous Don Pacifico speech, as he stood at that moment. He was spoken of as the rival of Peel, and the preference was generally given to his style of eloquence.

Alas! the brilliant prophecies then made as to Ireland have not been verified; for although the Catholic disabilities were removed, the spirit which had established them on the one side and resisted them on the other still remained; and up to this day there seems a difficulty in persuading those most interested in its welfare, that if you wish to govern Ireland as a statesman, you must not govern it as a sectarian, nor debate every political question with the predominant idea that you are dealing with the Protestant, the Catholic, or the Dissenter. It is this controversial feeling which poisons the Irish atmosphere; and until laws shall have changed manners, we must not expect to see any practical benefit from laws. But the glowing words of the orator were not chilled by any vision of distrust.

"I cannot sit down," said Lord Palmerston, "without expressing the satisfaction I feel, in common with the nation at large, at the determination which the government has at last adopted to give peace to Ireland. The measure now before us will open a career of happiness to that country which for centuries it has been forbidden to taste, and to England a prospect of commercial prosperity and national strength which has never yet been recorded in our annals. The labors of the present session will link together two classes of the community which have long been dissevered; they will form in history the true mark which is to divide the shadow of morning twilight from the brilliant effulgence of the risen sun; they will form a monument, not of the crime or ambition of man, not of the misfortunes or convulsions of society, but of the calm and deliberate operation of benevolent wisdom watching the good of the human race; and we ought to be proud to be employed on an act which will pass down to the latest posterity as an object of their respect, gratitude, and admiration."

I think I can see the smile of the incredulous critic who has just read these romantic sentences. But it is only through the alternate process of enthusiasm and disappointment that the visions of hope ripen into realities. And the day may yet come when, as the statesman of another generation foretold, the names of those who wrote the first pages in the history of reform in Ireland may be placed high among the far-seeing patriots of their country and the enlightened benefactors of mankind.

At all events, at the time Lord Palmerston spoke he expressed in eloquent language the sentiments on Catholic Emancipation common among the cultivated classes of his day, and this made him popular with those classes. His language respecting Don Miguel, however, was perhaps still more universally echoed by the public mind; for all classes—cultivated and uncultivated—feel a spontaneous horror for the despoiler of the child and the traitor to his word. Don Miguel was both. He had with unexampled treachery installed himself on the throne which he had acknowledged to belong to his niece, and suppressed the liberties that he had solemnly pledged himself to consolidate and protect. Common belief at that time accredited the accusation that the British ministry favored the usurper, although the young queen whose scepter he had seized was still treated and received at our court as the sovereign of Portugal.

It is but justice to observe that no man was so little likely to patronize disloyalty as the soldier-statesman who made honor and duty the guides of his life. Our great captain, however, was a man, and not without some of the small feelings of men in general. He had never pardoned Mr. Canning for the exclusive credit which he had obtained by his eloquence for the famous expedition of 1826. He had already, when the Canningites were in his Cabinet, declared—on withdrawing our troops from Portugal—that they had been sent to Lisbon in consequence of international obligations, and not in manifestation of any particular opinion. But, in his zeal to prove this more conspicuously, he went beyond the line which a nice appreciation of English feeling would have prescribed; and by an ostentatious parade of neutrality created a suspicion as to his not being really neutral.

It must be confessed, however, that appearances justified this suspicion. Don Miguel had been allowed to take forcible possession of Madeira; Donna Maria was not allowed to strengthen her garrison at Terceira: true, in one case the troops were sent from Portugal, where Don Miguel was for the moment supreme; in the other, it was proposed to send reinforcements from England, where Donna Maria was a guest and a stranger; but the public mind did not go into these particulars, nor consider what might have been the consequences of an opposite line of conduct; it saw the Duke of Wellington acting against a constitutional sovereign, permitting a tyrant to extend his authority; and the nation's heart went with Lord Palmerston when he thus expressed himself:

"The civilized world rings with execrations upon Miguel, and yet this destroyer of constitutional freedom—this breaker of solemn oaths—this faithless usurper—this enslaver of his country—this trampler upon public law—this violator of private rights—this attempter of the life of helpless and defenseless woman, is, in the opinion of Europe, mainly indebted for the success which has hitherto attended him to a belief industriously propagated by his partisans, and not sufficiently refuted by any acts of the British government, that the Cabinet of England looks upon his usurpation with no unfriendly eye.

"In the opinions of many this impression is confirmed by much that ministers have done, and very much that they have omitted to do. . . . .

"Their steady refusal to interfere in cases in which their interference would have been prejudicial to Don Miguel has been contrasted with their promptitude and vigor to interfere when their interference was subservient to his projects."

I have said that this attack upon Don Miguel, however severe, was in no wise an exaggeration of the general feeling respecting him; nor will it appear exaggerated or extraordinary now; but that which will appear extraordinary to many who knew Lord Palmerston in after-years as the most stanch protector of the integrity of the Ottoman empire, and the most resolute opponent of Russian ambition, is the fervor with which at this time he advocated the interests of Greece, and the indifference with which he seemed to regard the advance of a Russian army toward Constantinople.

Much, however, that the reader has been perusing sufficiently explains our complicated position at that time. We were parties to a treaty with Russia for establishing the practical independence of Greece, though for some time the form to be given to that independence was uncertain. We were undoubtedly not parties with Russia in her war against Turkey, and we were generally anxious, if we could not prevent, to limit the effects of that war. But it has been seen that from the commencement of the duke's first administration there were two distinct parties in his Cabinet, the one more especially desirous to see the treaty respecting Greece fulfilled, the other more especially desirous to prevent Turkey from being seriously enfeebled by a dangerous invader.

Lord Palmerston was evidently at this time among the first,—a generous champion of the country which had inherited so great a name and undergone so many humiliations.

He did not, however, believe that any temporary success of the Russian arms would effect any great or permanent diminution of the Sultan's power.

The Russian march, indeed, though victorious, had rather shown the weakness than the strength of that mysterious empire—so invulnerable on the defensive, but so crippled in the advance by an administration so corrupt and incapable that it can palsy the valor of a soldiery that rarely retreats, and the vigor of an ambition that never wearies. Russia, besides, had pledged herself at the commencement of her campaign not to make any extensive conquests; and an attempt to evade this pledge would have been resisted by a league too powerful to leave reasons for apprehensions. On the other hand, the idea which Lord Palmerston denounced in the House of Commons*—viz., that "of creating a Greece which should contain neither Athens, nor Thebes, nor Marathon, nor Salamis, nor Platæa, nor Thermopylæ, nor Missolonghi, which should exclude from its boundaries all the most inspiring records of national achievements, whether in ancient or modern times"—was sufficiently illiberal and

* Speech of 1st June, 1829.

unnatural to induce all generous minds to rejoice at any event that might thwart its accomplishment. This Philhellenism, however, on the part of Lord Palmerston is worth noticing, because it shows his original propensity, and that the policy he subsequently pursued was not caused by the preconceived prejudices founded on traditions, but by the results of practical experience, and a conviction maturely formed as to the possibilities of Greece and the interests of England. I may indeed observe here that Lord Palmerston—though generally desirous to keep England on the side of liberal opinions—had not any system of policy relative to foreign states. His notion was that every question should be treated on its own merits, without regard to the actual alliances it might dissolve, or the future dangers it might provoke. "England," he said to me once, "is strong enough to brave consequences;" a theory which has its inconveniences as well as its advantages.

The letter of the 14th June spoke of returning to Paris toward the end of the year; and nothing, perhaps, in the correspondence I have so freely drawn from is more interesting than the three or four letters which I now introduce.

To the Hon. Wm. Temple, St. Petersburg.

"Paris, Hôtel de Rivoli, Rue Rivoli,
"Dec. 4, 1829.

"My dear William,—

"I arrived here on Sunday morning at eight o'clock, not having stopped to sleep on the road; it is too much trouble to do so, and the roads were so heavy and rutty that one felt that if one did not keep moving one would never get to Paris. The snow lasted till rather more than half way, and then disappeared; here there was scarcely any. The weather has been mild, but the sky enveloped generally in a gray mist very like London and its neighborhood. I have got, however, what I think a very nice apartment; it is in the Hôtel de Rivoli, looking south, over the open part of the Tuileries Gardens, so that my opposite neighbors are the houses on the other side of the Seine; and as my room is not much higher than the top of the Monument, the labor of ascending to and descending from it is considerable; but then, in consequence of this elevation, the sun does not set for me till half an hour after he has taken leave of the inhabitants of the *rez de chaussée*; and, as I have whatever is to be seen of him all day long, the rooms are warm and cheerful.

"The public excitement continues unabated, but it seems pretty evident that the ministry must yield and go out, either when the Chambers meet, or before. Their only chance of staying in was by a *coup d'etat*, that is, by exertions of prerogative to alter the laws without consent or concurrence of the Chambers, and by supporting these exertions by armed force. This was what Labourdonnaye wanted, but Polignac and others demurred; Polignac was for management and waiting, by means of the priests, Labourdonnaye for using force. The latter sneeringly said, three of his gens-d'armes were worth more than a dozen Jesuits: these bickerings led to their separation, but the final rupture turned upon Polignac's appointment as President of the Council, that is to say, Prime Minister.

"When there is no President each minister is responsible for his own department, and the king or dauphin acts as President. When a President exists, he takes the king's pleasure whenever he pleases, with or without his colleagues, upon all matters; in short, he is what our duke chooses to be. Labourdonnaye, feeling himself an abler man than Polignac, and with more personal followers in the Chambers, thought that as long as there was no President he might gradually become the leading member of the government; and, accordingly, when he came in he stipulated that there should be no President. When, however, he and Polignac began to differ, the latter thought the best way of getting his troublesome colleague out, or of keeping him down while he stayed in, was to have himself invested with the authority of President. As soon as this was announced as about to be, Labourdonnaye declared it was a breach of compact, and he must resign. His party, consisting of about thirty members, will of course oppose the government, like Knatchbull and the Eldonites in our Parliament.

"As soon as Labourdonnaye was gone the rest began to consider whether a *coup d'état* was feasible; and they bethought themselves of an *ordonnance* that should alter the law of election by giving votes to government *employés* and to military officers on half-pay of a certain standing, independently of any qualification of property, which would reduce the age of admissibility to the deputies from forty to thirty years, and should modify the law of equal inheritance. This plan was, however, resisted by Chabrol, by Haussey, Minister of Marine, and by a third, and abandoned; and, to make sure of its defeat, it is supposed that these Cabinet objectors let out the secret; for on one and the same day all the newspapers were full of the project, and of denunciations against it. Thus, then, by the retreat of Labourdonnaye, and the relinquishment of this *ordonnance*, it is decided that the government do not dare to attempt violence; a majority in the Chambers, if ever possible, is out of the question with Labourdonnaye and the Ultra-Royalists against them; and therefore, though Polignac still swaggers, and the king knits his brows and clinches his fist, and talks of what he will do on foot and on horseback, and how the first Revolution was the child of the weakness of Louis XVI., and a second shall never spring from the weakness of Charles X., yet still, nevertheless, it is as certain as the return of the last comet, that either before the meeting or soon after it away will go the present ministry, and a Liberal one will succeed. What that Liberal one will be nobody but Mr. Moore, the Almanacker, can positively predict; but it is generally thought here that it will consist of Martignac, Hyde de Neuville, Pasquier, perhaps Châteaubriand, and people of that sort; and it seems not impossible that Polignac may be kept in, in a less important situation, by way of giving the government a hold upon the king. However, all this will be settled in an amiable manner, and there is no earthly possibility, or rather probability, of revolution or convulsion; *although if the king were, for the first time in his life, to carry his obstinacy up to the very hour of trial instead of dropping it, as he always has done hitherto, the night before; and if he was backed by a courageous and desperate ministry who were mad enough to bear the storm, not of public, but of national feeling, then and in that case the result would probably be a change of name in the inhabitant of the Tuileries, and the Duke of Orleans might be invited to step over the way from the Palais Royal; but as to any other change, it is out of the question. There are too many millions of proprietors of land and funds in France to let it be possible that anything should happen endangering the safety of either one property or the other.*

"*The army, however, would not support the government in any violent proceedings; they themselves say they cannot reckon upon the army, and can only rely on the Garde Royale;* the tribunals too, to whom in the first instance appeal would be made in any dispute between the government and the people, though not actually inspired with the devotion of martyrdom, are still disposed to do their duty, as they proved by a judgment the other day upon the editors of some newspapers. These editors had been accused by the government of publishing, with remarks, the 'Association Brétonne,' or resolutions not to pay taxes if the government imposed them illegally. The charge was, that these observations tended to bring the government into hatred and contempt, and to attack the just prerogative of the king; the verdict was, that the editors ought to be punished for *even supposing that the government could do so wicked an act as to attempt to levy taxes without the consent of the Chambers according to the Charter;* thus the sentence against the editors was a slap at the government. In the mean while public attention is riveted to home politics, and people think no more of foreign affairs than we did last year while the Catholic question was pending; excepting, always, that they still find time to talk about the duke and the English government for having brought upon France all this confusion and turmoil to serve foolish purposes of the English Cabinet, in which, after all, they have been disappointed. It seems, however, that Metternich was true to his double policy to the very last moment, and that up to the very signature of the Treaty of Adrianople he was writing to urge the Sultan to resist and hold out till winter, and promising then to make a coalition to support him before spring. The Turk, however, thought he had been bamboozled too long, and, when he found what a scrape he had been brought into by listening to Metternich and waiting for his help, became furious.

* * * * * *

"Nothing is known here as to the settlement of Greece; but Leopold seems rather to have risen in the odds as first favorite for the Athenian St. Leger.

"There are quantities of English here, some of whom I have seen, others only heard of; the Mintos, General Ramsay, Sir A. Barnard, Sir Thomas Hislop, King Allen, the Berrys, Poulett Thompson, Lord and Lady Ponsonby, the William Lockes, Wilmot Horton and his daughter, the Gally Knights, Pellew and his wife, are all scattered about the town; and the hotels are so full that I wandered nearly two hours about the streets before I could locate myself to my satisfaction. There is not much alteration in the town since last year, excepting that *trottoirs* are gradually creeping on in most of the principal streets; but you meet with them, like the houses in Washington City, dotted about here and there in little patches widely separated by immense blank intervals.

"Adieu, my dear William.

"Yours affectionately,

"PALMERSTON."

To Laurence Sulivan, Esq., War Office.

"PARIS, Dec. 9, 1829.

"MY DEAR SULIVAN,—

"The existence of the administration here is drawing rapidly to a close, and it seems highly probable that considerable changes will take place before another week has elapsed; the retirement of Labourdonnaye, followed as it was by a determination against violent measures, decided the fate of the ministry. The disputes between Polignac with Bourmont and the rest of his party on one hand, and Courvoisier, Chabrol, and Haussey on the other, have continued with increased asperity. Courvoisier last week appointed a Liberal lawyer to report upon the law which regulates the Council of State—corresponding with our Privy Council; upon which a violent attack was let off upon him in the government paper—a *slight* symptom of internal divisions. Courvoisier lost no time in taking his revenge, for in a Council a few days ago, upon some remark of the king as to some of the many difficulties they have to encounter, Courvoisier is said to have broken out, and to have declared that there was no use in attempting any longer to deceive themselves or his Majesty as to the state of affairs; that it was impossible the ministry could go on. Public opinion was against them, the press was against them, the Chambers were against them, all France was against them, and it was impossible they could stand. Polignac was amazed and furious, and was beginning to reply and explain, when the king cut the matter short and said, 'Since it seems, gentlemen, that you yourselves feel you cannot go on, or at least cannot agree together, I must take other measures and send for somebody else.' It is said he then sent for Roy, who was formerly Minister of Finance, and that Roy has for some days been in negotiation with different people endeavoring to make arrangements. The persons he communicated with were Martignac, Châteaubriand, Pasquier, etc Martignac declared he would have nothing to do with the government unless it was distinctly understood with the king, that those who are responsible for what is done should be allowed to do what they think best, so long as the king may choose to keep them. Châteaubriand did not choose to take the post of upper schoolmaster, or Chief of the Department of Public Instruction, which was proposed to him. Pasquier, I fancy, made no objections to any place that might be given him. The king demurred somewhat as to Martignac's theory of government, and moreover insisted upon keeping Polignac, to which arrangement, again, Martignac and Company vehemently objected, though it was said last night that they had been mollified on that point. The king hates Pasquier upon some personal grounds of offense, and abhors Châteaubriand as a renegade from Toryism, and wants Polignac as a *Herries* in the Cabinet, while the others object to him precisely in that capacity, not liking to have an avowed reporter at all their daily discussions. I dined at Polignac's the day before yesterday (Monday); there were forty people and more, and in the evening a large reception, fully attended. I thought Polignac was looking singularly beaten and cast down; but his soirée was attended by people of all colors. I sat between two charming Tory French country gentlemen, whose notions of things in general, and abhorrence of any change, reminded me greatly of some of my friends in England.

"The illness of Nicholas has caused great sensation here, and alarm among the friends of peace and quiet in Europe. It is quite astonishing how every Frenchman you meet raves about '*nos frontières*,' and declares he would cut off his two hands to get back the Rhine, Alps, and Pyrenees as boundaries; all this, however, is mere froth and vanity; and while they have Chambers who must levy taxes to carry on a war, nothing but egregious folly on our part can bring on a war between the two countries. Wilmot Horton is here, indefatigably hammering at emigration, and writing his short-hand scribe down to a skeleton. Gally Knight was to go back yesterday or to-day. Our weather is cold, but the frost is nothing to compare with that of last January. I saw a letter from Bologna, saying the Apennines were covered with snow; and *Soracte altâ nive candidum*, and the post had been interrupted for some days between Bologna and Florence.

"Adieu! yours affectionately,

"PALMERSTON.

"I wonder whether the word 'Private' will move the

curiosity of the French Post-Office to open and read this letter."

To the Hon. Wm. Temple, St. Petersburg.

"PARIS, Dec. 15, 1829.

"MY DEAR WILLIAM,—

"Thank you for your letter, which I received yesterday. The change of ministry, which was expected ten days ago, went off in smoke, and the present people remain till the Chambers turn them out—*which they are sure to do.* The negotiations of Roy failed; none of the Liberals would serve with Polignac, and the king would not give Polignac up; so on the king's return from Compiègne it was announced that Polignac was to continue. Violent measures are therefore again talked of, and *Polignac is a man likely to try them;* he is bold, obstinate, and determined. A man who has passed ten years in prison becomes either broken or hardened; he is the latter—he makes it also a matter of conscience and religion. If the king is as firm as his minister, there will be trouble in France; but there is every reason to hope he will not be, and will give in. They say Bourmont has had a large share in bringing about this revival of determination. The king is reported to have said at Compiègne, that the government could never be without a majority as long as he supported them, '*car la majorité c'est le Roi:*' this maxim has been well attacked in the papers. The report of the day is, that the government mean to issue proclamations changing the law of election, suspending the liberty of the press, and declaring the judges removable at pleasure; and then to dissolve the Chambers. *But all this would not do; the public feeling is too strong, and the army is too decidedly Liberal, to make it possible to carry through such a system; and if attempted it must end in the retirement of Charles X.* It is quite certain that Austria has promised to lead, in case of need, an army of observation into Piedmont and Sardinia, to back up this government and repress any rising; but this is preposterous. The mere entrance of an Austrian regiment would raise a flame all through France, and kindle a war of revolution all over Europe; they never will set foot within the frontier.

"Russia has, on the contrary, declared her anxious desire for the maintenance of those institutions which were established under the auspices of Alexander; and Prussia would probably side with Russia. It is to be hoped, however, that matters will not come to this, and that the legitimate means of resistance which the present Constitution gives will be sufficient to enable the French to upset their government quietly and without convulsion; and I am quite sure that not one in a thousand wishes for anything more than a rationally Liberal government. Some of the royalists whom one meets in society talk like fools and madmen: *il nous faut de la force, d'abord de la force, et puis on peut être raisonnable à loisir;* but when you ask them how their force is to be applied, and against what, they cannot tell you; but they say a free press is not applicable to France, and that it must be put down; that public opinion does not exist, except as far as it is created by the journals, and if these could be got rid of the government might be sure of the tribunals, and the army, and the electors, and the House of Peers—all stuff!

"I have been to hear some interesting lectures of Dupin,* and Villemain, and Guizot: the first, upon the State of Industry and Wealth in the nations of the earth; the second,

* Charles Dupin, author of several works, and brother to the celebrated lawyer, President of the Chamber of Deputies for a considerable time under Louis Philippe.

on the Progress of Modern Languages; the third, on the Progress of Civilization in Europe. These lectures are given twice or thrice a week, are open to the public, gratis, and are attended by many hundred persons, and must have a great effect in enlightening the public mind. The professors are paid by the government, but are entirely Liberal in their doctrines.

* * * * * * *

"I shall perhaps stay here till the 27th or 28th, so as to be able to get to Cambridge by the 31st, at night, which three days will easily enable me to do.

"Yours affectionately,

"Palmerston."

There are certain epochs in which the atmosphere of Europe, if I may so speak, seems to change—in a manner similar to that in which by modern contrivances the atmosphere is refreshed and renewed in our apartments. The old air, long pent up within narrow limits, and which has lost its life and vivacity, passes out on one side, and is replaced from another by fresh air, which the lungs receive and breathe out more freely than that from which they are delivered.

The first visible sign of this change is generally in writers and orators—in men of genius who seem to catch by intuitive sympathy the impressions which are germinating around them.

From 1820 to 1830 there was manifestly one of these epochs. In 1827 neither Mr. Canning nor M. de Châteaubriand were the Canning or Châteaubriand of earlier years. They had not abjured their former doctrines. Mr. Canning was still an anti-reformer, and M. de Châteaubriand was still a royalist; but they no longer represented the parties of which "opposition to parliamentary reform" and "fidelity to the crown" had been the watchwords. The circumstances of the times had created new questions, on which they had taken the popular side; and, lit up by the brilliant influence of their talents, these new questions had become conspicuous, whilst the old had ceased to be so. It is singular that in France, as in England, the main conflict of the moment was on matters connected with religion, and that in both countries the Conservatives were overborne in those battles which they attempted to fight under a theological banner. With the cry of "*A bas les Jésuites!*" the king's faction, the king himself being popular, was overcome in France; by the general impulse in favor of satisfying the Catholics the Tories were driven from power in England. The contest was apparently against the Catholics in one case, in favor of them in the other. But it was really and truly in both cases for religious liberty. Nor is it amiss to remark how the fortunes of the two nations were influenced by the characters of the two chiefs of the defeated parties,—the one of whom knew how to yield, whilst the other did not know how to resist.

But it is curious to see the soldier employing all his credit to prevent a civil war, which would have called forth his talents, and to find the civilian exercising all his influence to provoke a conflict, which proved his incapacity.

We know the result: it was that which Lord Palmerston had so sagaciously foretold. But, though the catastrophe which occùrred at Paris was one calculated to heighten esteem for the prudence which had directed the counsels of St. James's, the Tory party could not be so violently overthrown on the opposite side of the Channel without being shaken very rudely on this side.

The Duke of Wellington perceived this, and resolved to make sacrifices to persons if he could maintain principles;

for he was honestly attached to the ancient constitution of England, and saw in its alteration a social as well as a political transformation, which he condemned with the mind of a man bred up in ideas altogether different from those then coming into fashion.

The following extract from Lord Palmerston's autobiography will relate the steps which were taken to obtain support:

"In July, 1830, an overture was made to Melbourne from the duke to join the government, and he was given to understand that no objection would be made to Grant and myself. His answer was, that he could not join without Huskisson and Lord Grey. The duke's reply was, that he might perhaps consent to take back Huskisson, but that he could not act with Lord Grey, who had spoken of him in such unmeasured terms both in Parliament and private. We learnt a short time afterward, from pretty good authority, that the duke had made a proposal to Grey,* which had been declined before the communication made to Melbourne.

"Huskisson died September, 1830. At the end of September I received a letter from Lord Clive, dated from Powis Castle, saying he had been requested by the Duke of Wellington to propose to me to return to the Cabinet, and that he (Lord Clive) was coming purposely to speak to me on the subject, and would come either to Broadlands or London, according to a letter which he begged me to write to him to Salisbury.

"I was just starting for London when I received this letter, and appointed Clive to meet me in Stanhope Street, but said that in no case could I join the duke's government singly. Clive called at Apsley House with my letter be-

---

* There is probably some mistake in this.

fore he came to me, and was desired by the duke to ask who were my friends. I said the friends with whom I was politically acting were Melbourne and Grant; but that, to say the truth, I should be unwilling, and I believed they would be so too, to join the duke unless Lansdowne and Grey were to form part of his government. We knew that we differed on many points with those who were then in office, and we could have no security that our opinions would have due weight unless Grey and Lansdowne were in the Cabinet. Clive protested against this as an unreasonable demand, amounting to a surrender on the part of the duke; but said that there would be no objection to Melbourne and Grant, and that Goderich was understood to be a friend of mine, and would be taken in also if we liked. I said I had not lately had any political communication with Goderich, and could not by any means consider him as an equivalent for Grey and Lansdowne.

"To cut the matter short, and to avoid further communications, I set off immediately for Paris, to spend the fortnight previous to the meeting of Parliament.

"A few days after my return from Paris I got a note from the duke, asking me to step to him at Apsley House. I went immediately.

"He said he wished to speak to me on the subject on which Lord Clive had seen me—that he had understood that I had talked about friends, and he wished to know who were my friends.

"I said, as before, Melbourne and Grant, but that even with them I should be disinclined to enter unless his Cabinet was to be reconstructed.

"He said that he thought that for Melbourne and Grant he could find room, but that it was not so easy to get people out of a Cabinet as to put them in; and as to a larger change of his Cabinet, that did not enter into his intentions, and would be attended with too many difficulties.

"I said on leaving him—which I did at the end of the six minutes which our interview occupied—that what I had intended to say was, that I was flattered by his proposal, and was obliged to him for it, but that it would not suit me to join him unless he meant to reconstruct his administration, and that I purposely abstained from mentioning the names of any persons whom I might have in view in saying so.

"Croker called on me a few days afterward, to try to persuade me to reconsider the matter. After talking for some time, he said, 'Well, I will bring the question to a point. Are you resolved, or are you not, to vote for Parliamentary Reform?' I said, 'I am.' 'Well, then,' said he, 'there is no use in talking to you any more on this subject. You and I, I am grieved to see, will never sit again on the same bench together.'

"Melbourne, the two Grants, Binning, Littleton, Graham, Warrender, Denison, and one or two others, had met at my house a few days before, to consider what we should do on the motion that Brougham was to make in favor of Parliamentary Reform, and I and the Grants and Littleton had quite determined to vote for it.

"As soon as Lord Grey was commissioned to form a government, he sent for me."

The total failure of this negotiation turned, as it would appear, on Lord Palmerston's declaration that he should vote for reform in Parliament.

It was not, of course, known what reform, but the declaration was sufficient to show that the colors of the Canningites were changed with the times. They came into power with the Whigs, and were confounded with them ever after.

I add but one short letter, written after entering the Foreign Office, and which characteristically manifests the situation of a man entering for the first time that laborious department.

To Laurence Sulivan, Esq., War Office.

"STANHOPE STREET, Dec. 22, 1830.

"MY DEAR SULIVAN,—

"I send you the note you wish for; I have been ever since my appointment like a man who has plumped into a mill-race, scarcely able by all his kicking and plunging to keep his head above water.

"Yours affectionately,

"PALMERSTON."

In closing here the first volume of this biography, it may not be amiss to remark that my main endeavor throughout it has been to bring the man whom I undertook to describe before the reader.

In the next I shall have to speak of the statesman who exercised for so many years an important influence on public events, and whose life then becomes almost a European history. I shall thus be led into a fuller treatment of European affairs; and it so happens—a fact not without its peculiar interest at this time—that the first of those affairs is the creation of that prosperous little kingdom, the independence and neutrality of which we have lately manifested our determination to defend.

APPENDIX.

AUTOBIOGRAPHICAL SKETCH ENTIRE, AS GIVEN TO ME.—H. L. B.

I LEFT Harrow at sixteen, and went for three years to Edinburgh. I lived with Dugald Stewart, and attended the lectures at the University. In those three years I laid the foundation of whatever useful knowledge and habits of mind I possess.

In 1803 I went to St. John's, Cambridge. I had gone further at Edinburgh in all the branches of study pursued at Cambridge than the course then followed at Cambridge extended during the first two years of attendance. But the Edinburgh system consisted in lectures without examination; at Cambridge there was a half-yearly examination. It became necessary to learn more accurately at Cambridge what one had learned generally at Edinburgh. The knowledge thus acquired of details at Cambridge was worth nothing, because it evaporated soon after the examinations were over. The habit of mind acquired by preparing for these examinations is highly useful.

Dr. Outram, my private tutor at Cambridge, more than once observed to me that, as I had always been in the first class at college examinations, and had been commended for the general regularity of my conduct, it would not be amiss to turn my thoughts to standing for the University whenever a vacancy might happen.

My father died in April, 1802, and I lost my mother in January, 1805. The last misfortune delayed a few months the taking of my degree as master of arts, which it was usual at that time for noblemen to take as an honor, conferred without examination, at the end of two years after admission.

In January, 1806, Mr. Pitt died, and the University had to choose a new member, as well as the king a new minister. I was just of age, and had not yet taken my degree, nevertheless I was advised by my friends at St. John's to stand: the other candidates were Lord Althorp and Lord Henry Petty. I was supported by my own college, and by the exertions of the friends of my family; but the Pitt party in the University was broken up. Most men thought that the new government would for many years have the disposal of the patronage as well as the command of the power of the country; and I stood at the poll where a young man circumstanced as I was could alone expect to stand; that is to say, last, and by a large interval the last of the three.* It was an honor, however, to have been supported at all, and I was well satisfied with my fight.

I continued to reside at Cambridge a few weeks, and then came to London. I tried to get into Parliament; but no opening presented itself.

In November, 1806, Parliament having been dissolved, a general election took place. Lord Fitz-Harris and I stood for Horsham. The borough was burgage-tenure, and the right of voting disputed. There was a double return; each party petitioned, and the committee seated our opponents. Fitz-Harris and I paid about £1500 each for the pleasure of sitting under the gallery for a week in our capacity of petitioners. We thought ourselves unlucky in being unseated; but in a short time came the change of government, and the dissolution in May, 1807, and we rejoiced in our good fortune in not having paid £5000 for a three-months' seat.

I was at Broadlands at Easter, 1807, when, on 1st April, I received a letter from Lord Malmesbury, desiring me to come to town immediately, as he had found me a seat, if not in Parliament, at least at the Admiralty. The Duke of Portland had been appointed First Lord of the Treasury. He was an old and intimate friend of Lord Malmesbury, who had been one of my

---

* Petty	331
Althorp	145
Palmerston . . .	128

guardians, Lord Chichester being the other. Lord Malmesbury had obtained from the duke that I should be one of the Junior Lords of the Admiralty.

When Parliament was dissolved I stood again for Cambridge; and, having entered the lists when nothing could be hoped for but an honorable defeat, I had established a kind of right to support from the government and its friends in preference to any other ministerial candidate. It was voted, however, by the government, that one candidate against two would have no chance; and Sir Vicary Gibbs was sent down to assist me against Lord Euston and Lord Henry Petty.

I soon found that my colleague was almost as dangerous as my opponents, and that every supporter of the government who had but one vote to give was requested to give it to Gibbs. Our committees canvassed separately, and there was no coalition; but, the night before the polling began, Gibbs and myself and the chairmen of our committees met to go over our returns. It appeared doubtful from the books which was the strongest, and there was no sufficient evidence to show which ought to give up in order to bring in the other; for Lord Euston was known to be stronger than either, and the only question was whether one of us could beat Lord Henry Petty. We therefore agreed to coalesce, and that each should give to the other the second votes of all his disposable plumpers.

Toward the end of the polling Sir Vicary Gibbs came up to me in the Senate House and said that my friends were not acting up to our agreement, and were going to plump for me. I said I would immediately see that this was not done. I went and placed myself at the bar through which the voters went up to poll, that I might beg each man as he went to vote for Gibbs as well as for me.

Dr. Outram, my tutor, was standing there. He urged me to do no such thing, and to let my friends do as they chose. He said that they wanted to bring me in, and not Gibbs; that the votes had been counted by people in the gallery, posted for that purpose; that Euston was far ahead, and Gibbs was running me hard; that my committee and a few more stanch friends had reserved their votes, and if they plumped for me I should certainly come in, but if they split for Gibbs I should be thrown out; that they were no parties to the agreement of the night before, and were not to be bound by it. I said this would not do; I was bound in honor. Gibbs's friends had, I believed, given me their second votes; but be that as it might, and be the result what it might, I must insist upon it, if they had the slightest regard for me, that they would, every man of them, give a second vote to Gibbs. They consented, though with much ill humor and grumbling, and Gibbs beat me by four votes. It turned out that I had no reason to complain of want of good faith by Gibbs, as he had only seven plumpers, while I had twelve.

Soon after this I came into Parliament for Newtown, in the Isle of Wight, a borough of Sir Leonard Holmes'. One condition required was that I should never, even for the election, set foot in the place; so jealous was the patron lest any attempt should be made to get a new interest in the borough.

In September of this year Copenhagen was taken, and the Danish fleet carried off.

The Danish expedition was the great subject of debate at the beginning of the session in 1808. Papers relating to it were laid before Parliament. At that time lay Lords of the Admiralty had nothing to do but to sign their names. I had time therefore to study the Copenhagen papers, and put together a speech, upon which I received much praise and many compliments.

Robert Milnes, better known as "Orator Milnes," had made a splendid speech on the first night of the discussion. He chose to make a second speech on a following night, to show that he was as good in reply as on preparation. His speech was a bad one, and mine was luckily thought better than his bad one.

In October, 1809, the Duke of Portland died; and the government having broken up in consequence of that event, and of the duel between Mr. Canning and Lord Castlereagh, Mr. Perceval was made Prime Minister. I was at that time at Broadlands, and received a letter from Perceval, desiring me to come to town immediately, as he had a proposal to make to me which he thought would be agreeable. I came to town immediately, and called on him next day, when he offered me the Chancellorship of the Exchequer. He said he had proposed it to Milnes, who had declined it, and he wished me to take it. I was a good deal surprised at so unexpected an offer, and begged a little time to think of it and to consult my friends. Perceval said that if I declined to be Chancellor of the Exchequer, he should perhaps be able to offer me the War Office; but he felt bound to offer it first to Milnes. I wrote to Lord Malmesbury, then at Park Place, and consulted with Lord Mulgrave, then First Lord of the Admiralty. The result was that I declined the Exchequer, as too hazardous an attempt for so young and inexperienced a man, and accepted the office of Secretary at War, which Milnes had declined. Perceval had offered me a seat in the Cabinet with the Exchequer, but said that such a seat would not go with the War Office.

In 1812 Wellesley Pole resigned the office of Chief Secretary for Ireland, and Lord Castlereagh offered me that office. It was more important, more active, and more likely to lead to distinction than the office of Secretary at War which I held; but particular circumstances and considerations led me to decline it at once, and without the least hesitation. It was then offered to Peel, who was Under-Secretary of State, and he accepted it.

Some years afterward, when Peel was Secretary for the Home Department, he asked me, by Lord Liverpool's desire, whether I should like to go to one of the minor East Indian presidencies, then about to become vacant, with the understanding that I should be Governor-General of India upon the next vacancy. I thanked him, but declined. The proposal was afterward renewed to me by Lord Liverpool, when the office of Governor-General actually became vacant, but I said I had no fancy for such latitudes.

Charles Long, upon some changes of administration that were taking place, asked me from Lord Liverpool whether I should like a peerage and the Post-Office. I said I preferred remaining in the House of Commons.

From the death of Perceval, in 1812, the Catholic question disunited the government. From that time it became impossible to form an anti-Catholic administration, because both Canning and Castlereagh were for Emancipation, as were all the Whigs; and against such opponents no government could be formed in the House of Commons. It was therefore determined that it should be an open question, on which every man should vote as he chose.

The Duke of York, the chief leader of the anti-Catholics, was generally expected to outlive his elder brother; and it is hard to say to what degree some ambitious men may have been led to espouse his side of the question, in expectation of becoming the ministers of Frederick the First. In 1811, upon the death of the late Duke of Grafton, Lord Euston made a vacancy at Cambridge, and I stood against Smyth, his nephew, and was elected.

From 1812 downward I constantly voted for Catholic Emancipation, and was re-elected in 1812, 1818, and 1820, at the general elections in those years, with the full knowledge on the part of the University as to what my opinions on that subject were.

Smyth, though beat by me in 1811, had afterward been elected on the death of Gibbs; and on the death of Smyth, in 1822, William Bankes was elected.

In November, 1825, it being generally understood that Parliament would be dissolved in the next summer, Sir J. Copley, then Attorney-General, wrote to me to say that he was going to begin to canvass the University, with a view of turning out Bankes; and shortly afterward Goulburn, who was Chief Secretary for Ireland, announced himself as a fourth candidate. Bankes, Copley, and Goulburn were all anti-Catholic; I was the only one of the four who voted for Emancipation. The canvass lasted from the end of November, 1825, till the dissolution in June, 1826, and a most laborious task for myself and my friends it became.

It was soon manifest that the object of certain parties was to eject me as well as Bankes; and the active influence of the anti-Catholic members of the government was exerted in favor of Copley and Goulburn, and therefore, as there were but two to be returned, against me.

The Church, the Treasury, and the Army were in anti-Catholic hands; and though the Duke of Wellington and Peel condemned the cabal, and Liverpool himself did not join in it, yet Eldon, Bathurst, the Duke of York, the Secretaries to the Treasury, and many others, did all they could against me. I stood upon my personal interest at Cambridge, and threw myself on my political opponents, the Whigs, for support against my political friends, the Tories. The support which I asked upon the ground of our accordance upon Catholic Emancipation was handsomely granted, and it enabled me to triumph. Copley, indeed, headed the poll; but I beat Bankes by 122, and Goulburn by 192.

I had complained to Lord Liverpool, the Duke of Wellington, and Canning of my being thus attacked, in violation of the understanding upon which the government was formed, and by which the Catholic question was to be an open one, and not a ground for the exclusion of any individual; and I told Lord Liverpool that if I was beat I should quit the government. This was the first decided step toward a breach between me and the Tories, and they were the aggressors.

In February, 1827, Lord Liverpool was taken ill; and in April of that year Mr. Canning was declared minister, and commanded to form a government. Upon this the Tories retired in a body. Lord Eldon, the Duke of Wellington, Peel, Lord Bathurst, Lord Westmoreland, Lord Melville, Lord Bexley (who, however, retracted), Wallace, Beckett, Wetherell, Duke of Dorset, Duke of Montrose, Lord Londonderry, all sent in their resignations, leaving Canning "alone in his glory"

Canning had, some little time before, desired me not to leave town for Easter without letting him know; and upon this break-up he sent for me to offer me a seat in the Cabinet and the office of Chancellor of the Exchequer. He said he wished to keep the Foreign Office as Prime Minister, instead of being First Lord of the Treasury; but he found that there were official attributes attached to the First Lord of the Treasury which rendered it necessary that the Prime Minister should be First Lord; that he wished, however, to have a separate Chancellor of the Exchequer, to relieve him both in the Treasury Office and in the House of Commons, and to leave him more leisure for general matters, and should be glad to have my assistance.

I accepted both offers.

Canning gave a great dinner at his house at the Foreign Office just before the recess; and after dinner he proposed to me to take immediately the office of Chancellor of the Exchequer, in order that I might be re-elected during the holidays, and to be ready to start again as soon as the House met. Croker, who had *not* resigned, but who remained in office, and who was standing by, artfully suggested that there was going to be a contest at Cambridge between Goulburn and Bankes for the seat vacated by Copley—made Chancellor and created Lord Lyndhurst—and strongly advised me to wait, in order that I might not incur the danger of being mixed up with that contest; adding that, by the usual courtesy of the University, I should have no contest if I vacated upon changing office, but might be in danger if I ran my head into a battle begun by other people.

Canning said that I must take the Exchequer *then*, or else wait till the end of the session, as it would not be convenient that I should be out of Parliament for a fortnight during the session. It was then agreed that I should remain Secretary at War till the end of the session, and then go to the Exchequer.

In the mean while intrigues were set on foot. George IV., who personally hated me, did not fancy me as Chancellor of the Exchequer. He wanted to have Herries in that office. There were questions coming on about palaces and crown lands which the king was very anxious about; and he wished either to have a creature of his own at the Exchequer, or to have the office of Chancellor of the Exchequer held by the First Lord, whose numerous occupations would compel him to leave details very much to George Harrison, the Secretary, and to Herries, Auditor of the Civil List.

Toward the end, or rather about the middle, of the session, Canning sent for me, and, evidently much embarrassed, said that he wished to speak to me about the Chancellorship of the Exchequer. That it had been arranged that I was to have it, and he had at that time much wished that I should; but that since then it had been strongly pressed upon him by all the financial department that it was extremely important that the First Lord should also be Chancellor of the Exchequer; and that the union of the two offices in the person of the Prime Minister, when that minister was in the House of Commons, was attended with great official convenience; and the result, he said, was that he felt himself unable to carry our intended arrangement into effect.

Having finished his statement, he walked to the other end of the room, like a man who wishes to hide from another the emotions of embarrassment which for a moment were shown upon the countenance. I was a little surprised, and saw that there was something behind which he did not choose to tell. I said that my only wish was to be useful to his government, and that I had no selfish objects in view; that if he thought it better for the public service that I should remain as I was, I was perfectly contented to do so; that, moreover, as the office of Commander-in-Chief had been vacant since the death of the Duke of York in January, and as I was administering the discipline and patronage of the army by virtue of my office of Secretary at War, I might well, for the present at least, be satisfied with the importance of my functions.

Canning seemed much relieved by the manner in which I took his communication, admitted the justness of my last remark, and said that he would take care that when my double functions ceased, by the appointment of a Commander-in-Chief, some arrangement should be made that would be satisfactory to me. I told him that I thought there ought to be a military man as Commander-in-Chief; but that he should well consider who that man should be, as he had the power of doing much mischief, military and political, as well as good.

Some weeks after this, Canning sent for me again, to say he had a proposition to make to me, which he should not himself have thought of, but that the king had said he knew, and was sure, that it was just the very thing I should like; and that was to go as Governor to Jamaica. I laughed very heartily, and assured Canning I preferred England and the War Office to Jamaica and the negroes. But I laughed so heartily that I observed Canning looked quite put out, and I was obliged to grow serious again.

Not long afterward he again sent for me, and said he had an offer to make which might be more worth my consideration, and in making which he had only one difficulty, and that was lest I should think he wanted to get rid of me, which he could very sincerely assure me was far from being the case. The offer was the Governor-Generalship of India. I thanked him very kindly for his offer, assured him I was not insensible to the splendor of the post which he was now proposing; that I felt what means it afforded for increasing one's fortune, for gratifying one's love of power, for affording scope for doing good upon a magnificent theater of action; but my ambition was satisfied with my position at home. I happened not to have a family for whom I should be desirous of providing, and my health would not stand the climate of India. I had already, I said, declined the office when offered me by Lord Liverpool at a time when I was not in the Cabinet, and the same motives which influenced me then still operated now.

On Canning's death Goderich was appointed First Lord of the Treasury, and he immediately requested me to be his Chancellor of the Exchequer. I accepted. On the day of Canning's funeral we assembled, in a darkened room in Downing Street, previously to proceeding to the Abbey. Goderich, as he stood next me, whispered that a difficulty had arisen about the Chancellorship of the Exchequer, and that the king insisted upon its being given to Herries, for whom (if my memory does not deceive me) he said the king had wanted it in Canning's time. I said that we were old friends, and I never would allow any claim of mine, or promise made to me, to embarrass him in his dealings with the king; and that I fully released him from his own spontaneous offer if my doing so would facilitate his arrangements. I said I had luckily mentioned his offer to nobody, and therefore my honor was not committed in any way. He said this was very kind and handsome on my part, but he should do his best to adhere to the first arrangement.

Herries, on being spoken to by Goderich, affected to decline, pleaded bad health, and begged to be excused. The king, between whom and Herries Goderich was made to suppose himself the only channel of communication, said he would not give up the chance of having so able a man as Herries without at least seeing and talking to him.

We had, on the 12th of August, a council at Windsor Castle. Herries was in attendance. When he arrived he told Goderich he still declined. Goderich went into the king's closet to report this unfavorable decision. Herries, in the mean while, *jouait la victime.* The king insisted upon seeing Herries. Herries was too loyal a subject to refuse to obey the summons. He entered the closet, remained half an hour, and came out Chancellor of the Exchequer,—but the king's Chancellor of the Exchequer, and not Goderich's. Goderich then asked the king if he would not see me, to explain the matter to me. I went in, and George assured me how much esteem and regard he felt for me, and how happy he should have been to have had my services at the Exchequer if he had not had the good fortune of obtaining those of Mr. Herries, unquestionably the fittest man in England for the office. I bowed, entirely acquiesced, and thanked his Majesty for the gracious and flattering manner in which he had spoken to me. Huskisson blamed me for not having stood out: he said, if I had insisted upon the fulfillment of Goderich's promise, that promise would not have been retracted, especially as it was spontaneously made, and Herries would not have been thrown like a live shell into the Cabinet to explode and blow us all up.

At the appointed time he did explode. He picked a quarrel with Huskisson, who, having been abroad at Canning's death, returned soon afterward and took the Colonial Office. Goderich had not energy of mind enough to determine in favor of one or the other, though the question was literally nothing more than who should be proposed as chairman of a finance committee to be appointed next session. Instead of going to the king, and saying, "Sire, Mr. Huskisson and Mr. Herries have differed, and cannot serve together, and therefore I propose to you to appoint A B instead of one or the other," Goderich stated the quarrel, the impossibility of the two going on as colleagues, and gave the king to understand that he had no advice to give, and did not know what to do. But George knew very well what he had to do: he bid Goderich go home and take care of himself, and keep himself quiet; and he immediately sent for the Duke of Wellington to form a government.

One of the first acts of Goderich's administration had been to ask the Duke of Wellington to be Commander-in-Chief—Lord Anglesey had been sent to make the offer. He traveled without stopping, arrived at some country house in the west, where the duke was staying, about three in the morning; found the duke in full uniform just come home from a fancy ball; obtained his immediate acceptance, and arrived with it at Windsor, while we were sitting in council on the memorable day in August, at which Lord William Bentinck also was present, to be sworn in Governor-General of India. Lord Anglesey said to us, "Well, gentlemen, I have done what you sent me to do. I have brought you the Duke of Wellington's acceptance as Commander-in-Chief, and, by God, mark my words, as sure as you are alive, he will trip up all your heels before six months are over your heads."

Before the six months were well over the duke was in, and our heels were up; but what share he had in that I cannot say. The king was the great plotter, and Holmes and Planta worked upon Goderich, and persuaded him he could never overcome the difficulties he would have to encounter.

When the duke came in he sent for Huskisson to Apsley House, as head of the Canning party, and asked him to join his government. The inducements held out were these:—The Catholic question to be as before an open question, and to have, therefore, the benefit of the influence belonging to a portion of the Cabinet being in its favor. The Greek Treaty to be faithfully executed, and Dudley to be left as Foreign Secretary to watch over its execution. Huskisson's principles of trade to be acted upon, and Charles Grant to be left at the Board of Trade as a pledge and security on that point. Huskisson, Grant, Dudley, and myself to have seats in the Cabinet; Lamb to remain as Irish Secretary, as a guarantee that an impartial system would be pursued toward the Catholics. Eldon and Westmoreland to be excluded from the Cabinet, they being the representatives of the most illiberal opinions. Dudley, Lamb, Binning, Grant, and myself met at Huskisson's house in Somerset Place, which he still occupied, he being still very unwell, in order to take these proposals into consideration. We discussed the matter fully with reference both to the personal question between Herries and Huskisson, and to the public interests and political questions involved; and our determination was that the offer ought to be accepted. We did accept it, not as individuals, but as a party representing the principles and consisting of the friends of Mr. Canning.

We joined the new government in January. We left it in May. The causes which led to our retirement, and the manner in which that retirement took place, are well known. We joined as a party; as a party we retired, The only one who hesitated was Dudley; and he would willingly have given £6000 a year out of his own pocket, instead of receiving that sum from the public, for the pleasure of continuing to be Secretary for Foreign Affairs.

The evening that Huskisson's correspondence with the duke was brought to a close, and that his resignation was laid before the king, Dudley and I had dined with Sir Thomas Farquhar; we went down to Huskisson, who was then living at the Foreign Office, and met Lamb there.

After learning the result of the correspondence, we walked away. As soon as we had left the door, arm in arm, and Dudley in the middle, Dudley said, "Well, Huskisson is out, and now that we are all alone in the street, and nobody to hear us but the sentry, let me ask what other people mean to do." "I go out, for one," said I. "And I for another," said Lamb. Dudley was embarrassed, talked of the difficulty of deciding, the pain of separating himself from so great a man as the duke, etc.; but everybody told him he ought to go out, and at last out he went.

In 1829 I supported the government on the Catholic question, and opposed them on the East Retford Bill, on which he had gone out.

In 1830, as in 1829, I opposed them on foreign policy.

In July, 1830, an overture was made to Melbourne from the duke to join the government, and he was given to understand that no objection would be made to Grant and myself. His answer was, that he could not join without Huskisson and Lord Grey. The duke's reply was, that he might perhaps consent to take back Huskisson, but that he could not act with Lord Grey, who had spoken of him in such unmeasured terms both in Parliament and in private. We learnt a short time afterwards, from pretty good authority, that the duke had made a proposal to Grey, which had been declined, but a short time before the communication made to Melbourne.

Huskisson died in September, 1830, at a place near Liverpool

At the end of September I received a letter from Lord Clive, dated from Powis Castle, saying he had been requested by the Duke of Wellington to propose to me to return to the Cabinet, and that he (Lord Clive) was coming purposely to speak to me on the subject, and would come either to Broadlands or London, according to a letter which he begged me to write to him to Salisbury. I was just starting for London when I received his letter, and appointed him to meet me in Stanhope Street, but said that in no case would I join the duke's government singly.

Clive called at Apsley House with my letter before he came to me, and was desired by the duke to ask who I considered my friends. I said the friends with whom I was politically acting were Melbourne and Grant; but that, to say the truth, I should be unwilling, and I believed they would be so too, to join the duke unless Lansdowne and Grey were to form part of his government. We knew that we differed on many points with those who were then in office, and we could have no security that our opinions could have due weight and consideration unless Grey and Lansdowne were in the Cabinet. Clive protested against this as an unreasonable demand, amounting to a surrender on the part of the duke, but said that there would be no objection to Melbourne and Grant, and that Goderich was understood to be a friend of mine, and would be taken in also if we liked.

I said I had not lately had any political communication with Goderich, and could not by any means consider him as an equivalent for Grey and Lansdowne.

To cut the matter short, and to avoid further communications, I set off immediately for Paris, to spend there the fortnight previous to the meeting of Parliament. A few days after my return from Paris I got in the morning a note from the duke, asking me to step to him at Apsley House. I went immediately. He said he wished to speak to me on the subject on which Lord Clive had communicated. That I had talked about friends, and he wished to know who were my friends. I said, as before, Melbourne and Grant, but that even with them I should be disinclined to enter unless his Cabinet was to be reconstructed. He said that he thought that for them he could find room, but that it was not as easy to get people out of a Cabinet as to put them in, but that as to a larger change of his Cabinet, that did not enter into his intentions, and would be attended with too many difficulties. I said on leaving him—which I did at the end of the six minutes which our interview occupied—that what I had intended to say was, that I was flattered by his proposal, and was obliged to him for it, but that it would not suit me to join him unless he meant to reconstruct his administration, and that I purposely abstained from mentioning the names of any persons whom I might have in view in saying so.

Croker called on me a few days afterward to try to persuade me to reconsider the matter. After talking some time, he said, "Well, I will bring the matter to a point. Are you resolved, or are you not, to vote for Parliamentary Reform?" I said, "I am." "Well, then," said he, "there is no use in talking to you any more on this subject. You and I, I am grieved to see, shall never again sit on the same bench together."

Melbourne, the two Grants, Binning, Littleton, Graham, Warrender, Denison, and one or two others, had met at my house a few days before to consider what we should do on the motion which Brougham was to make in favor of Parliamentary Reform, and I and the Grants and Littleton had quite determined to vote for it.

As soon as Lord Grey was commissioned by the king to form an administration he sent for me.

MEMORANDUM BY THE LATE LORD PALMERSTON WHEN SECRETARY AT WAR.

War Office, 16th August, 1811.

SIR DAVID DUNDAS, having submitted to H. R. H. the Prince Regent certain papers and memoranda relative to discussions which have taken place between him and Lord Palmerston, Lord Palmerston humbly avails himself of the permission given him, to state on his part such circumstances as he may think necessary to explain and justify his conduct.

Sir D. Dundas states that for a considerable time past the Secretary at War has assumed powers and exercised an authority which do not of right belong to his office, derogatory to the dignity of the Commander-in-Chief, and subversive of the discipline of the army. The immediate ground and foundation of this charge are three circumstances which have occurred since the appointment of Lord Palmerston as Secretary at War; and it might, therefore, perhaps appear sufficient for Lord Palmerston to give that explanation of these three cases which, he trusts, would exculpate him from any blame on those points; but as Sir D. Dundas's memorandum contains some general positions respecting the relations of the Commander-in-Chief and Secretary at War, it will be necessary in the first instance to give a short summary of the history and progress of the office of the Secretary at War, and a view of the nature and extent of the duties which that officer has heretofore discharged.

Sir D. Dundas seems to imagine that the Secretary at War is, like the Adjutant and Quartermaster-General, subordinate to and dependent upon the Commander-in-Chief, and he founds this idea chiefly upon the wording of the commission of the Secretary at War,* which directs him "to observe and follow such orders and instructions as you shall receive from Us or the General of Our forces, according to the discipline of war." It is, however, conceived that there will be no difficulty in proving that, in the first place, "the General of Our forces" does not mean a Commander-in-Chief, but a Captain-General; and that in point of practice, in matters of finance, and as a civil servant of the Crown, the Secretary at War never has been in the habit of receiving orders and commands from any person but the king himself.

Lord Palmerston has, with this object, examined with great care the records of the War Office from the earliest times, particularly directing his attention to those periods when there existed Captains-General, or Commanders-in-Chief; the substance of the information which he has collected will be stated in this memorandum; but he has added, as an appendix, more particular

---

* See 6 and 7 W. and M., c. 8, sec. 5, which refers to "the Secretary of the Commander-in-Chief of the Army."

notes, taken from the perusal of upwards of fifty folio volumes of records of the office.

Although much stress cannot be laid upon precedents previous to the revolution in 1688, yet it appears that even as early as the reign of Charles II. the civil and financial business of the army was understood to be distinguished from that which was purely military; and we find accordingly that warrants and orders connected with the former were countersigned and issued by one of the Secretaries of State. There are in the War Office numerous documents of this sort, signed by the king himself, and countersigned by Arlington, Clifford, Coventry, Williamson, and Sunderland; one of the most remarkable of which is a warrant* ordering that "no military establishment, or alterations thereof, shall be presented for Our signature without having been previously approved by Our Lord High Treasurer, and one of Our Secretaries of State, to whom We have referred the care and consideration thereof:" and this warrant, which makes no mention either of the Captain-General or Commander-in-Chief, has been annually renewed down to the present time.

The first Secretary at War, or, as he was at that time indiscriminately called, Secretary to the Forces, was Mr. Locke, who is supposed to have been detached from the office of the Secretary of State, with a view of relieving that officer from a part of his labors. Mr. Locke's commission cannot be found, but it seems that he did not at first countersign the king's warrants, which still for some time bore the signature of the Secretary of State.

But by a warrant† addressed to the Duke of Monmouth, who was Commander-in-Chief at the time, the king directed that "Whereas We continue to issue from Ourself some kinds of Warrants and Military Orders which did belong to the office of Our late General, and which he was wont to despatch and sign, We being desirous to distinguish such Warrants and Orders from other affairs of Our Crown, passing Our Signet and Sign Manual, have thought fit, and it is Our will and pleasure that all such kinds of Warrants and Orders as formerly issued from George

* 21st January, 1669.

† 27th September, 1676.

Duke of Albemarle, Our late General deceased (in regard of that office), and which we continue to issue from Ourself, shall pass Our Sign Manual only, and shall be countersigned by the Secretary to Our forces, as by Our command."

And accordingly from that period downward there is no instance of any warrant or order, signed by the king, being countersigned by any military officer, but always by the Secretary at War, a Secretary of State, or the Lords of the Treasury.

In 1679,* the Duke of Monmouth, then Commander-in-Chief, was, by a warrant addressed to the Attorney-General, appointed Captain-General, with powers of a very ample and extraordinary nature, which have never been granted since.

He was authorized to arm, muster, apportion, quarter, and pay the army; to disperse and pardon rebels; and all officers, soldiers, and persons whatsoever were required to be obedient and assisting to him.

On the 18th August, 1683, and, as it should seem, during the continuance of this commission, Mr. Blathwayte was appointed to succeed Mr. Locke as Secretary at War. The entry of Mr. Blathwayte's commission has been found, and it is couched very nearly in the same words as that of the present Secretary at War, the only material difference being the statement in the beginning of Mr. Blathwayte's of the resignation of his predecessor, Mr. Locke. Mr. Blathwayte, therefore, as far as the wording of his commission went, was equally bound to obey the commands of the Captain-General.

It appears, however, that Mr. Blathwayte communicated and transacted his business with the king before and after the revolution, in the same manner as the Secretaries of State.

He took and signified the pleasure of James II. upon all sorts of military subjects, and as an instance of the manner in which he conceived himself attached to the person of the king, he deemed it necessary to ask specially his permission to go for a month into the country,† and in November, 1688, he attended him to Salisbury with his army.

Mr. Blathwayte seems indeed to have regulated almost all the

---

* 3d June. † 20th Jan. 1687.

affairs of the army, as well with regard to discipline as finance, and down to the conclusion of the reign of James II. he issued orders of almost every description, for paying, mustering, quartering, marching, raising, and disbanding troops, and also upon various points of discipline, such as the attendance, duty, and comparative rank of officers and regiments.

Upon the accession of William III., Mr. Blathwayte was continued in office, and transacted business with him in the same manner as with James II.

In the year 1690, the Earl of Marlborough was made Commander-in-Chief, and was afterward succeeded by the Dukes of Leinster* and Schonberg,† the latter of whom continued in office till the beginning of 1696.

In 1690 we find the Treasury referring to Mr. Blathwayte for his opinion, and report all claims and applications made to them connected with military finance.

In 1692, Mr. Blathwayte accompanied the king when he took the command of his army in Flanders, and acted during that and the subsequent campaigns as Military Secretary to the king. He issued in his name and by his command orders and regulations of every description to the army, signed proclamations, safeguards, and passes to persons, and protections to towns and villages, and gave orders even to the naval force forming part of the armament.

During the absence of Mr. Blathwayte upon the Continent, Mr. George Clarke, the Judge-Advocate-General, was appointed with a temporary commission and inferior powers to act as Secretary at War at home,‡ and it is remarkable that by his commission he is required "to follow such orders and instructions as you may receive from Us, the General of Our forces, or the Commander-in-Chief of Our said forces." The insertion of these last words in this temporary commission marks in the strongest possible manner that the General mentioned in Mr. Blathwayte's commission was not a Commander-in-Chief, and that the permanent Secretary at War was not liable to the authority of such an officer.

* 1691. † 1694. ‡ 7th March, 1692.

Mr. Clarke, however, seems to have exercised very nearly the same powers, and to have used them in the same manner, as Mr. Blathwayte, and his commission does not appear to have rendered him in practice more dependent upon and subordinate to the Commander-in-Chief than Mr. Blathwayte himself had been to the Captain-General.

Accordingly we find that Mr. Clarke constantly signified the pleasure of the queen regent, and afterward of the Lords Justices, and in some cases even that of the king, upon communication with him during his absence.

The most remarkable instances of this sort are those in which he signed a Proclamation for pardoning deserters, granted leave of absence to officers, issued a circular to the army, by the king's command, about levy money, signed orders for apprehending deserters and enlisting debtors; and, what is very remarkable, an order from the Lords Justices* to the Duke of Schonberg, the Commander-in-Chief, directing him to reprimand certain officers for neglecting to fill up their regiments and to have them properly clothed and armed.

Mr. Clarke's commission was only valid during the absence of the king, and when William used to return to England in the winter months, Mr. Blathwayte came with him, and resumed the functions of his office, being again succeeded by Mr. Clarke whenever the king took the field in the summer.

During these periods of temporary resumption, Mr. Blathwayte continued to act nearly in the same manner as he had before done, and issued all kinds of orders to the army. He called for states and returns of effectives, granted leaves of absence, and ordered officers to repair to their posts, pardoned deserters, disposed of prisoners of war, ordered colonels to account with their regiments, directed embarkations, and the raising and disbanding of regiments.

In 1695† an expedition was sent to the Straits of Gibraltar, and Mr. Blathwayte issued its orders and instructions upon embarkation. The most remarkable points of these instructions are that the land officers were to command their men on shipboard,

* 6th Sept. 1695. † 7th March.

as well as on shore; that the commanding officer was empowered to hold courts-martial; and that the Spaniards, with whom the expedition was destined to co-operate, were to have precedency in their own dominions.

At the end of this year Mr. Blathwayte issued by order of the king a general code of regulations for the dress and arming of the foot, and regulated in many instances the succession and promotion of officers.

In 1702,* Mr. Blathwayte being still Secretary at War, the Duke of Marlborough was appointed Captain-General, and continued to hold that commission till the end of the year 1711, when he was succeeded by the Duke of Ormond.

This, therefore, is a period most particularly in point for the purposes of the present inquiry, as there existed the General, who is mentioned in the commission of the Secretary at War.

But Mr. Blathwayte, from this period till his resignation in 1704, appears to have acted in the same independent manner as before, and to have constantly communicated with and signified the pleasure of the queen.

He gave numerous orders by the queen's command for the embarkation of troops and horses for Portugal; for the disposal of recruits; for making detachments from some regiments, and for completing others for service; and, among other things, issued a circular to the army† directing patterns of the clothing of each regiment to be sent to General Churchill to be inspected.

In April, 1704, Mr. St. John was appointed Secretary at War, and one of his first acts was to send to the Transport Board a list which he had received from his predecessor of the forces to be transported to Holland, with orders from the queen that they should be immediately embarked and conveyed to their destination.

During the four years he continued in office, he seems to have acted very much in the same manner as his predecessors, laying the matters of his office before the queen, receiving her pleasure upon them, and communicating it to persons concerned.

He gave orders, by the queen's command, relative to marching,

* March. † 20th January, 1704.

quartering, mustering, pardoning, recruiting, embarking, and the hiring of transports; directed officers to join their corps; appointed escorts for treasure; ordered the invalids to do duty at Kensington, in the absence of the Guards; superseded officers for absence without leave; called upon the Governor of Guernsey to explain his conduct in discharging, without authority, some prisoners of war, and signified to him the queen's pleasure upon his explanation; transmitted to Mr. Secretary Hedges a list of the staff for Lord Peterborough's expedition, as settled by the Committee of Lords; ordered the commanding officer at Lichfield to prohibit mass, and to confine the French prisoners to the distance of one mile from the town; called for a return of effectives of the several regiments under the immediate command of the Duke of Marlborough, Captain-General, as they stood before and after the battle of Blenheim, and for returns from all recruiting parties in England; corresponded with Mr. Secretary Hedges on proposals for raising regiments and relieving troops on foreign stations; signified the queen's pleasure to the Ordnance for the delivery of stores, and countersigned a warrant by the Queen, ordering all commissions to be entered in the office of the Secretary at War, and another strictly prohibiting their sale.

The Duke of Ormond, who succeeded the Duke of Marlborough as Captain-General, held that situation till December, 1719, and was also Commander-in-Chief.

Mr. William Pulteney was made Secretary at War in 1714, and we find that all matters of finance and claims of officers were referred to him by the Treasury and the king; and he reported, among other things, on various claims for half-pay and augmentations of allowances; on applications of officers to be restored after supersession; on a complaint of the inhabitants of Dunkirk of damage done to their town, and of the non-payment of supplies afforded by them; and upon a proposal for new regulating the general rate of subsistence for the army.

Mr. Craggs, who succeeded in 1717, seems to have had the same exclusive control over the finance of the army; and to him all applications touching that subject, made either to the king or the Treasury, were constantly referred; he reported upon all sorts of claims for pay, allowances, clothing, etc.; and in 1718 he summoned a Board of General Officers, and signified to them the queen's pleasure that they should consider and report upon the state of military affairs in the island of Minorca.

Mr. Pringle and Mr. Ireby, who succeeded to the office in 1718 and 1719, seem to have followed in all respects the practice of their predecessors.

From 1720 to 1744 it does not appear from the records of the War Office that there was any Captain-General or Commander-in-Chief; and during that period the whole management and government of the army, both at home and abroad, seem to have devolved upon the Secretary at War.

In 1744,* Lord Stair was appointed Commander-in-Chief, with very ample and extensive powers, the warrant of his appointment being countersigned by Sir William Yonge, then Secretary at War. Lord Stair's commission continued in force till June, 1746; and in the mean time, in 1745,† the king appointed another Commander-in-Chief, Marshal Wade, and a Captain-General, the Duke of Cumberland. The first ceased to hold his commission in December, 1745, but the latter continued Captain-General till October, 1757. There were thus at one time a Captain-General and two Commanders-in-Chief.

This seems to be another period particularly deserving of attention, and the precedents of which bear strongly upon the point at issue between Sir D. Dundas and Lord Palmerston, inasmuch as they prove that a Commander-in-Chief is an officer not only inferior to, but coexistent with, a Captain-General, and the transactions which took place at that time show that in matters of finance at least, and as a civil servant of the Crown, the Secretary at War is independent even of the Captain-General.

The Treasury appear to have referred to the Secretary at War, at this time as much as before, all military financial matters, sometimes to him singly, and at others to him jointly with the Paymaster-General, or the Comptrollers of Army Accounts, but never to have thought that the Captain-General was in any degree entitled to interfere in such matters.

Some very striking instances of this occurred at that time.

---

* 24th February.

† 11th March.

In 1746, Lord Henry Beauclerk and General Huske memorialized the Duke of Cumberland, Captain-General, for compensation for accouterments lost by their regiments at the battle of Fontenoy, praying that his Royal Highness would be pleased to move the king to grant the same. The duke, however, transmitted these memorials to the Treasury, and that Board, instead of granting immediately the compensation asked for, referred the memorials to the Secretary at War, desiring him to consider the same, and report to them a state of the matter therein set forth, with his opinion what was fit to be done therein.

In the same year the army in the North was in want of clothing, but the Captain-General, instead of giving orders himself to have a supply provided, stated the fact to the Secretary at War, and he signified to the agents of the several regiments the king's pleasure that the clothing should immediately be supplied.

In 1753 an estimate of the expense of making certain roads and bridges in the Highlands was laid before the Treasury, but, though the engineer told them that he had submitted his plan and estimate to the Captain-General, who had given it his approbation, the Treasury did not choose to act upon it till they had referred it to the Secretary at War for his report.

These three cases clearly prove that, according to the opinion and practice of government at that time, the Secretary at War was the responsible adviser of the king on matters connected with the finance of the army and military expenditures.

Sir William Yonge, who was appointed in 1735, and continued in office till 1746, exercised the same sort of powers as were vested in his predecessors.

He issued orders for marching, drafting, recruiting, completing, raising, augmenting, and disbanding regiments; discharged men, ordered officers to join their corps, and recruits to be forwarded to their regiments in Flanders; regulated the pay and allowances and forage of general and staff officers serving in Flanders; issued a general order, fixing the bounty to be given to recruits for the Guards; countersigned warrants of appointment to commands; signed a warrant empowering General St. Clair to order money for his hospitals, and sent him instructions for their management; others relative to stoppages from soldiers, assignments of off-reckonings, regulations for the full pay and half pay of corps and officers, and one in particular regulating the honors to be paid by his Majesty's forces to the Master-General of the Ordnance.* He issued circular letters to the army† calling for returns of effectives upon honor; he informed certain colonels that his Majesty was not well pleased that so little progress had been made in recruiting their regiments, notwithstanding former orders, and desired that any officers who might have been negligent might be reported to him, that he might lay the matter before the king; he sent instructions to certain colonels that they might give them out in orders to their regiments; gave leave of absence to officers; signified the king's pleasure that an officer should be pardoned, but dismissed the service; and called for returns periodically of the progress made in recruiting; and in May, 1746, he signified to the duke the king's pleasure that certain regiments were to be reduced, in order that the duke might send officers to re-enlist such of the men as might choose to enter again into the service.

Mr. Henry Fox succeeded Sir William Yonge in May, 1746, with undiminished powers and authority, and continued in office nine years, during the whole of which time, the Duke of Cumberland remaining Captain-General, the practice of the War Office seems to have been uniform and unchanged,— all matters relating to the financial and civil affairs of the army, and many, more apparently connected with its discipline, being conducted by the Secretary at War under the immediate orders of the king.

Lord Barrington was appointed Secretary at War in 1755, and transacted the business of his office in the same manner as his predecessors; was in every respect entirely independent of the Captain-General, and had a separate and complete control over every part of the army.

In 1757, the Duke of Cumberland ceasing to be Captain-General, Lord Ligonier was appointed Commander-in-Chief, and he continued so till the end of the year 1763, beyond which time he cannot be traced in the books of the War Office.

About this time a transaction took place which strongly illustrates the independent and authoritative manner in which, during

---

* 5th October, 1745.

† August and October, 1744.

the existence of a Commander-in-Chief, the Secretary at War was accustomed to act in matters connected with military finance.

In the summer of 1759, some great irregularities having prevailed respecting the delivery of forage to the troops encamped, the Secretary at War, by the king's command, summoned a board of General Officers to inquire into the circumstances, and he laid their report before the king. The result was that double charges to a great amount were discovered, and in June, 1760, Lord Barrington signified the king's pleasure upon the subject.

He informed certain colonels "that the king hoped that the circumstance had arisen from inadvertence in the officers; but as inadvertence in matters of duty is in itself highly culpable, that it was his Majesty's pleasure that they should severely reprimand all the officers of their regiment who had been in any ways concerned in the transaction, and caution them in the strongest manner against a negligence and inattention which might subject them, as in the present instance, to the severest censures of military law, and which would not a second time be passed over with the same lenity by his Majesty." He added also, that the money overcharged for forage was to be paid back to the contractor.

He wrote at the same time letters to other colonels, informing them of what had been done, and adding: "though your regiment and many others were not in any way concerned in this transaction, his Majesty hath thought fit to order that the like caution should be given them, and accordingly I am to signify to you his Majesty's pleasure that you do take this opportunity of recommending to all your officers the strictest fidelity and exactness in their returns of all kinds, and of reminding them that it is of the highest importance to his Majesty's service that he should be able to depend as securely upon the care and fidelity as upon the honor of his officers."

Many similar instances occurred in which the Secretary at War was the channel through which the king's pleasure was signified to the army, and he seems to have been the regular and usual organ for such communications on all subjects in any way connected with finance or law.

The Secretary at War, indeed, appears to have stood and acted formerly very much in the situation of the Secretary of State, and to have transacted some kinds of business which, since the finance of the army has increased to its present extent, have been transferred to the Secretary of State for the War Department; and accordingly we find that everything relative to the exchange of prisoners passed through him; and in 1759 he conducted a long negotiation upon that subject with the Court of France, and at all times corresponded with all the governors and commanders-in-chief on foreign stations.

A very complete chain of documents appears in the books of the year 1758, showing the sort of business transacted at that time by the Secretary at War, during the existence of a Commander-in-Chief.

Lieut.-Gen. Bligh was selected to go on service in command of a body of cavalry. Lord Barrington first wrote to him, informing him, by the command of the king, that he was appointed to that service. He then wrote to the Treasury to tell them that five regiments of cavalry were to go on foreign service, that their lordships might give orders for a supply of bread and forage. He next sent orders to each regiment to hold themselves in readiness to embark. He then wrote to the Paymaster-General, signifying to him the king's pleasure that he should issue subsistence to the men, and twelve months' off-reckonings to the colonels; and, lastly, a letter to the Apothecary-General, desiring him to send immediately a supply of medicines for the expedition,—thus carrying through, by the immediate orders of the king, every detail connected with the financial arrangements of the expedition.

Lord Barrington, too, continued to issue many orders apparently much more connected with discipline than finance.

He communicated to corps distinctive appellations granted them by the king; he signified the king's pleasure upon points of rank and precedency, when disputes arose between officers; reprimanded officers for improper conduct; granted or refused leave of absence to those whose regiments were abroad (the Commander-in-Chief at home having formerly no authority out of the kingdom); called for returns of effectives whenever he wanted them; and regulated in many cases the promotion of officers.

In January, 1760, Lord Barrington wrote to Mr. Adair, the agent, expressing his surprise that the sale of an adjutancy should have been transacted without his having been consulted; ordered the arrangement to be stopped if the money had not been paid, and if it had, the bargain to be annulled, and the money paid back again; and in another letter, a few days afterward, he said it was the king's positive command that no commission of staff officers should for the future be sold.

In 1760, also, Lord Barrington wrote to General Holdsworth, Governor of Dartmouth, in answer to a letter received from him, informing him that as governor he certainly had a right to call for a return of all troops in his garrison, and to order such guards as he might think proper; but that the troops in town were not within his command.

All matters connected with the increase or diminution of military establishments, and bearing therefore upon the public expenditure, seem to have been peculiarly under the direction of the Secretary at War, and accordingly he signified the king's pleasure upon all augmentations, reductions, and drafts, and on all proposals for raising new corps.

In September, 1760, Lord Barrington issued a circular letter to several officers who were employed in raising independent companies, informing them that, having reason to apprehend that his Majesty's confidence might be abused by the recommendation of persons not properly qualified as officers, it was the king's pleasure that they should make particular inquiry about those persons whom they might propose for commissions in their corps.

In January, 1761, he desired Commandant Johnson to acquaint him whether he had any reasons to allege in excuse why his Majesty should not supersede him for having failed to raise the stipulated number of men for his independent company.

In March of the same year, Lord Ligonier being still Commander-in-Chief, Lord Barrington wrote to Lord George Beauclerk, Commander-in-Chief in North Britain, to state to him "that he had laid before the king the trial of certain officers at Edinburgh, that the king was highly displeased with their conduct, but, as they had been punished by law, he would not try them by court-martial; but that it was his Majesty's pleasure that Lord

G. Beauclerk should reprimand them as officers, in his Majesty's name, in the strongest terms for their breach of military discipline as well as of civil duties."

In March, 1761, Lord Ligonier being still Commander-in-Chief, Mr. Charles Townshend succeeded Lord Barrington, and the authority and independence of the office were kept unimpaired in his hands. Some altercation, indeed, took place between Lord Ligonier and Mr. Townshend; but as the latter continued in the full exercise of all the authority of his predecessors, the points at issue were effectually decided in favor of the Secretary at War; whether expressly so decided by his Majesty, or whether the opposition on the part of Lord Ligonier was withdrawn, does not appear.

Mr. Welbore Ellis succeeded Mr. Townshend in 1763, about which time Lord Ligonier ceased to be Commander-in-Chief, and Mr. Ellis conducted from that period till his resignation the whole business of the army, including promotions of every description.

In 1766 the Marquis of Granby was appointed Commander-in-Chief, and continued so till 1770, during which time Lord Barrington was again Secretary at War.

The same observations which have been made upon former periods apply equally to this; the Secretary at War at all times acted under the immediate orders of the king, to whom alone he was accountable, and from whom only he received directions; and all matters in any way related to the civil and financial concerns of the army were under his exclusive control.

It should be added that this applies to the army at home, because with regard to the troops on foreign stations, the Secretary at War transacted everything relative to them, as well discipline as finance. He corresponded with all the Commanders-in-Chief and Governors abroad, and conveyed to them the king's pleasure on all points of promotion, exchanges, leaves of absence, financial arrangements and claims of all sorts; drafts, reductions, augmentations, disbandments, and recruiting; the disputes of officers about rank and precedency; and the arrangements and appointment of the foreign staff.

An instance, unimportant in its subject, but tending, in proportion to its minuteness, to illustrate the present inquiry, may be found in a letter from Lord Barrington to Lord Lorne, in

August, 1769, Lord Granby being at the time Commander-in-Chief. Lord Lorne applied for a piper to his regiment (the Royal), and Lord Barrington refused it, pipers not being allowed to other regiments. But the language of the letter is worthy of attention, inasmuch as it shows that Lord Barrington conceived that however he might, for his own satisfaction and information, advise with others, the responsibility of deciding upon a question involving an increase of establishment rested with him alone. He said: "I have considered your application, and consulted with those whose opinions have most weight in my judgment. . . . I should be sorry that at any time, but particularly when I was Secretary at War, the Royal should be deprived of any honorary distinction belonging to it, but no person whom I have consulted is of opinion that a drum-major or piper can add to, or take away from, the honor of that most respectable corps."

In 1778,* Lord Amherst was appointed General on the Staff, and his appointment was communicated to the army by the Secretary at War. Lord Barrington, on the 25th March, wrote a circular letter, informing the army that the king had been pleased to appoint General Lord Amherst to serve as a General on the Staff, and that it was his Majesty's pleasure that all matters respecting his military service which were to be transacted at home should pass through his hands, conveying also the king's commands that each colonel should communicate the same to the regiment under his command, and direct his officers to govern themselves accordingly.

It appears, however, that this appointment was confined to matters of discipline, and that Lord Barrington still gave orders relative to marching, embarking, recruiting, reductions, augmentations, raising of corps, leaves of absence, resignations, supersessions, and in some cases the promotion of officers.

In 1782,† Marshal Conway was appointed Commander-in-Chief, and on the following day Mr. Townshend (afterward Lord Sidney) succeeded Mr. Jenkinson as Secretary at War. Marshal Conway continued in his appointment till December, 1783.

Mr. Townshend, and Sir George Yonge, who succeeded him in

* 25th March. † 27th March.

July, 1782, seem, during the continuance of Marshal Conway as Commander-in-Chief, to have acted in the same manner as their predecessors, and to have been equally independent in all matters of law and finance, and to have communicated the pleasure of the king upon all subjects which came officially before them.

As an instance of the manner in which they acted, it appears that in May, 1782, certain pirates were condemned to be executed, and the Admiralty, being apprehensive that some tumult might take place, applied to the Secretary at War for military assistance to attend the execution and preserve order. Mr. Townshend does not seem to have thought it necessary to have recourse, officially at least, to any authority but his own upon this occasion, but made the following reply to the Admiralty:

"There has not for many years been an instance of employing the military on a duty of this kind; the objection to it must strike their Lordships in a general view, and I do not find that any particular and certain information has been laid before them which might convince them that such a measure is necessary on the present occasion. I hope, therefore, their Lordships will agree with me that a proper exertion of the civil power will prevent any disturbances to-morrow."

In August, 1782, the invalids petitioned the Commander-in-Chief to be placed on the same footing as the rest of the army in point of pay and allowances. Marshal Conway, not considering himself authorized to decide upon the point, referred the petition to the Secretary at War, who returned it to him, stating at some length his reasons for not granting the prayer of the petition.

In January, 1793, Lord Amherst was again placed upon the Staff as General, and his appointment was communicated to the army by the Secretary at War in the same manner as in 1778, excepting that matters relative to the Foot Guards were ordered not to pass through Lord Amherst's hands, but were still to be transacted between the Secretary at War and the king.

Sir George Yonge, who was at this time Secretary at War, did not, however, in any respect surrender his financial control over the whole of the army, but exercised, in all matters involving expense, the same authority as before.

In February, 1793, he issued a circular to the colonels of regiments of dragoons, by the king's command, stating that, it being of the utmost importance that the late augmentations of men and horses should be completed, it was desirable, with that view, that the new commissions should be given to officers who would raise a certain number of men, and "that in the execution of this arrangement, it was his Majesty's particular order that the commanding officers should render every requisite assistance for recruiting," etc.

As the complaint of Sir D. Dundas is that "for a considerable time past" the Secretary at War has assumed powers and used an authority that do not properly belong to him, it might perhaps appear to be sufficient for Lord Palmerston to have proved, by tracing the proceedings of the office in former times, that these powers and this authority have always heretofore been attached to it, and to allow the fact of their having continued to be exercised of late years, and before Lord Palmerston's appointment, to rest upon the admission which the very charge itself contains. But it is, however, equally certain that neither by Mr. Windham nor by any of those persons who have succeeded him has the authority or independence of the War Office been in any degree surrendered or compromised. To prove this, it is only necessary to refer to the Book of Regulations, which consists almost entirely of circular letters, orders, and instructions upon every subject connected with law or finance, issued at different times within the above-mentioned period to the army by the Secretary at War, under the immediate orders of the king; and this book does not, as Sir D. Dundas seems to suppose, show merely the power of the Secretary at War to issue orders to the printer, but is the code by which the whole army is governed in respect of the subjects to which it relates. Lord Palmerston, indeed, does not observe in Sir David Dundas's statement any answer to the references which, in a letter to Mr. Perceval, he made to these regulations, excepting that the collection is imperfect, because some of them are altered or rescinded by others of a later date; but as the later regulations making these alterations were issued by the same authority as those which they amend, this circumstance, however it may affect the utility of the book, does not disprove the authority of the Secretary at War, and Lord Palmerston cannot but think that the pages referred to as instances are important to the question.

In page 567 is an order from Mr. Windham to Generals Commanding on all foreign stations to transmit to him quarterly returns of the staff under their command.*

In page 563 is a circular from Mr. Yorke to the commanding officers of regiments in India, ordering the regular transmission of monthly adjutants' rolls, and containing instructions as to the effects and credits of deceased soldiers.†

In page 577 is a circular from General FitzPatrick, requiring a quarterly return of the name, age, and description of every soldier in the army.‡

In page 37 is a circular from General FitzPatrick, communicating to the army at large the increase of pay and of pension which was granted in 1806;§ and he concludes his letter by saying, "I have great pleasure in being the channel of communicating to you these instances of his Majesty's gracious consideration for the army."

The very first page, indeed, contains a very important communication to the army by Mr Windham,‖ in which he informs them that the part of the pay of the officers, previously withheld under the name of arrears, would in future be regularly issued with their subsistence.

In 1802, on the formation of the Royal Garrison battalions from the invalids and out-pensioners of Chelsea, a difference of sentiment arose between his Royal Highness the Commander-in-Chief and Mr. Yorke, Secretary at War, upon the four principal points connected with the arrangement, namely:

1st. As to the numbers of which the establishments were to consist.

2d. As to the pay the men were to receive.

3d. As to the manner in which the clothing was to be furnished, whether government were to provide it, or to allow off-reckonings to the colonels.

* 24th July, 1799. † 6th April, 1803. ‡ 21st Feb. 1807. § 15th July, 1806. ‖ 25th Jan. 1798.

4th. As to the right to be given to the officers to retire upon full or half pay, in the event of reduction.

Upon all these points his Majesty's confidential servants concurred in the opinion which was entertained by the Secretary at War; and the measure, as it was afterward submitted by Mr. Yorke to Parliament, was founded upon the principles he had recommended.

Lord Palmerston trusts that the statement already given might of itself be sufficient to establish the independence of the Secretary at War, and his separate control over matters of law and finance; but fortunately the books of the War Office not only have enabled him to collect what has been the ancient and invariable practice of his predecessors, but also afford several records of the opinions which they entertained, and deliberately expressed, upon the nature and extent of the authority which they possessed; and he therefore considers it to be important to add a few extracts from those books, illustrating the view which Secretaries at War have heretofore taken of their situation and powers.

Lord Barrington, who, from the length of time he held the office, may be considered as a valuable authority on this subject, wrote to the Treasury in 1759,* remonstrating against subjecting the pay of General and Staff officers to the pension tax, and added, "It being equally the duty of my station to oppose any encroachments made on or by the officers of the army."

In the same year,† on a complaint to the Secretary at War by the Postmaster-General, of some irregularities which had taken place in the War Office in regard of franks, the Deputy Secretary at War stated "that the business of the Adjutant-General is so closely connected with the department of the Secretary at War, that it is almost always necessary that his lordship's orders to the troops should be accompanied by others from the Adjutant-General, whose letters, therefore, upon his Majesty's service, are often forwarded from this office."

In 1759,‡ General Jeffreys having applied to Lord Barrington for leave of absence for an officer, Lord Barrington informed him,

---

* 3d March. † 5th September. ‡ 24th December.

in reply, that he never himself gave leave of absence to any officer without the consent of the commanding officer of the regiment to which he belonged.

In the same year* Lord Barrington informed the Treasury that the Judge-Advocate was in respect of taxes in the same situation with himself, and some other civil officers upon the Military Establishment, who are at present obliged to pay 5 per cent. in their civil and another 5 per cent. in their military capacity.

In 1761,† Mr. Townshend informed Sir Henry Erskine that he found it was usual, when officers wanted leave to be absent from their corps, that the application should come to the Secretary at War from their colonel, or at least with his approbation.

Mr. Fane having in the same year‡ applied respecting the quarters of a regiment, Mr. Townshend informed him that he had added several places to the Blandford quarters, but that he could not by the practice of his office extend them so far as Dorchester and Shaftesbury, without the consent of the Commander-in-Chief.

It has already been stated that some discussion took place between Mr. Townshend and Lord Ligonier. Very soon after Mr. Townshend's appointment a difference seems to have arisen between them upon the arrangements for quartering some regiments of militia, and the following is an extract of a letter from Mr. Townshend to Lord Ligonier upon the subject:

"I am extremely sorry that anything should happen in which I have the misfortune to differ in my judgment from your lordship, but I flatter myself I reason in support of my opinion on this point upon the principle of equality, the only rule that can preserve harmony in the militia, or justify public office in any regulation relating to them."

In 1761,§ Lord Ligonier recommended to the king that a Captain Thompson should succeed to a commission that happened to be vacant, and it was settled that he should do so. Mr. Townshend, however, represented to the king in so strong a manner the superior claims of Major Appleton, of the regiment in which the

* 24th December. † 22d March.
‡ 11th April. § 26th July.

vacancy arose, that the first arrangement was rescinded, and Major Appleton obtained the commission.

Lord Ligonier was extremely offended at this change, and wrote in very strong terms to Mr. Townshend upon the subject, and a good deal of correspondence passed between them, of which the two following extracts are important:

Mr. Townshend, in one letter,* said "that he had no further share in this alteration than as he represented to his Majesty the situation, service, and character of Major Appleton, a duty which he thinks annexed to his office, and which he shall never omit."

In another note he said,† "Mr. Townshend shall always think it his duty, till he learns it is not from the king himself, to represent the situation and claims of any officers in the natural succession upon any vacancy, not by way of remonstrance against arrangements taken, as Lord Ligonier suggests, but merely by way of representation for his Majesty's information, and in discharge of what Mr. Townshend imagines to be a part of the duty of the Secretary at War."

In August of the same year, Mr. Townshend wrote a letter to Lord Strange, which is strongly expressive of his ideas of the authority of his office:

"Your lordship having made your application to me upon the rank in question between your lordship and Lord Denbigh, I consulted Lord Ligonier upon the point, but the War Office in no instance decides by any other authority than the directions of his Majesty, or the opinion of the Secretary at War; the latter of these I did myself the honor to transmit to your lordship some time past, and, hearing that opinion was not held decisive, I by the last post signify to your lordship his Majesty's directions."

In September following, Mr. Townshend wrote to his brother, Major-General Townshend, ... "It were endless to enumerate the other officers whom I have without knowing them sometimes saved, and at other times promoted, upon the single consideration of duty, a pleasing, though a thankless office. I wish to do more; I hope to succeed."

This letter, written after the altercation with Lord Ligonier in

---

* 26th July. † 28th July.

the same year, seems to show that the king decided the point then at issue in favor of the Secretary at War.

In a letter to Lord Scarborough, Mr. Townshend says: "Jealousy of me and a variety of motives prevent my having any weight in the department of the Commander-in-Chief. . . . The constitution of rival offices often exposes me to a variety of mortifications and disappointments, whenever friendship leads me to express a wish, or any method of obviating a difficulty."

Mr. Townshend informed Lord Tyrawley,* who was appointed Commander-in-Chief of the Forces in Portugal, that he was not a little surprised that he should think of taking out of the War Office the nomination of the Hospital Staff of his expedition.

To General Leighton, Lord Barrington wrote † . . . "But it is my duty to take what care I can of the half-pay. . . . I am of opinion that all vacancies at home shall go on in this way, but regiments like yours in the West Indies will meet with more indulgence."

In 1766,‡ Lord Barrington wrote to a Board of General Officers, signifying to them the king's approbation of a report they had made, and adding some long observations about the sale of commissions. He concludes: "But the officer of the Crown who is intrusted with the important charge of the whole army cannot be too vigilant. . . . But the poor though deserving officer should always find at the War Office a constant assertor of his rights, and faithful guardian of his interests." It is to be observed that there was not at that time any Commander-in-Chief, and this letter proves that when such an officer does not exist, the whole management and superintendence of the army devolve upon the Secretary at War.

In March, 1769, Lord Barrington wrote to a Mr. Lee a very striking and important letter, bearing as strongly upon the object of this Memorandum as that of Mr. Townshend of August, 1761:

"I have received your letter of the 21st instant, and the papers therein inclosed. Without entering into a detail of the business to which they relate, it is sufficient that I inform you that I never had the least idea of your being paid an annuity for life, as appears

* 8th March, 1782. † 19th November, 1765. ‡ 8th February.

by my warrants; that Mr. Ellis* never had, as appears by his; that the Commander-in-Chief has no business with, or authority in, transactions which relate to the public money; and that I do not think proper to advise the king to allow you anything further."

In March, 1782, Mr. Jenkinson (afterward Lord Liverpool) gave the same strong and decided opinion in a letter to Lieutenant-Colonel Goldsworthy, in which he said, "I think it right at the same time to say that in articles of public expenditure it is, in my judgment, the duty of the Secretary at War alone to decide."

In 1802, some correspondence took place between his Royal Highness the Duke of York and Mr. Yorke, then Secretary at War, with regard to the nature of the appointment of regimental paymasters, in the course of which Mr. Yorke stated it to be his opinion† "that the War Office was perfectly warranted in considering the paymaster as a public officer who was to look for the rule of his conduct to the existing Regulations, and to the instructions which he should receive from this department, as having the exclusive control of the expenditures intrusted to his administration."

It has been shown by references already made from the books of the War Office, that the Treasury have in all times past considered the Commander-in-Chief or Captain-General to have, according to Lord Barrington's expression, "no business with, or authority in, transactions which relate to the public money;" but even if that opinion could not be sufficiently collected from the history of the office, there is a recent decision of that Board which places the point beyond the possibility of a doubt.

On the 21st August, 1807, Mr. Huskisson transmitted to the Secretary at War a minute of the Treasury, dated the 19th of the same month, desiring him to take it into his serious and attentive consideration, and report his opinion thereupon to the Board.

This minute recites that the Board of Treasury have read the first report of the Committee of Public Expenditure of the United Kingdom, and taken into their most serious consideration the

---

* The last Secretary at War.

† 26th March.

several suggestions which it contains, and thereupon propose the adoption of certain regulations.

The most important of these are, that large sums of money shall be placed in the hands of the Paymaster-General by warrants from the Treasury; that the power of applying any moneys placed in the hands of the Paymaster-General by these warrants shall be vested in the Secretary at War and Lords of the Treasury, and in no other authority whatsoever.

That the application of these sums for ordinary services shall be made by the Secretary at War alone, upon his sole authority and responsibility, and under his warrant.

That in all cases in which the Secretary at War shall think it requisite to recommend any increase of establishment or salary, or to alter or add to the regulations now in force with respect to the allowances to the army or any part thereof, he shall communicate the same to the Treasury, and obtain their sanction before he submits the same to the king or to Parliament, as the nature of the case may be.

It is difficult to conceive anything more strongly decisive on the point now under discussion than this deliberate opinion of the Treasury, pronounced in consequence of a report from a Select Committee of the House of Commons, specially appointed to inquire into and consider of the checks existing or necessary to be imposed upon the expenditure of the public money.

It has been shown in the preceding pages that from the revolution down to the beginning of the last war, by the course of office, by the recorded opinions of Secretaries at War, by the opinions and practice of the Treasury, and by the sanction given to all these by the several sovereigns of the country, the independence of the Secretary at War, and his exclusive control and jurisdiction over all matters of law and finance, may be fully collected and proved; nothing therefore remains but to add the authority of the Legislature, and that can also be adduced in support of those above mentioned on this point.

Parliament has at various times passed Acts imposing distinct duties and responsibilities upon the Secretary at War, thereby incontrovertibly proving that in their opinion he is a civil servant of the Crown, liable to no orders but from his sovereign; because to impose responsibility where there is not liberty of action is impossible. and it is obvious that no officer who is subordinate to and dependent upon another can by possibility be a free and independent agent.

The Acts of Parliament in which the Secretary at War is mentioned, and in which duties and responsibilities are imposed upon him, or powers and authorities given him, are Mr. Burke's and other Pay Office Acts, by which he is required to lay before Parliament annual estimates of the expenses of the army, and to examine and settle regimental accounts ; the annual Mutiny Act, the Innkeepers' Act, the Pay and Clothing Acts of the Army and Militia, Militia Acts, Volunteer Acts, the Act regulating the office of Agent-General, and, in short, almost all Acts relating to military matters, require or authorize him to do or not to do certain things.

In an Act of the 19th George III., cap. 10, directing men to be forthwith raised for the army, the superintendence and direction of that service were placed in the hands of the Secretary at War, and it is remarkable that there is a special clause prohibiting any military officer from being one of the commissioners who were in the several counties to carry the Act into execution. The operation of the Act was also to be superseded whenever his Majesty thought fit, by notice from the Secretary at War.

But the most remarkable Act of this sort is that of the 8th of George II., regulating the quartering of soldiers during elections. The object of the Legislature was to secure the freedom of election from any interference on the part of the military, and for that purpose it was necessary to compel some responsible and ostensible officer, who had the power to do so, to remove all troops from places where elections were to be held. Accordingly, the Secretary at War was fixed upon for that purpose, and he is bound by this Act to move troops from such places one day previous to the election, and to keep them away till one day after the election is over, under pain, should he omit or neglect to do so, of forfeiting his office, and of being incapable of ever again serving his Majesty in any capacity whatever, civil or military.

If the Secretary at War were impeached at the bar of the

House of Lords, for having violated the provisions of this law, would he be suffered to plead that he had been prevented from moving the troops by the order of the Commander-in-Chief, or Captain-General, or by his not being able to obtain their concurrence and consent? or would he not be told that such was precisely the case against which the Act intended to guard the liberty of the subject, that to him alone Parliament and the country looked for the execution of its law, and that even the royal authority could not release him from an obligation which it had concurred with the other two branches of the Legislature to impose?

The Secretary at War seems, indeed, to be the officer who stands peculiarly between the people and the army, to protect the former from the latter, to prevent their public revenue from being drained by any unauthorized increase of military establishments, and their persons and property from being injured by any possible misconduct of the soldiery; and upon him would Parliament and the country justly fix the responsibility for any neglect of this part of his duty.

Everything, therefore, which relates not only to the finance of the army, but also to those matters in which soldiers come in contact with the civil inhabitants of the country, such as the quartering, billeting, and marching of troops, requires the sanction and authority of the Secretary at War; and although, as these matters are also closely connected with those general arrangements of the military force, which must of necessity be requested by the Commander-in-Chief, or the militia officer in command of the army, they are, therefore, in general settled and determined by him; yet this is only an arrangement and understanding which has been made for the convenience of office, and the more easily to carry on the public service; because orders of this sort are in fact issued by the Secretary at War, although the arrangement is made and communicated privately to him by the Commander-in-Chief. But if in any case the Secretary at War saw reason for objecting to any such arrangement, the Commander-in-Chief could not compel him to issue the orders, and without the orders of the Secretary at War, and of the magistrates acting under the provisions of the Mutiny Act, although the troops might be bound by military discipline to march, in obedience to the commands of the Commander-in-Chief, they would be entitled to no quarters or billets or subsistence on their march; and would be liable to the severest punishments of criminal law for any attempt to provide these things by force for themselves.

The same reasoning holds good also in matters of finance. The Commander-in-Chief cannot by his own authority order the issue of money to any individual. His warrant would not be noticed by the Paymaster-General, and no officer who should pay money by his order would be reimbursed, unless he obtained also the authority of the Secretary at War.

Independently, therefore, of its being inconsistent with the spirit of the Constitution, and the undeviating practice of office from the revolution downward, that the Commander-in-Chief should issue orders affecting the public expenditure, there is an inconsistency inherent in the thing itself; because his order is by itself of no authority, and if the arrangement which he proposes and orders is afterward approved by the Secretary at War, or through him by the Treasury, and the Secretary at War issues his order in support of that of the Commander-in-Chief, it is the order of the War Office, and not that of the Commander-in-Chief, that is the efficient authority, and in that case the latter is at least useless; but if the Secretary at War or Treasury should refuse to concur with the Commander-in-Chief, and should not sanction the arrangement which he had proposed or promulgated, then the order of the Commander-in-Chief is powerless, and would not indemnify the persons who might have acted under it; and it is obvious that nothing can tend more directly to lower the authority of any officer than his issuing orders which he has not legally the power to enforce.

Lord Palmerston therefore submits that, according to the principles which regulate the British Constitution, power cannot be vested where there is no responsibility, or responsibility be imposed where authority does not exist. The Legislature have imposed a responsibility upon the Secretary at War from which he cannot discharge himself; and it would be placing him in a situation perfectly anomalous and unknown to any one office in the

Constitution to deprive him of that independence by which alone he can secure to himself the power of faithfully performing his duty.

It is therefore submitted, that to quote the wording of the commission of the Secretary at War is not sufficient for the purpose of proving that he is subordinate to, and dependent upon, the Commander-in-Chief in any matter of law or finance connected with the army; because, in the first place, setting aside every other consideration, it is quite clear from the commission of Mr. Clarke, that "the General of our Forces" mentioned in it is the Captain-General, and not the Commander-in-Chief; and that the addition of the words "according to the discipline of war" (words which, it is to be observed, Sir David Dundas does not notice in his argument) prove that the orders he was so liable to receive from the Captain-General were in his military capacity as a staff officer, and not in his civil character as a political servant of the Crown; and as a staff officer he has now only a nominal existence. It must be remembered, too, that Mr. Blathwayte's commission, in which those words were first inserted, was made out before the revolution, when constitutional principles and ideas of civil liberty were not understood as they have been since those days; and when there existed a Captain-General, whom not military officers alone, but all persons whomsoever, were ordered to obey, and possessed of powers unknown in later times. It is not, therefore, fair to infer from a form of words made out originally under such circumstances and in such times, and copied, as was natural they should be, on each successive appointment, the situation and powers of the officer at the present day, after all the changes and improvements that have since taken place in the constitution and government of the country. And because, in the second place, whatever might have been the intention of those who originally made out the commission, it is quite certain that for more than a century it never has, in practice and in fact, borne the construction which Sir David Dundas now attempts to put upon it.

The commission of Secretary at War is certainly in its nature, in some degree, a military commission, but it is also a civil one. It enjoins him to take the place into his charge, and the appointment, even in the case of a General Officer, to whom it is not a first commission, vacates a seat in the House of Commons.

He is therefore a civil servant of the Crown, and as such has of late years sat, at times, to advise his Majesty in the Cabinet. It seems, then, clear that the obedience which this civil officer is on any supposition to render to the Captain-General, according to the discipline of war, cannot relate to the administration of the public business which, in his political capacity, passes through his hands.

Lord Palmerston most humbly trusts that the preceding detail and observations, and the extracts in the Appendix from the books of the War Office (which have indeed run into a length much greater than he wished, but which the nature and importance of the subject rendered unavoidable), will satisfy the mind of his Royal Highness the Prince Regent, that the Secretary at War never could, by any construction of his commission, be dependent upon or subordinate to the Commander-in-Chief, as distinguished from the Captain-General; that he never has, in point of fact, been so even to the Captain-General in matters of law and finance; and that over these subjects he has always hitherto exercised an independent jurisdiction under the immediate orders of his sovereign, whose commands alone it is his duty to obey; and Lord Palmerston founds this position upon the ancient practice of his office, upon the recorded opinions of Secretaries at War and of the Treasury, upon the sanction of the successive sovereigns who have sat upon the throne, and upon the Acts of the Legislature of the country.

Lord Palmerston, however, while asserting his official independence in those matters which belong to his department, would wish most distinctly to be understood as not blending with that question, in any degree, the consideration of the relative dignity or importance of the Commander-in-Chief and Secretary at War; and fortunately, indeed, for this part of his purpose, the alteration which since this Memorandum was originally begun has taken place in the former office, must effectually secure him from the possibility of misconception on that head.

It may also be necessary to say that in the preceding detail of the history of the War Office Lord Palmerston has necessarily been led to state things as he found them recorded; that in some particulars, however, the arrangement of former times has been altered, that part of the business of a political nature which was formerly transacted in the War Office has, since the separate establishment of a Secretary of State for the War Department, been conducted by him, while the Secretary at War has also of late years made it a point, while a Commander-in-Chief exists, not to interfere in the patronage of the army, or in matters purely connected with its discipline; and it is most foreign from Lord Palmerston's intention to wish in any degree to recall the practice of former times in those respects in which it has been altered for the convenience of the general arrangements of the government, or by the sanction of competent authority deciding upon a full consideration of the subject.

Nor would he think of contending that the independence which the Secretary at War has always enjoyed should be exercised by making innovations in the service, or taking steps altering or affecting the interests of the army, without previous communication with the Commander-in-Chief, because he is persuaded that without a good understanding and cordial co-operation and concert between the two offices the public service cannot be well and advantageously carried on. But, on the other hand, he must beg leave humbly to submit to his Royal Highness that it never has belonged to the Commander-in-Chief to issue by his authority orders and regulations affecting the expenditure of the public money, and that the Secretary at War is the accustomed and, as he humbly submits, the proper channel for any signification of his Majesty's pleasure upon such subjects; and that if it should be his Royal Highness's pleasure to make the office of Secretary at War dependent upon that of Commander-in-Chief, it would in some important particulars require the authority of Parliament to alter those laws which have imposed special duties on the Secretary at War.

TREATY FOR THE PACIFICATION OF GREECE, BETWEEN ENGLAND, FRANCE, AND RUSSIA, SIGNED AT LONDON, JULY 6, 1827.

Art. I.—The contracting Powers will offer to the Ottoman Porte their mediation, with the view of bringing about a reconciliation between it and the Greeks.

This offer of mediation shall be made to this Power immediately after the ratification of the Treaty, by means of a collective declaration, signed by the plenipotentiaries of the allied courts at Constantinople; and there shall be made, at the same time, to the two contending parties, a demand of an immediate armistice between them, as a preliminary condition indispensable to the opening of any negotiation.

Art. II.—The arrangement to be proposed to the Ottoman Porte shall rest on the following bases: the Greeks shall hold of the Sultan, as of a superior lord (*suzerain*); and, in consequence of this superiority, they shall pay to the Ottoman Empire an annual tribute, the amount of which shall be fixed, once for all, by a common agreement. They shall be governed by the authorities whom they shall themselves choose and nominate; but in the nomination of whom the Porte shall have a determinate voice. To bring about a complete separation between the individuals of the two nations, and to prevent the collisions which are the inevitable consequence of so long a struggle, the Greeks shall enter upon possession of the Turkish property, situated either on the continent or in the isles of Greece, on the condition of indemnifying the former proprietors, either by the payment of an annual sum, to be added to the tribute which is to be paid to the Porte, or by some other transaction of the same nature.

Art. III.—The details of this arrangement, as well as the limits of the territory on the continent, and the designation of the islands of the Archipelago, to which it shall be applicable, shall be settled in a subsequent negotiation between the High Powers and the two contending parties.

ART. IV.—The contracting Powers engage to follow up the salutary work of the pacification of Greece, on the bases laid down in the preceding articles; and to furnish, without the least delay, their representatives at Constantinople with all the instructions which are necessary for the execution of the Treaty now signed.

ART. V.—The contracting Powers will not seek in these arrangements any augmentation of territory, any exclusive influence, any commercial advantage for their subjects which the subjects of any other nation may not equally obtain.

ART. VI.—The arrangements of reconciliation and peace, which shall be definitely agreed upon between the contending parties, shall be guaranteed by such of the signing Powers as shall judge it useful or possible to contract the obligation: the mode of the effects of this guarantee shall become the object of subsequent stipulations between the High Powers.

ART. VII.—The present Treaty shall be ratified, and the ratification shall be exchanged, in two months, or sooner, if possible.

In faith whereof the respective plenipotentiaries have signed and sealed it with their arms.

Done at London, 6th July, 1827.

DUDLEY.
POLIGNAC.
LIEVEN.

Additional and Secret Article.

In case that the Ottoman Porte does not accept, within the space of one month, the mediation which shall be proposed, the High Contracting Parties agree upon the following measures:

1.—It shall be declared, by their representatives at Constantinople, to the Porte, that the inconveniences and evils pointed out in the public Treaty as inseparable from the state of things subsisting in the East for the last six years, and the termination of which, through the means at the disposal of the Sublime Porte, appears still remote, impose upon the High Contracting Parties the necessity of taking immediate measures of an approximation with the Greeks.

It is to be understood that this approximation shall be brought about by establishing commercial relations with the Greeks, by sending to them for that purpose, and receiving from them, consular agents, so long as there shall exist among them authorities capable of maintaining such relations.

2.—If, within the said term of one month, the Porte do not accept the armistice proposed in the first article of the public Treaty, or if the Greeks refuse to execute it, the High Contracting Powers shall declare to that one of the two contending parties which shall wish to continue hostilities, or to both, if such become necessary, that the said High Contracting Powers intend to exert all the means which circumstances may suggest to their prudence to obtain the immediate effect of the armistice; the execution of which they desire by preventing, in as far as may be in their power, all collision between the contending parties; and, in fact, immediately after the aforesaid declaration, the High Contracting Powers will conjointly employ all their means in the accomplishment of the object thereof, without, however, taking any part in the hostilities between the two contending parties.

In consequence, the High Contracting Powers will, immediately after the signature of the present additional and secret Article, transmit eventual instructions, conformable to the provisions above set forth, to the admirals commanding their squadrons in the seas of the Levant.

3.—Finally, if, contrary to all expectation, these measures do not yet suffice to induce the adoption by the Ottoman Porte of the propositions made by the High Contracting Parties; or if, on the other hand, the Greeks renounce the conditions stipulated in their favor in the Treaty of this day, the High Contracting Powers will nevertheless continue to prosecute the work of pacification on the bases agreed upon between them; and, in consequence, they authorize from this time forward their representatives in London to discuss and determine the ulterior measures to which it may become necessary to resort.

The present additional and secret Article shall have the same force and value as if it had been inserted, word for word, in the Treaty of this day. It shall be ratified, and the ratifications thereof shall be exchanged, at the same time as those of the said Treaty.

In faith whereof the respective plenipotentiaries have signed and sealed it with their arms.

Done at London, the 6th day of July, in the year of grace 1827.

DUDLEY.
POLIGNAC.
LIEVEN.

CORRESPONDENCE BETWEEN MR. HUSKISSON AND THE DUKE OF WELLINGTON.

DOWNING STREET, May 20,
Tuesday morning, 2 A.M.

MY DEAR DUKE,—

After the vote which, in regard to my own consistency and personal character, I have found myself from the course of this evening's debate compelled to give on the East Retford question, I owe it to you, as the head of the administration, and to Mr. Peel, as the Leader of the House of Commons, to lose no time in affording you an opportunity of placing my office in other hands, as the only means in my power of preventing the injury to the king's service which may ensue from the appearance of disunion in his Majesty's councils, however unfounded in reality, or however unimportant in itself the question which has given rise to that appearance.

W. HUSKISSON.

MY DEAR HUSKISSON,—

Your letter of two this morning, which I received at ten, has surprised me much, and has given me great concern. I have considered it my duty to lay it before the king.

WELLINGTON.

Downing Street, May 20, 1828,
Half-past 6 p.m.

My dear Duke,—

Having understood from Lord Dudley and Lord Palmerston that you had laid my letter of last night before the king under a different impression from that which it was intended to convey, I feel it due both to you and to myself to say, that my object in writing that letter was, not to express any intentions of my own, but to relieve you from any delicacy which you might feel toward me, if you should think that the interests of his Majesty's service would be prejudiced by my remaining in office after giving a vote in respect to which, from the turn which the latter part of the debate had taken, a sense of personal honor left me no alternative.

W. Huskisson.

May 20, 1828.

My dear Huskisson,—

I have received your letter of this evening. I certainly did not understand your letter of two this morning as offering me any option; nor do I understand the one of this evening as leaving me any, except that of submitting myself and his Majesty's government to the necessity of soliciting you to remain in your office, or of incurring the loss of your valuable assistance to his Majesty's service. However sensible I may be of this loss, I am convinced that in these times any loss is better than that of character, which is the foundation of public confidence.

In this view of the case I have put out of it altogether every consideration of the discredit resulting from the scene of last night—of the extent of which you could not but have been sensible when you thought proper, as a remedy for it, to send me the offer of "placing your office in other hands."

Wellington.

Colonial Office, May 21, 1828.

My dear Duke,—

In justice to myself I cannot acquiesce for a moment in the construction which your letter of last night puts upon my conduct. You cannot refuse to me the right of knowing the motives of my own actions; and I solemnly declare that in both my letters I was actuated by one and the same feeling. It was simply this:—That it was not for me, but for you, as head of the government, to decide how far my vote made it expedient to remove me from his Majesty's service. I felt that I had no alternative, consistently with personal honor (in a difficulty not of my own seeking or creating), but to give that vote; that the question in itself was one of minor importance; that the disunion was more in appearance than in reality; but I also felt that possibly you might take a different view of it, and that in case you should I ought (as I had done on a similar occasion with Lord Liverpool) to relieve you from any difficulty arising out of personal consideration toward me, in deciding upon a step to which you might think it your public duty to resort on the occasion.

It was under this impression alone that I wrote to you immediately upon my return from the House of Commons.

If you had not misconceived that impression, as well as the purport of my second letter, I am persuaded that you could not suppose me guilty of the arrogance of expecting "that you and his Majesty's government should submit yourselves to the necessity of soliciting me to remain in my office," or do me the injustice of believing that I could be capable of placing you in the alternative of choosing between the continuance of my services, such as they are, and the loss to your administration of one particle of character, which, I agree with you, is the foundation of public confidence.

If, understanding my communication as I intended it to be understood, you had in any way intimated to me, either that the occurrence, however unfortunate, was not one of sufficient moment to render it necessary for you, on public grounds, to act in the manner in which I had assumed that you possibly might think it necessary, or that you were under that necessity, in either case there would have been an end of the matter. In the first supposition, I should have felt that I had done what in honor and fairness toward you I was bound to do; but it never would have entered my imagination that I had claimed or received any sacrifice whatever from you or any member of his Majesty's government.

On the other hand, nothing can be further from my intention than to express an opinion that the occasion was not one in which you might fairly consider it your duty to advise his Majesty to withdraw from me the seals of office, on the ground of this vote. I do not, therefore, complain; but I cannot allow that my removal shall be placed on any other ground. I cannot allow that it was my own act; still less can I admit that when I had no other intention than to relieve the question on which you had to decide from any personal embarrassment, this step on my part should be ascribed to feelings the very reverse of those by which alone I was actuated, either toward you or his Majesty's government.

W. Huskisson.

London, May 21, 1828.

My dear Mr. Huskisson,—

In consequence of your last letter, I feel it to be necessary to recall to your recollection the circumstances under which I received your letter of Tuesday morning.

It is addressed to me at two o'clock in the morning, immediately after a debate and division in the House of Commons. It informs me that you lose no time in affording me an opportunity of placing your office in other hands, as the only means in your power of preventing an injury to the king's service, which you describe. It concludes by "regretting the necessity for troubling me with this communication."

Could I consider this in any other light than as a formal tender of the resignation of your office, or that I had any alternative than either to solicit you to remain in office contrary to your sense of duty, or to submit your letter to the king?

If you had called on me the next morning after your vote, and had explained to me in conversation what had passed in the House of Commons, the character of the communication would have been quite different, and I might have felt myself at liberty to discuss the whole subject with you, and freely to give an opinion on any point connected. But I must still think that if I had not considered a letter couched in the terms in which that letter is couched, and received under the circumstances under which I received it, as a tender of resignation, and had not laid it before the king, I should have exposed the king's government and myself to very painful misconstructions. My answer to your letter will have informed you that it surprised me much, and that it gave me great concern. I must consider, therefore, the resignation of your office as your own act, and not as mine.

WELLINGTON.

DOWNING STREET, May 25, 1828.

MY DEAR DUKE,—

On Tuesday last I wrote to the king to solicit an audience; his Majesty has not yet been pleased to grant me this honor.

In the expectation (not unnatural for me to entertain in the situation which I hold) of being afforded an opportunity of waiting upon his Majesty, I have deferred acknowledging your letter of the 21st, which, passing by altogether all that is stated in mine of the same date, you conclude in the following words: "I must, therefore, consider the resignation of your office as your own act, and not as mine."

I will not revert to the full explanation which I have already given you on this subject. Not denying that my first letter might be capable of the construction which you put upon it, I would ask you whether it be usual, after a construction has been from the first moment explicitly disavowed, to persist that it is the right one? It being, however, the construction to which you adhere, I must assume, as you laid the letter before his Majesty, that you advised his Majesty upon it, and that his Majesty is, therefore, under the same misapprehension as yourself of what I meant—the more especially as I have no means of knowing whether any subsequent letters have been laid before his Majesty.

It was for the purpose of setting right any erroneous impression on the royal mind that I sought to be admitted as soon as possible into his Majesty's presence.

I was then, as I am still, most anxious to assure his Majesty that nothing could have been further from my intention than that the letter in question should have been at all submitted to his Majesty; to make known to his Majesty the circumstances and feelings under which it had been written; to point out to him that I had taken the precaution (usual between ministers in matters of a delicate and confidential nature, when it is wished to keep the subjects as much as possible confined to the respective parties) of marking the letter "private and confidential;" that I understood that this letter, so marked specially to guard its object, had been, without previous communication of any sort with me in respect to the transaction referred to but not explained in the letter itself, laid before his Majesty, as conveying to the foot of the throne my positive resignation.

I should further have had to state to his Majesty the great pain and concern which I felt at finding that a paper should have been submitted to his Majesty, and describing (*sic*) to him as conveying my resignation of the seals, in a form so unusual, and with a restriction so unbecoming toward my sovereign as is implied in the words "private and confidential;" that in a necessity so painful (had I felt such a necessity) as that of asking his Majesty's permission to withdraw from his service, my first anxiety would have been to lay my reasons, in a respectful but direct communication from myself, at his Majesty's feet; but that most certainly, in whatever mode conveyed, the uppermost feeling of my heart would have been to have accompanied it with those expressions of dutiful attachment and respectful gratitude which I owe his Majesty for the many and uniform proofs of confidence and kindness with which he has been graciously pleased to honor me since I have held the seals of the Colonial Department.

If I had been afforded an opportunity of thus relieving myself from the painful position in which I stand toward his Majesty, I should then have entreated of his Majesty's goodness and sense of justice to permit a letter so improper for me to have written (if it could have been in my contemplation that it would have been laid before his Majesty as an act of resignation) to be withdrawn. Neither should I have concealed from his Majesty my regret, considering the trouble which has unfortunately occurred, both to his Majesty and his government, that I had not taken a different mode of doing what, for the reasons fully stated in my letter of the 21st, I found myself bound in honor to do, so as to have prevented, perhaps, the misconception arising out of my letter written immediately after the debate.

I have now stated to you frankly and without reserve the substance of all that I was anxious to submit to the king. I have done so in the full confidence that you will do me the favor to lay this statement before his Majesty; and that I may be allowed to implore of his Majesty that he will do me the justice to believe that, of all who have a right to prefer a claim to be admitted to his royal presence, I am the last who, in a matter relating to myself, would press that claim in a manner unpleasant to his Majesty's wishes or inclinations. I bow to them with respectful deference, still retaining, however, a confidence, founded on the rectitude of my intentions, that in being removed from his Majesty's service I may be allowed the consolation of knowing that I have not been debarred from the privilege of my office in consequence of my having incurred his Majesty's personal displeasure.

W. Huskisson.

London, May 25, 1828.

My dear Huskisson,—

It is with great concern that I inform you that I have at last attended his Majesty, and have received his instructions respecting an arrangement to fill your office.

I sincerely regret the loss of your valuable assistance in the arduous task in which I am engaged.

Wellington.

Downing Street, May 25, 1828,
Half-past 9 P.M.

My dear Duke,—

Lord Dudley has just sent to me, unopened, my letter to you, which I forwarded to Apsley House about five o'clock this afternoon.

This letter was written as soon as I was given to understand by Lord Dudley, who called here after an interview with you this morning, that his Majesty had not signified any intention of granting me the honor of an audience. No other mode, therefore, remaining open to me of conveying my sentiments to the king, I address myself to you for the purpose of bringing before his Majesty, in the shape of a written communication, what I am prevented from stating to his Majesty in person.

I feel confident that you will not deny me this favor, and you will be satisfied by the contents of my letter (which I now return) that in writing it nothing was further from my intention than to intrude myself between you and the arrangements which, upon my removal from office (for such I have considered the result of our correspondence since your letter of the 21st), you have received his Majesty's instructions to make.

Your letter communicating this fact reached me about half-past seven this evening. I thank you for the information, and for the kind manner in which you advert to any feeble assistance which I may have been able to give to your administration, as well as for the expression of the concern with which you have advised his Majesty to place my office in other hands.

W. Huskisson.

London, May 26, 1828.

My dear Huskisson,—

I have received your letter of yesterday, accompanied by another letter from you, dated also yesterday, which I had returned to Lord Dudley, under the impression that I ought not to open it without your previous consent, under the circumstances that existed at the time I received it.

I have laid both before the king. In answer, I have only to repeat that I considered your letter of the 20th as a formal tender of the resignation of your office, and that the circumstance of its being marked "private and confidential" did not alter the character of the letter, or relieve me from the painful duty of communicating its contents to his Majesty, as I did, in person.

Your subsequent letters did not, according to my understanding of them, convey any disavowal of your intention to tender your resignation. I laid them before his Majesty, and my answers to them, and communicated to Lord Dudley that I had done so.

The king informed me, I think on Wednesday the 21st, that you had desired to have audience of his Majesty, and that he intended to receive you on the day but one after. I did not conceive it my duty to advise his Majesty to receive you at an earlier period.

It is scarcely necessary for me to observe that your letter to me of the 20th was entirely your own act, and wholly unexpected by me. If the letter was written hastily and inconsiderately, surely the natural course was for you to withdraw it altogether, and thus relieve me from the position in which, without any fault of mine, it had placed me—compelling me either to accept the resignation which it tendered, or to solicit you to continue to hold your office.

The latter step was, in my opinion, calculated to do me personally, and the king's government, great disservice; and it appeared to me that the only mode by which we could be extricated from the difficulty in which your letter had placed us was, that the withdrawal of your letter should be your spontaneous act, and that it should be adopted without delay.

The interference of his Majesty pending our correspondence would not only have placed his Majesty in a situation in which he ought not to be placed in such a question, but it would have subjected me to the imputation that that interference had taken place on my suggestion, or with my connivance. I did not consider it my duty to advise his Majesty to interfere in any manner whatever. His Majesty informed me this day that he had written to you this morning, appointing an audience in the course of the day.

WELLINGTON.

END OF VOL. I.

Bulwer's Novels. Globe Edition. Complete in twenty-two volumes. With Frontispiece to each volume. Beautifully printed on fine tinted paper. 16mo. Extra cloth, $33 extra cloth, gilt top, $38.50; half calf, neat, $55; half Turkey, gilt top, $66; half calf, gilt extra, $66. Each novel sold separately as below, in extra cloth, at $1.50 per volume.

The Caxtons	1 vol.	Zanoni	1 vol.
My Novel	2 vols.	Pelham	1 vol.
What will He Do with It?	2 vols.	The Disowned	1 vol.
Devereux	1 vol.	Paul Clifford	1 vol.
Last Days of Pompeii	1 vol.	Ernest Maltravers	1 vol.
Leila, Calderon and Pilgrims	1 v.	Godolphin	1 vol.
Rienzi	1 vol.	Alice	1 vol.
The Last of the Barons	1 vol.	Night and Morning	1 vol.
Harold	1 vol.	Lucretia	1 vol.
Eugene Aram	1 vol.	A Strange Story	1 vol.

"The Globe edition of Bulwer is very neat and satisfactory—more satisfactory than any other issued in this country."—*Philada. North American.*

"The Globe edition is remarkable for a judicious combination of cheapness, legibility and beauty."—*Charleston Courier.*

"We have repeatedly borne witness to the pre-eminence of the Globe over all other editions, in respect to cheapness, neatness and convenience of size."—*Cincinnati Gazette.*

"The clear-cut type, delicately-tinted paper and tasty binding of this Globe edition of Bulwer's works cannot be awarded too much praise."—*Rural New Yorker.*

"We repeat what we have so often before stated—that the Globe edition is the best ever issued on this side of the Atlantic."—*New Orleans Times.*

"The Globe edition of Bulwer furnishes a model well worthy of imitation."—*Philada. Age.*

"As to execution and price, there is no better edition in the market."—*Chicago Evening Journal.*

"We congratulate this well-known Philadelphia publishing house upon furnishing so complete, so legible, so compact and so beautiful an edition of the writings of this great novelist. The American book-buying and book-reading public will not fail to place this fine edition upon their library shelves. It is the best cheap edition of Bulwer that we have ever seen. It is offered at the low price of $1.50 per volume, at which price the purchaser gets the best part of the bargain."—*Providence Evening Press.*

Reade's Novels. Illustrated Standard Edition of Charles Reade's Novels. Complete in ten vols. 12mo. With Engraved Frontispiece and Vignette Title to each. Handsomely bound in extra cloth. Price, $15 per set. Extra cloth, gilt top, $17 per set. Sold separately, in extra cloth, as follows:

Hard Cash	$1.75	The Cloister and the Hearth	$1.75
Love me Little Love me Long	1.50	Griffith Gaunt	1.50
Never too Late to Mend	1.75	Peg Woffington	1.25
White Lies	1.50	Christie Johnstone	1.25
Foul Play	1.50	The Course of True Love Never did Run Smooth	1.25

www.ingramcontent.com/pod-product-compliance
Lightning Source LLC
LaVergne TN
LVHW020124110826
845151LV00001B/272